THE DARTMOOR PONY

—— *A History of the Breed* ——

Joseph Palmer

DEVON BOOKS

First published in 1990 by Devon Books

ISBN 0 86114-863-0

British Library Cataloguing-in-publication Data

CIP Catalogue Record for this book is available from the British Library

Typesetting by P&M Typesetting Ltd, Exeter

Printed and bound in Great Britain by BPCC Wheatons Ltd, Exeter

DEVON BOOKS

Official Publisher to Devon County Council
An imprint of Wheaton Publishers Ltd
A member of Maxwell Communication Corporation plc

Wheaton Publishers Ltd
Hennock Road, Marsh Barton, Exeter, Devon EX2 8RP
Tel: 0392 411131; Fax: 0392 425274

SALES

Direct sales enquiries to Devon Books at the address above

Photographs are reproduced by kind permission of the following:

Richard and Carol Gilson pp. 116, 134, 134, 166
Tracey Eliot Reep p. 32
Anthony Reynolds pp. 57, 106, 111, 136 (bottom right)
Solo Photographics p. 119
Equestrian Services Thorney p. 100
Sally-Anne Thompson pp. 91, 95
All other photographs are from private collections

ACKNOWLEDGEMENTS

The author records his warmest thanks to all those who have helped, guided and, occasionally, admonished him in his task of planning and writing this book. Aware of his own limitations in that he neither breeds, owns, exhibits nor judges Dartmoors, he has drawn heavily and often on the deep knowledge of those that do.

In the first place he is grateful to the Chairman and Council of the Dartmoor Pony Society: for commissioning the work and for agreeing that he should enjoy a free hand in the actual writing. Within the Society, his especial thanks go to the Book Committee, without whose detailed information and guidance he would have been lost indeed: Ann Jones (also for her loan of early volumes of the NPS Stud Book), Elizabeth Newbolt-Young, Peter Upton, Patricia Robinson.

Thanks are also due to Peter Upton on a second front, as a contributor: a comprehensive appendix on foundation stock and a most generous *gift* of a large number of line-drawings plus several full-colour illustrations. Not for the first time the DPS has reason to be grateful to Peter Upton.

The author also acknowledges the kindness of Robert Hale & Company in allowing him to quote from *High Dartmoor* by the late Eric Hemery.

Finally he thanks the National Pony Society for the generous help and information exactly and swiftly supplied, but especially for allowing him to quote extensively from the Society's Stud Books; the only readily accessible written record of the early days of the century.

DUCHY *of* CORNWALL

10 BUCKINGHAM GATE   LONDON SWIE 6LA   ·   TELEPHONE: 01-834 7346

**FOREWORD BY HIS ROYAL HIGHNESS THE PRINCE OF WALES,
DUKE OF CORNWALL**

Dartmoor has long been an important part of the Duchy of Cornwall and the Dartmoor Pony is as much a part of Dartmoor as the tors and mires.

The Dartmoor Pony Society Moor Scheme, in which the Duchy of Cornwall, the Dartmoor Pony Society and the Dartmoor National Park have combined to re-establish the pure-bred pony on the Moor, continues this association.

This book, produced by the Dartmoor Pony Society, records the history of the breed since the mid-nineteenth century and is a story known to only a few.

With the co-operation of all concerned, the Dartmoor Pony will have a secure future on the Moor.

Charles

LIST OF SUBSCRIBERS

Diana Alford, East Week, South Zeal, Okehampton, Devon
Mrs M. R. Ashby, 4 Trafalgar Court, Uffculme, Devon
Miss June Axon, Eves Cottage, Magham Down, Hailsham, Sussex
Miss Denise Aylmer-Aylmore, 7 Thorne House, St Peters Street St Albans, Herts
J. A. Baldwin, 43 Woodlands Road, Baughurst, Basingstoke, Hants
Martin Ball, 59 Earls Court Square, London SW5
Mrs J. I. Barber, Wynhill Stud, Eye Kettleby Hall, Melton Mowbray, Leics
Mr and Mrs A. Barclay, Hopelaws Stud, Leetside Farm, Whitsome Duns, Berwickshire
Mrs Mary Basset, Broomells Farm, Beare Green, Nr Dorking, Surrey
Mrs J. J. Beale, Lurgecombe Farm, Ashburton, Devon
Anne Belam, Fore Stoke Farm, Holne, Newton Abbot, Devon
Gaynor Berridge, Deep Mill Farm, London Road, Great Missenden, Bucks
Mary Bienkowska, Mayfield, Whitestone, Exeter, Devon
Mrs Audrey Billiau, M. S. 342 Roadvale, Queensland, Australia
Joyce Blair, 11 Uphill Way, Hunston, Chichester, Sussex
Mrs Sandra Bliesner, Heise Road, Boonah, Queensland 4310, Australia
The Booth Family, Hurstock Lodge, Cardynham, Bodmin, Cornwall
Gillian Boyer, Byrdland Park Stud, Glenridge, Mountain Ridge Rd, Jimbooba, Queensland 4280, Australia
Mrs Trudy Bressow, M. S. 21 Kalbar, Queensland 4309, Australia
Miss Lizzie Briant, Park View Farm, Lower Assendon, Henley-on-Thames, Oxon
Mr T. L. Brown, Forge Cottage, 65 High Street, Warboys, Cambs
Mr and Mrs G. R. Bubear, Redwoods Pony Stud, Westwood Farm, Leigh, Surrey
Mrs I. N. Burrell, Breamish Stud, Ingram Mill, Powburn, Alnwick, Northumberland
Mrs G. Buss, 41 The Mount, Cranleigh, Surrey
Mrs John Caldwell, Kelk Cottage, Crosshouse, Kilmarnock
S. D. Cambage, Roecliffe Stud, Willowgarth, Roecliffe, Boroughbridge, Yorks
Mrs G. K. Cameron, Shorts Lane Cottage, Middlemoor, Tavistock, Devon
A. J. C. Campbell, Watersmeet Farm, Five Oak Green, Tonbridge, Kent
Mrs T. R. Campbell, Nimrods, Membury, Axminster, Devon
Mrs Julia Carne, Meldons, Winkleigh, Devon
Merwe Carstens, Wiedall 30, D-4715 Ascheberg, West Germany
Mrs Frances Carter, Millcroft Farm, Dawlish, Devon
B. R. Churchill, 5 Belvedere Avenue, Hockley, Essex
Mrs L. M. Colley, Micklehill Stud, Aldbrough, Hull, East Yorks
Miss N. Colley, Micklehill Stud, Aldbrough, Hull, East Yorks
Miss Ann Corbishley
Denise Cowan, 14 Oakford, Scots Gap, Morpeth, Northumberland
Mrs J. A. Crafer, Malthouse Woodchurch, Ashford, Kent
Mrs M. E. Danford, Fordans, Clare Court, Newbiggen Street, Thaxted, Essex

Sara Davey, Teragram, Doddiscombleigh, Exeter, Devon
A. V. L. Davies, Orchard Hill, Oakfordbridge, Tiverton, Devon
David Osmond Davis, Barley Corn, Vines Lane, Hildenborough, Tonbridge, Kent
Peter and Susan Deutermann, Single Tree Farm, Milledgeville, Georgia, U.S.A.
'DIBS', Pupums, North Lane, Norham, Berwick upon Tweed, Northumberland
Mrs A. Dixon, Scotland House, Ingoldsby, Nr Grantham, Lincs
Mrs G. F. Dod, Stonehouse Farm, Halstead, Sevenoaks, Kent
Mrs A. Doughty, The Old Rectory House, Wilby, Wellingborough, Northants
Mrs D. M. Dudley, Tudhay, Hawkchurch, Axminster, Devon
Mr and Mrs Dudley-Croker, Drybridge, South Zeal, Devon
P. and M. G. Earl, 'Bimbimbi', Bowning, New South Wales 2583, Australia
Mrs Irene Edvardsson, Raquaqen 10,76040 Vaeldo, Sweden
Mrs Gillian Ellis, Rosemount, Wroxhall, Ventnor, Isle of Wight
Rita Elwell, Wanneroo Farm, Timberscombe, Nr Minehead, Somerset
Mrs Sue Everest, Redroofs, 106 Station Road, Stanbridge, Leighton Buzzard, Beds
Mrs G. D. Faraday, Briars Stud, Top Farm, Streatley, Luton, Beds
Miss S. E. Ferguson, Timbercroft, Timber Lane, Wick, Pershore, Worcs
Mrs Jenny Franklin, 2 Foxham Lock, Foxham, Nr Chippenham, Wilts
Rosemary Freegard, The Bungalow, 53 Hawkstreet, Bromham, Chippenham, Wilts
Mrs June M. Freeman, Murrayton Exmoor Pony Stud, Reeves Green, Wareside, Herts
Suzanne Frewin, 'Welshes Cottage', Ashill, Cullompton, Devon
A. G. Fuller, Rossway Stud, Hargreaves Fold Farm (N), Lumb Rossendale, Lancs
Mrs Patricia A. Gibson, Little Yedbury Farm, Pennymoor, Tiverton, Devon
Mrs H. Goodwin, Blacknest Cottage, Brimpton Common, Reading, Berks
Mrs Joanna Van Gorkum, Coreley Farm, Coreley, Ludlow, Shropshire
Meg Gould, Boveycombe Stud, Nutcombe, Lustleigh, Devon
Mrs M. I. Gould, Boveycombe Stud, Nutcombe, Lustleigh, Devon
Tessa Gowan-Morgan, Ham Farm, Whitestone, Exeter, Devon
Miss Gemma Gower, 60 Rowan Road, Denvilles, Havant, Hants
Mr and Mrs I. M. Graham, Delf Field Farm, Triangle, Sowerby Ridge, West Yorks
Mrs. P. M. Grayson, Prunus Cottage, Crudwell, Malmesbury, Wilts
Mrs M. E. Grayston, Green-Acres, Warleggan, Bodmin, Cornwall
Mrs. J. I. L. Green, Broxbridge Cottage, Exbridge, Dulverton, Somerset
Mrs Susan Green, 9 Alliance Street, Baxenden, Accrington, Lancs
Charlotte Emma Harrison, Lower Stunts Green Farm, Stunts Green, Herstmonceux, East Sussex
Penny Harrison, Lower Stunts Green Farm, Stunts Green, Herstmonceux, East Sussex

Mrs P. Harrison, Lower Stunts Green Farm, Stunts Green, Herstmonceux, East Sussex

Mrs P. A. Harrison, The Glebe House, Bucknowle, Wareham, Dorset

Mrs Ann Hart, Amber's Oast, Biddenden, Ashford, Kent

Mrs J. Healey, Orchard Cottage, Wimble Hill, Crondall, Farnham, Surrey

Patricia C. M. Heath-Caldwell, The Pound House, Cattistock, Dorchester, Dorset

Mrs J. Hibbert, 'Cataln Stud', The Stables, Barrington Hall, Hatfield Broad-Oak, Bishops Stortford

David Hinde, 'Pumphill Stud', Becca Farm, Aberford, Leeds

Linda Hingley, Wits End, 33 North View Road, Brixham, Devon

Mrs A. E. Hobby, 36 Ashcroft, Chard, Somerset

Heidi Hobson, 18 Clifford Street, Chudleigh, Newton Abbot, Devon

Betty Holman, 62 Comeytrowe Lane, Taunton, Somerset

Mark Holman, Great Widefield, Inwardleigh, Okehampton, Devon

Peter Holman, Bude Farm, Sticklepath, Okehampton, Devon

Mr and Mrs K. Hopkinson, 105 Booth Street, Tottington, Nr Bury, Lancs

Mrs Caroline House, Bincombe, Over Stowey, Bridgwater, Somerset

Mrs J. Hull, Appleacre, The Hale, Wendover, Bucks

Mrs Hunter, Cross Hills, Sutton under Whitestone Cliffe, Thirsk, North Yorks

Mr and Mrs D. W. Hutchinson, 60 Gorse Lane, Oadby, Leics

A. R. J. Van Ingen, Broenenbergweg 4, 7256 KK, Keyenborg, Netherlands

Victoria M Jackson, Little Knowle, Lustleigh, Newton Abbot, Devon

Mrs A. Jones, Lower Hisley, Lustleigh, Devon

Mrs Scilla Jones, The Ranch, Two Gates Lane, Bellingdon, Chesham, Bucks

Peter Keeble, Spring Vale, Curdridge, Hants

Mrs Margaret A. Kidman, Romans Farm, Rettendon Common, Chelmsford, Essex

Mary Korn, Dinmor, Penmon, Beaumaris, Anglesey

Eva Kornhall, Nysatra Vagen 5, 190 63 Orsundsbro, Sweden

Tansy Kucharsky, North View, Wolds Lane, Wolvey, Warks

Rita Langton, 2 Orchard Drive, Wooburn Green, Bucks

Sybil and David Lee, Waltroyd Farm, Waltroyd, Halifax, West Yorks

Mrs C Lightfoot, Hampton Farm, Hampton Lane, Brook, Ashford, Kent

Mrs G. N. Little, The Lane, Guilsfield, Welshpool, Powys

Mr D. K. S. and Mrs E. D. Locke, Niases, Jacobstowe, Okehampton, Devon

Albert H. W. Lockefeer, Panel Judge, Netherlands Dartmoor Pony STDB, Smedekensbrugge 18, 4527 G. E. Aardenburg, Holland

Dr. W. L. A. Lockefeer, Hon Chairman Netherland Dartmoor Pony STDB, Domaine du Moulin d'Olenne, 76 Rue De France, 5582 Felenne, Belgium

Miss Pat Lyne, Coombe Cottage, Presteigne, Herefordshire

Mrs D. M. Marshall, Pear Tree Farm, The Boyle, Barwick-In-Elmet, Nr Leeds

Mrs W. Martens-Joannes, Loostraat 10, 5641 J S Eindhoven, Holland

Gina Martlew, Tamborough Glen Road, Oadby, Leics

Mrs Maria McCulloch, Gilchristland, Closeburn, Thornhill, Dumfries

Marilyn McGregor, Glynton Park Dartmoor Pony Stud, Lot 63 Glynton Road, Jimboomba, 4280, Australia

F. H. McMillan, Trianon, Stocklinch, Ilminster, Somerset

Rosamond Mills, The Dower House, Upton Grey, Basingstoke, Hants

Bina Milton, Ddol Bach, Afonwen, Mold, Clwyd

Mrs J. Montgomery, White Willows, Yelverton, Devon

Tamzin Morphy, Bracken Cottage, Hartgrove, Shaftesbury, Dorset

Miss J Muggleton, 35 Thorney Lane South, Iver, Bucks

James and Anne Munton, Westgate Lodge, Manor Street, Ruskington, Lincs

Necta Stud, Little Walstead Farm, Lindfield, Haywards Heath, Sussex

Mrs Louise Nilsson, Lindvagen 4, 76040 Vaddo, Sweden

The Oakfield Dartmoor Pony Stud, Lower Bitchfield, Grantham, Lincs

Mrs D. W. J. O'Brien, Hills Place Farm, Blackboys, Uckfield, East Sussex

Jeanette Osborne, M. S. 342, Roadvale, Queensland, Australia

Phoebe Palmes, South Hooe Farm, Bere Alston, Yelverton, Devon

Michelle Parkes, 18 Highfield Road, West Cheshunt, Herts

Mrs V. P. Parkinson, Stourton Leaze Farm, Holnest, Sherborne, Dorset

Miss J. E. Paterson, Redlands Farm, Stanwick, Wellingborough, Northants

Marilyn Pawson, 2 Sandpit Cottages, Ripe, Nr Lewes, East Sussex

Mrs Sarah Peters, 20 Knappe Close, Henley-on-Thames, Oxon

Elizabeth Polling, Cross Farm, Bovingdon, Herts

Guus Pynenburg, Driehoven 21, 5076 B A Haaren, Holland

Mrs Sheila De Quincey, Ca'n Mestransa, Pollensa, Mallorca, Balleares, Spain

Jan C. Rabuszko, St Albans, Herts

Miss S. M. Raphael, Maunby Gates, Maunby, Thirsk, N. Yorks

Miss Judith Redburn, Breach Farm, Limbym Hall, Swannington, Leics

Pam Harvey Richards, 2 Home Farm Cottages, Bramshaw, Hants

Miss A. C. Rigby, 7 The Dykes, Yealand Conyers, Carnforth, Lancs

Mr and Mrs R. Rigby, Monarchs Meadow, Hindley Road, Daisy Hill

Mrs Diny Ring, 1 Moffett Street, Kalbar, Queensland 4309, Australia

Mrs A. M. Robathan, Tredower, Goonhavern, Truro, Cornwall

Julie Helen Roberts, Greenbanks, New School Road, Histon, Cambs

Miss P. Roberts, Lower Hisley, Lustleigh, Devon

Mrs M. Robertson, Nash Farm, Marshwood, Bridport, Dorset

Mr and Mrs John Robinson, Rull Cottage, Ashill, Cullompton, Devon

Mrs W. E. Robinson, Hackpen Barton, Ashill, Cullompton, Devon

Mrs J. C. Rodd, Parlby Arms Cottage, Huckworthy Bridge, Yelverton, Devon

Mr and Mrs D. B. Rodi, Hill House, Heather Way, Chobham, Surrey

Mr J. S. Roles, 37 Manor Farm Road, Tredington, Shipston-on-Stour, Warks

Alexander Rollo Esq, Kilbees Stud, Lovel Road, Winkfield, Windsor,

Mrs V. C. Sainty, 63 Park Walk, London, SW10

Beatrice Sandbach, Leesden, Beneden, Kent

Margaret Saunders, Whinberry Dartmoor, Millfield Cottage, Long Marston, York

Tamarin Sauver, Kerourio, 56400 Brech, France

Sequin Arabian and Pony Stud, Oakdene, High Road, Great Finborough, Stowmarket, Suffolk

Miss Pep Sherman, Alston Farm, Ovington, Thetford, Norfolk

Mr W. G. Shillibeer, Bellever House, Postbridge, Devon

Mrs A. A. Silvester, The Oast, Stunts Green, Herstmonceux, East Sussex

Natasha Silvester, The Oast, Stunts Green, Herstmonceux, East Sussex

Karen Yvonne Sinclair, Greenfields Farm, St Martins, Oswestry, Shropshire

Christina Sjölander-Johansson, Balleboväg 5, 51700 Ballebygd, Sweden

Janice Skippings, 103 Spencer Road, Emsworth, Hants

Mrs S. A. Squires, Cotswood, Stockend Edge, Stroud, Glos

Mrs V. A. Stace, Brynewen Uchaf, Llanboidy Road, Whitland, Dyfed

Miss Lena Stenquist, Alusjogard, 76124, Norrtalije, Sweden

Mrs M. Stevenson-Young, The Leal Stud, Wylam, Northumberland

Mrs Hedy Sumption, Craddock Cleve, Cullompton, Devon

N. P. Sutherland, Whitestones Farm, Holden, Bolton By Bowland, Clitheroe, Lancs

Jean and Michael Syddall, The Old Rectory, Lower Bitchfield, Grantham, Lincs

David Sykes, The Red House, Froxfield, Petersfield, Hants

Vice Admiral Sir Fitzroy Talbot, Wooton Fitzpaine Manor, Bridport, Dorset

Lucinda Talbot, Meadoway, Etling Green, East Dereham, Norfolk

Mr and Mrs Paul Taylor, Broad Carr Farm, Langfield, Todmorden, Lancs

Mrs R. M. Taylor, 17 Adelaide Square, Windsor, Berks

Mr and Mrs Rupert Thornely-Taylor, Stone House, Oldlands Hall, Heron's Ghyll, Uckfield, East Sussex

Caroline Tiley, Quaives Cottage, Wickham Lane, Ickham, Kent

Susan Tolfree, The Manor House, St James, Shaftesbury, Dorset

Miss Marygold Turner, Podkin Farm, High Halden, Ashford, Kent

Mrs Nicola Tyler, Springwater Stud, North Yorkshire

Peter Upton, The Old Vicarage, Clun, Shropshire

Sonia Watkins, Ridgewood, Clayhidon, Cullompton, Devon

Judith M Watson, Marsida, High Street, Marden, Tonbridge, Kent

Mr Clarence White, Lambe Farm, South Zeal, Okehampton, Devon

Miss Eileen White, 3 Lynton Gardens, Fareham, Hants

Judith E. A. Williams, Beaux Aires Cottage, Yelsted, Stockbury, Kent

Mrs E. C. M. Williamson, Weston Maror, Corscombe, Dorset

Chris Woodward, Holyrood Farm, Balne, Goole, North Humberside

Mrs Roma E. Wright-Smith, Solway Cottage, Main Street, Upton, Newark, Notts

CONTENTS

Preface:

THE DARTMOOR PONY AND ITS ORIGINS

This is the story of the Dartmoor pony: of its origins, known or surmised; its evolution; what it is today; with, perhaps, some tentative forecast of its prospects; the story of a tough, intelligent, strong-willed but friendly and amenable little animal, small of its species but large of heart, for many centuries the servant, companion and friend of Man.

The Dartmoor, like all other true moorland stock, is the product of an exceptionally tough environment, thus offering a striking demonstration of the force of one of Nature's inexorable laws: that the inhabitant must adapt to its habitat; with outside help if it is lucky (or exceptionally skilful, as in the case of Man), otherwise without. It adapts and survives. Or it goes under.

The Dartmoor pony has not gone under. Far from it. Nor, in general, has it received all that much help from Man. When things are really rough on the moor, it might be brought in or given a little extra to eat, but usually it fends for itself, just as it always has done; a bona fide moorland pony, out in all weathers and the year round; not just surviving but thriving in any but the bleakest conditions.

In all those centuries the moor has been, as it were, at work on the pony: moulding its sturdy, independent character, building up its physique, even determining its size. In addition to this process of natural selection must be considered the other aspect of heredity, man-sponsored selective breeding. The results of the latter are more quickly apparent, but it has been the slow, unrelenting, long-term pressure and influence of its surroundings that have made the Dartmoor pony what it is. It is fitting, therefore, that its story should start with a brief survey of this upland from which it has acquired a great deal more than simply a name.

Saddle Tor

1 THE LAST WILDERNESS

Every story, like a deep-sea voyage, should take its departure from a recognizable and fixed point. For that of the Dartmoor Pony the natural choice must be the land from which it takes its name – and which has moulded much of its character. Dartmoor is, in several senses, the central feature of the county of Devon, occupying no less than one-seventh of the total area of the county. It is called 'Dartmoor', but in addition to fathering the two branches of the River Dart it is also the source of every other stream of consequence apart from the Exe, Tamar and Torridge.

The reason for this is not far to seek. Dartmoor is well placed to intercept the rain-clouds sweeping in on the prevailing south-westerly winds. It certainly rains on the moor. Princetown, for instance, receives an annual average of 82 inches compared with the 30 inches falling on the Exe estuary little more than 20 miles away. Dartmoor is certainly beautiful, but equally certainly it is wet.

Dartmoor is not only wet, but wild; to the extent of acquiring the title of 'The Last Wilderness in the South'. And so it is, by any reckoning. There may be *wider* open spaces in the south (Dartmoor ranks eighth for sheer size among the National Parks), but it would be hard to find any *wilder*. The stranger would do well to bear this in mind. Here is no tame, man-made, man-ruled, open recreation space on which the honest burgesses and their broods may disport themselves as they might in Hyde Park or St James's, safe within touching distance of a public road; nor is it territory on which the tenderfoot or the townsman may strike out on a day's hike; not, that is, with any certainty of returning.

The moor might seem to be smiling, but for how long? That sunny afternoon with those enchanting vistas all the way across to Bodmin 30 miles away can, in the batting of an eye, transform itself into a mist-shrouded twilight with visibility down to 10 feet; a situation when even the moorman must have his wits about him, carefully noting exactly where he is (in an apparently uniformly blank landscape) and which way to turn; schooled to detect and skirt the bog on the crown of the tor as easily as he can pick his way across the equally lethal mire in the valley below.[1]

Indeed, this is no fable to scare the children into obedience, but based on unhappy fact. Why otherwise the Dartmoor Rescue Teams? The moor is by no means a hostile place, but it *is* wild, not to be treated otherwise than with respect; even by modern Man. Here Nature rules and that is all there is to it.

Ponies, however, are close to nature; none closer than the Dartmoor. They find no great difficulty in coming to terms, asking in any case for no more than the three basics: food, shelter and water. Given these, they can – and do – put up with hardship that would daunt their more pampered cousins in their heated stables. They receive all three; not lavishly, but enough to satisfy those born and bred to frugality. The grass, for a start, is not the lush, cultivated, fertilized stuff grown with such care lower down, but simply – grass; rough, but of a species that calls for no husbandry at all. Then there are the evergreen shrubs: the heather and the furze. Unappetizing? In point of fact they are highly nutritious. Added to that, they are there for the asking all the year round. Even in deep snow – apart from heavy drifts –

---

[1] *Not that every moorman knew his way everywhere, even near home. A former Master of the Dartmoor Hunt was reputed to be one of the few able to cross Fox Tor Mires. And, if you went in, the odds were you stayed in.*

there will always be some part of them showing the ponies where to dig for their dinners. And water? At least there's no need to worry about that on the moor.

The ponies have also learnt to make the best use of the land – and there is plenty of it – available to them. In winter they will mostly be found down in the valleys, which combine the best grass and such shelter as there is. As the weather becomes warmer they will work their way uphill, one incentive being to escape from the flies that swarm in bracken country. This bracken is one of the hazards that they have learnt to avoid. When dried it makes excellent bedding, but it is poisonous if eaten in quantity, which ponies might be impelled to do if really hungry. Also it tends to spread and smother the grass. On it the farmers wage an endless war; cutting it if they can reach it with a powered mower. Bracken is not an easy growth to subdue, for it laughs at the business known locally as 'swaling', another name for the controlled burning on the heathland, the accent being on the control. Swaling burns the grass but not the bracken. Good fun for the spectators, of course, but not popular with the Fire Brigade. One can understand their point of view.

Thus the pony out on the moor ekes out its existence, as it has done for many centuries. There are, of course, Dartmoor ponies that have never been within a hundred miles of Postbridge (reputedly the very centre of Dartmoor). At this juncture all that is required is to note that a 'pony on Dartmoor' is not necessarily of the Dartmoor breed; nor is a pure-bred Dartmoor (in the sense of either being in the stud book or eligible for inclusion) necessarily to be found on the moor. In the meanwhile, however, let us confine our interest to the actual terrain.

Just as the moor is often shrouded in mist, so is its early history, although recent discoveries have considerably added to our knowledge; and, it seems, overturned a number of previously accepted beliefs. It therefore behoves the outsider to speak warily.

There is no firm evidence that there were ponies there before the Romans came. Indeed, it is not yet clear how far the Romans themselves penetrated. Until recently it was thought that Exeter, at the end of the Fosse Way, was a frontier town. Now it seems there are Roman sites on the Dart and Plym, even in Cornwall.

By the time of the Saxon Invasion (c.660–c.710) we are on firmer ground, for there was a monastery at Exeter by 680. Perhaps 'invasion' gives a false impression. It is more accurate to say that, around then, the Saxons were being driven westwards across the country by the real invaders from Scandinavia. When they found themselves on the shores of the Bristol Channel, some bore right to find safety in the Welsh mountains, others left

to end up on and around Dartmoor. There was some fighting with indigenous tribes; as there usually is when tribes meet, then as now; but to call what was, in reality, a flight an 'invasion' hardly accords with the facts. The Saxons migrated. And, when they found both space and safety, they settled. Timid, but realistic.

And, of course, they brought their livestock with them. It would be pleasant to think of these ancestors of our Dartmoor Ponies as the descendants of the little horses that had hauled the chariots of the Iceni six hundred years before, when those valiant but foolhardy, queen-led warriors tried conclusions with the Legions of Rome.[2] There is, however, no firm basis for this belief.

This, then, seems a good starting point for studying the long connection between the pony and the moor which gave it its name – and much else besides. Its name? Here, right away, lies danger for the unwary. 'Dartmoor' as a place-name clearly meant nothing to the compilers of the Domesday Book, for it does not merit even a passing reference. Indeed, we have to wait a further century for its official debut; on an Exchequer Pipe Roll dated 1181. By 1239, however, it has arrived, for in that year Henry III included 'the Forest of Dartmoor' in land granted to his brother Richard[3] on creating him Earl of Cornwall. This land lay entirely in the parish of Lydford and comprised about 56 000 acres of what we should nowadays call 'the high moor', being largely about 1500 feet above sea-level.

In 1337 it had apparently reverted to direct royal ownership, for Edward III made it over once more, only this time permanently, to Edward the Black Prince, the first Duke of Cornwall (indeed, the first duke to be made in all England). This Duchy, including the Forest of Dartmoor, was to remain the estate of the heir apparent, only reverting to the Crown temporarily during any period when no such direct, male heir existed (as, for instance, during the reign of George VI, when

---

[2] *To discover, not for the first time in history nor for the last, that cavalry, however glamorous, is no match for properly handled, well-armed, disciplined infantry. Pace, inter alia, Napoleon himself at Waterloo.*

[3] *Not to be confused with his uncle Coeur de Lion, albeit the new earl also had a liking for overseas adventures, ending up as (of all things) King of the Romans, though it should be remembered that in those days royalty was above mere nationality – so far as the latter existed at all. Perhaps it is on this account that he has left no lasting mark on the history of Dartmoor – or anywhere else in the realm. Nevertheless, the event is of interest, for it marks the first link between what became the Duchy of Cornwall and the moor: a link that has lasted – and been strengthened – over seven centuries to this day.*

Princess Elizabeth was heir presumptive and therefore ineligible to be Duchess of Cornwall in her own right). Another curiosity: although the older title of Prince of Wales must be specifically conferred on each individual, that of Duke of Cornwall is by inheritance. At all events, there was the Forest of Dartmoor in 1337 safely in the strong hands of the greatest captain of the age. It would be pleasant to think that its future was well assured. Such, however, was not the case.

Down the ages, ever since King David's deplorable snatching of Naboth's Vinyard, owners of land have cast covetous eyes across their boundaries. Despite the fact that the exact extent of Dartmoor Forest was carefully laid down by the Sheriff's Perambulation of 1240, those around the edges of Dartmoor, or holding tenancies within it, have lost no opportunity to grab what they could; sometimes with a show of legality, sometimes not even that. Nor has the Duchy itself entirely refrained from claiming common land clearly outside its boundaries as being 'in the King's Forest'. The picture is confused, to say the least. Those eager to discover who filched which land from whom should consult such scholarly works as *Dartmoor, a New Study* (edited by Crispin Gill)[4] or Eric Hemery's magisterial *High Dartmoor*[5]. With their help he will not only be able to disentangle the subtleties of Venville (as adjusted by Foldage) and to differentiate between Incountry and Intakes, but can follow in authentic detail the progressive erosion of 'The Moor' to become private property. Let a single statistic suffice here. In 1898 it was stated in a parliamentary reply that 'over 15 000 acres of Dartmoor' had been enclosed *since 1820*. Which, when set against the original 56 000 acres mentioned and discounting any similar depredations before the date quoted, is what countrymen would call 'a tidy slice'.

Nor was enclosure the only agency at work. In 1873 the town council of Okehampton wrote to the War Office actually suggesting that northern Dartmoor would be an excellent place for the forthcoming summer manoeuvres. That was in January. In August, 12 000 men and 2100 horses got off several special trains at Exeter, sorted themselves out and then marched across the moor to Roborough Down; 34 miles as the crow flies, a great deal further as the infantryman plods. They came, they saw and, even though that year rain stopped play, they liked. It was true that the army had at first favoured ground a longish way from Okehampton, but the seed had been sown (or, as the War Office

had put in its first acknowledgement, they had 'taken note'). The word went round Whitehall that the moor had plenty of wide open spaces and, even if the rainfall might not be such good preparation for the burning sands of the Sudanese desert or for the High Veldt, you could not have everything. The important thing was that there they could march, manoeuvre, even fire their guns to their hearts' content. And that Postern Gate had been opened from within: first by the councillors of Okehampton, later by those willing (or wishing) to sell otherwise unproductive land, as instanced by sales of Okehampton Park (3000 acres) and Willsworthy Manor (3200 acres). The point here is that the War Office did not *take* the land; it acquired possession from willing sellers. Indeed, on one occasion when more Draconian methods were mooted sharp opposition was at once evident. The Military Manouevres Bill was laid before Parliament in 1901. This proposed to grant power to the soldiers to take over very large areas for twenty days a year, at a fortnight's notice and with no allowance for discussion. During this occupation – a most appropriate word – even the normal occupiers would be kept out. If the purpose was to test the heat of the opposition – and not only on the moor – then it certainly succeeded. The bill was dropped. Owners and other interested parties were willing to be seduced, provided the price was right; but no more than that.

By then, powerful voices were raised in defence of Dartmoor: as a site of ancient remains, as a place of beauty and recreation. The Dartmoor Preservation Association was formed in 1883 to protect it against the triple threat of army training, destruction of antiquities and further enclosure. It is sufficient here to note that this centenarian thrives, with spokesmen neither to be cowed by minor officials quoting vaguely defined authority, nor to be placated by specious promises.

Oddly enough, the First World War brought little increase of army activity. It was very different in the Second, with ranges for both small arms and artillery, an airfield at the north end of Roborough Down, even an area for training for the war in the Far East. All very well when the country was fighting for its life, but 1945 saw little eagerness to hand anything back. The Government's announcement in the autumn of 1946 that it was holding onto 72 000 acres (from three-quarters of which the public would be kept out) was greeted with such an outcry that this was eventually pared down to around 30 000; with which the elected representatives of the people have had to make do.

For some while – since the late-nineteenth century – there had been talk of turning Dartmoor and other open spaces into 'national parks'. Finally, in 1949, this came about with the

---

[4] *David & Charles, first published 1970, third impression 1983*
[5] *Hale, 1983*

National Parks Act. This declared that certain areas in England and Wales were 'marked out for special care (so as to) conserve and enhance their natural beauty and to promote their enjoyment by the public'; purposes at which the moor's most ardent lovers and conservers could hardly cavil. And, no more than two years later, 'Dartmoor National Park' came officially into being.

Another benefit came along as part of this package; welcome, no doubt, to tidy-minded folk. At long last the actual extent of the moor was laid down officially. The excellent map at the front of *Dartmoor, A New Study* shows it as roughly circular and running close up to (though not including) Okehampton in the north, Bovey Tracey in the east, Ivybridge in the south and Tavistock in the west. This takes in Moretonhampstead, which can hardly be called moorland, but painted as it is with a good broad brush it gives an excellent general definition of what before had been no more precise than 'the West Country' itself. This area comprises some 365 square miles (233 600 acres) and for a start it is interesting to compare this with Earl Richard's 'Forest' of 56 000 (now more or less forming the northern quarter of the park) and, of course, the 30 000-odd acres in the hands of the Ministry of Defence.

So is the moor safe at last? Protected by Act of Parliament, delineated, given its purpose of affording Us-the-People enjoyment. Perhaps. But what Parliament has done Parliament can, with equal ease, undo. The price of preserving this, our last wilderness in the south, and with it the natural home of its fauna would therefore seem to be, in the words of John Philpot Curran, no less than 'eternal vigilance'.

Haytor

2 FOREBEARS

*'The history of the Dartmoor pony,
prior to a century ago, must
be largely one of conjecture.'*

So wrote Sylvia Calmady-Hamlyn in 1953, after twenty-six years as Honorary Secretary of the Dartmoor Pony Society and a great many more as herself a breeder of ponies of exceptional quality. She gave as her reason for this sweeping statement that this period covered her own personal knowledge and the evidence of reliable witnesses known personally to her. This much she knew or accepted; the rest was guesswork.

A cautious approach, to be sure. But over-cautious? We should remember that there was no National Pony Society in 1853, nor anything like it. Hence records, if any, were compiled by individual breeders, not necessarily at the time of actual foaling. Is it not prudent, then, to cast doubt on the claims of our forebears for stock outside the General Stud Book? On the other hand, we can gather a pretty clear *general* picture of the pony on the moor in the many centuries leading up to the appearance of the Dartmoor section in Volume V of the *Stud Book of the NPS* in 1899.

Aficionados of the horse must, however, reconcile themselves to the sad fact that the noble animal *(Equus caballus)* is not, strictly speaking, indigenous to the British Isles. It was imported; no one can say confidently when, but a long time BC. At all events, it was well established by the time Julius Caesar stepped ashore at Pegwell Bay, for he mentions it most favourably in his *Commentaries*. Unfortunately, this normally meticulous observer neglects to record its height, although it is evident that it was small (probably under 13 hh), nimble and wiry.

Caesar, the infantry-soldier *par excellence*, may have approved of these sturdy little beasts (while dealing briskly with their owners), but later, more cavalry-minded, military men were less enthusiastic. They demanded weight-carriers, remaining unconvinced by such demonstrations of infantry firepower as Crecy

and Agincourt. Henry VIII viewed 'little horses and nags of small stature' with disgust, setting about their supplanting with his usual heavy-handed vigour. In 1535 he curtly directed all occupiers of land 'to the extent of one mile in compass' to keep 'two mares apt and able to bear foals of the altitude or height of 13 handfuls at least upon pain of 40s'. Moreover, there was a further 40-shilling fine lying in wait for those 'who shall willingly suffer any of the said mares to be covered or kept with any stoned horse under the stature of 14 handfuls'.

Worse was to come. Only six years later these rules were stretched to apply to all horses in no fewer than twenty-six shires and other breeding areas across the country. The war against 'the little horses' was on. Authority was, as it might have known, fighting a losing battle, the end-product being almost exactly contrary to what this bossy bit of legislation had intended. The Act did indeed prescribe fining the offenders and putting down the illicit progeny – always assuming that the former could be identified and the latter caught. Dartmoor – only one of the areas to be affected – was even wilder then than it is today. The King's writ, when it ran at all, did not excite a great deal of awe. Likewise, there must have been many occasions when the court's officials stood in impotent fury as they saw their quarry high-tailing it to some fastness even less accessible; there incidentally, to preserve the purity of their breed.

For all that, authority did not give up. An Act of 1740 proclaimed two intentions (a bad start). It sought to eliminate races between 'poneys', by fixing the lowest match-prize at £50 (except at Newmarket and Black Hambleton) and the weights to be carried at 10 stone for five-year-olds, 11 stone for six-year-olds and 12 stone for seven-year-olds. These restrictions, the Act

Opposite page: **Hisley Pedlar (1970) at Langfield**

proclaimed, would 'not only prevent the encouragement of a vile and paltry breed of horses, but likewise would remove all temptation from the lower class of people who constantly attend these races, to the great loss of time and hindrance of labour, and whose behaviour still calls for stricter regulations to curb their licentiousness and correct their manners'. It is pleasant to record that the licentiousness and manners of racegoers, high and low, remained exactly as they were before; very much like everyone else's.

Such was the strength of what would today be called the anti-pony lobby. However, during the latter part of the eighteenth century and continuing throughout the nineteenth new demands were making themselves felt; not all at once, but gradually over more than a century. First came the Industrial Revolution (very approximately 1750-1850). This, paradoxically, called for horsepower in its literal sense. Newcomen's steam-pump and later George Stephenson's similar but improved machine made deep mining possible by pumping out the water. The output could now meet the increased demand, provided the coal could be brought from the coal-face to the surface. The answer to that was the pit pony.

Sport followed fast on the heels of industry. In 1869 the 10th Hussars returned from service in India, bringing polo with them. And with it a problem for horse breeders. For two centuries these had bent all their energies to increasing the height of the racehorse,[1] now they were invited to produce, in addition, a quality animal, able to carry, say, 13 stone through a period of an arduous game and yet be under the prescribed height. Writing in the last year of the century when the limit had been raised from 11.3 to 14.2 hh, Sir Walter Gilbey saw no quick, easy answer, pointing out a number of practical snags. First, the impossibility of breeding to an ordered height, neither less nor more; second, that a 'worn-out' polo mare sent to stud after an active career of four or five seasons was no answer, in view of the well-known fact that a big mare threw a big foal, even to a small horse. On the other hand, he believed, with skill and care it could be done. His suggestion ran on the following lines: a sire for the foundation stock to be a small and compact Thoroughbred or Arab; the dam for such foundation to be from 'the best of our Forest or Moorland Ponies'. Given a start on these lines, he recommended the following as antidotes to undue increase in height: in the individual pony, as free and natural a life as the climate permitted; in the breed, further infusions of forest or moorland blood when necessary.

The foregoing, culled from Sir Walter's *Ponies Past and Present,*[2] thus adds a demand for quality (for polo, to be sure, but with spin-off for riding and driving) to the previous acceptance of mere quantity (for which there would always be some kind of market). So, while the Empire as a vast whole was celebrating the Great White Queen's jubilees, a few devotees were taking in hand the matter of 'the small horse'.

The following milestones mark their way — and that of their successors:

1869 Polo introduced from Manipur via India
1874 Hurlingham Club draws up rules for the game, thus highlighting its growing importance
1893 National Pony Society formed (a retrospective date). Then and for some years it continued to be known as 'the Polo Pony Society' (or variant), but this is as good a date as any for taking departure
1899 Mountain and Moorland sections opened in *Polo Pony Stud Book*
1925 Dartmoor Pony Society formed

Thus, roughly coinciding with the century referred to by Sylvia Calmady-Hamlyn, the quality (and hence the status) of the Dartmoor Pony steadily improved; largely thanks to the realization by breeders that this sturdy little animal could not only contribute to the creation of ponies for polo but was also something very desirable in its own right. No longer was it to be seen as just another native running wild on the moor, picturesque no doubt but not to be taken very seriously. Now it was a recognized and properly recorded breed; a breed, moreover, by no means casting aside the qualities of hardiness and intelligence which had enabled it to survive (and thrive) over the centuries, but now also enjoying the benefits of careful, selective breeding under expert and dedicated direction. All this, together with judicious out-crossing, soon demonstrated the very real improvement that could be achieved. In short, the 'pony on Dartmoor' was yielding place to the Dartmoor Pony.

---

[1] *Estimated by Admiral Rous in 1860 to be at the rate of 1 inch every twenty-five years.*

[2] *Vinson & Co (London, 1900).*

Princetown

U'86

3 INTO SOCIETY

Of all the interconnected events listed towards the end of the previous chapter, two in particular signally contributed to the translation of the Dartmoor from, in effect, poor relation to full member of the pony branch of the horse family. These were the formation of a nationwide pony society and the resultant introduction of registration for mountain and moorland ponies as such.

The end of the long Victorian Age was indeed a time of change. It saw the virtual completion of the transition from horse-dominated transport to steam and the internal-combustion engine. Not that this spelt curtains for the horse. Far from it. Indeed, now that it had, as it were, regained its amateur status, it was admired, cherished and esteemed as highly as ever. In its continuing and expanding role as a beautiful and useful partner for Man it was, and still is, irreplaceable; a continuing role, but with a shift of emphasis; no longer merely transport for Man and his goods, but an integral part of Man's amusement, recreation and sport, with status and organization to match.[1]

The National Pony Society was founded in 1893. At least, so it is said, though there is some confusion of identity between it and the Polo Pony Society. Polo had come to England with the 10th Hussars in 1869. At all events, the society that started in 1893 can claim to be the foundation stock of the present-day NPS. Things moved slowly in those days; slowly maybe, but with an unrelenting momentum.

The NPS may have been slow to start, but once assembled it got to work with commendable speed. Before following these activities, however, it would be wise to survey for a moment the situation as it then was and seen to be by people at the time. For instance, are we referring to this new society by its correct title; that is, the name by which it was currently known, officially or otherwise? Maybe the answer to this and other matters – or, at any rate, some answers – can be interpreted from the early volumes of the Stud Book, starting with Number One issued in 1894. First its list of president, vice-president and members of council. Impressive, to be sure, and no doubt engendering gratifying touching of forelocks among the generality. Today, on the other hand, while admiring their enterprise we are not obliged to accept their utterances (under 'Resolutions and Rules', pp. 9-10) as *ex* any kind of *cathedra*, for these are some way from completeness or – dare one add – consistency.

The resolutions lead off, as they should, with a purpose: 'that a Society be formed for the improvement and encouragement of the breeding of high-class Riding Ponies.' So far, excellent; first things first. But what then? Disappointingly, an omission, then a contradiction. After such a start, should not resolution two have laid down the society's title? Nor is this mere pedantry, for what a thing is called is what it is – or should be. Here it is called – nothing. Worse than nothing, if we are to pay any regard to resolution one, for in the same paragraph it is further resolved that ' … a stud book be formed … and that it be called 'The Polo Pony Stud Book.' All of which leads the reader to enquire what exactly this society is about. Riding ponies in general as in the first resolution, or polo ponies in particular, as slips out in the name of the new stud book?

---

[1] *Modern sport being, as we know, strictly business (though it has not yet sunk quite so low as to become an industry), the wheel has come full circle. We write, however, of an earlier, less Midas-minded age.*

There is much to support an uneasy feeling that polo is still strongly entrenched, if not enthroned. The Introduction to Volume I of the Polo Pony Stud Book refers unblushingly to the Polo Pony Society, as though it and it alone were the parent of what it introduces; likewise the Preface, by President Lord Harrington. Only once around this area does one hear a whisper of actual support for the broader implication of that original first resolution, when council member John Hill, having noted (with irony?) that the publication is 'dedicated to polo ponies', makes the point that it has, in fact, been 'formed for the registration of all ponies suitable for *riding*'. And the italics are his.

A voice in the wilderness? For the time being, it would seem so, for the *Resolutions and Rules* are reprinted verbatim in Volumes II–IV. Well, not quite, for in Volume IV we find that the resolution about the stud book has been slightly amended, so that it now reads ' … and that it (sic) be called the Polo Pony *Society*'.

So where are we? In the dark, so far as discovering anything precise on 'the society' from the stud book, but in a slow dawn with regard to the book and its contents. The light increases, but we have to wait a further seventeen years for full NPS sunrise. The sequence was as follows.

The first four volumes did not evoke any wild response from the world of the native pony. Indeed, writing to Miss Calmady-Hamlyn many years later,[2] the then Secretary of the National Pony Society declared that 'he could trace no entries of Mountain and Moorland stock in Volumes I–IV'. Perhaps not as such, but recent research suggests that this sweeping statement requires some qualification. Nevertheless, it is entirely clear that the editing committee was disappointed at the lack of interest on this side; especially as it was well aware of the mutual benefit of closer and better informed contact. It quickly – that is, within a few years – took steps to put matters right.

The results of their efforts can be found in Volume V, which claimed 'to mark a new phase in the scheme of registration'. It did indeed, for it introduced 'separate Divisions for the various native British Breeds', adding that 'its object was two-fold: first, to save from extinction and endeavour to improve the native breeds; second, to establish a stock of approved mares easily accessible to the breeders of Polo Ponies'. We should note the order: first, ponies in their own right, for riding, driving and so on; second, ponies as breeding stock, a recognition that allows the mountain and moorland world to overlook the slightly

[2] *Letter dated 14 January 1957.*

Molly Croft's May Queen VII, Coronet II (grey) and foal at Jurston

patronizing reference to saving them from extinction. The 'improvement' is another matter. There is no gainsaying the fact that native ponies have been greatly improved by judicious out-crossing over these last ninety years. Improved, but by no means spoilt.

The native pony was coming into its own, but it took a long time, as such affairs tend to. But one by one the bastions fell. We can trace the process on the title pages of successive stud books. Volumes I–IV were simply entitled *The Polo Pony Stud Book* (no wonder they got no takers from mountain and moorland). Volumes V and VI added (in smaller and plainer type) a subtitle running ' … and of British Ponies of the Mountain and Moorland Breeds'. Then Volume VII was entitled *The Polo and Riding Pony Stud Book*. Finally, with Volume XIII (published in 1915), it became *The National Pony Stud Book*. In this volume we also find, for the first time and twenty years after its foundation, that 'the Society' refers to itself as 'the National Pony Society'. At long last.

From now on all ponies were to be ponies. Or were they? The objects of the NPS (as we may now call it) are given as: ' … to promote the breeding of ponies for polo, riding and military purposes and to encourage the native breeds'; as nice a distinction as you'd meet on a day's march. The mountain and moorlands had arrived, though it had taken those twenty years and a (possibly coincidental) European war to do it.

In tracing this tangled skein of titles we have strayed a little in advance of our main theme. Let us return to 1899 and see how these excellent intentions were actually put into effect. And there is no better place to do so than in the pages of Volume V of the stud book, especially in the Editorial Chairman's Introduction and the Report of the Council to the A.G.M. (20 June 1899). It would appear that the ball had been given an initial shove by John Hill, the same who had five years earlier drawn council's attention to the fact that ponies meant *all* ponies. The report mentions his proposal 'at a previous meeting', though without saying what this was. It must have concerned native ponies, for the upshot was, the report goes on, that the council had 'enlisted, in each district, the aid of local Committees, composed of gentlemen intimately acquainted with the peculiarities and requirements of (their respective breeds) … in this initial attempt to register ponies of the Mountain and Moorland type.' This was decentralization at its best: to enthusiastic experts.

It worked splendidly. So well that the council could point with justifiable pride to the entries in Volume V of 20 Mountain and Moorland stallions and 158 mares from the 7 breeds so far enrolled;[3] each one inspected and passed as 'true to type'.

But what was 'type' for each breed? And who did the inspecting? Once again, it was a case of decentralizing. Local committees were invited to provide the society with 'descriptions of points' of their respective breeds, to appoint inspectors, then to leave them to get on with the job, guided by the 'descriptions' mentioned above. The Chairman of the Editing Committee had his own firm opinion of a general yardstick: 'the power of the animal to live and thrive in the winter time without any adventitious sustenance'. In other words, registration and the encouragement of skilful and selective breeding must never be allowed to soften their character or physique; they remained *moorland* ponies, a point frequently recalled by the society and, even more strongly, by the local committee.

From the general to the Dartmoor in particular. First the Introduction lists the members of the local committee. There it is good to see that six of the seven live on or within a stone's throw of the moor. The seventh, Lord Lionel Cecil, is shown as living in Lymington, a hundred miles away as the crow flies, but making up for this by being a member of a family both influential and much concerned with ponies.[4]

For the Dartmoor's 'points', we are referred back to those for the North Wales Division, with 'amendments and additions'; a little ruffling to the Dartmoor *amour propre*, but reflecting the close relationship. It is also worth noting that these various features, what might be called 'the portrait of the Dartmoor', have altered very little since then; with two important exceptions: colour and height. 'Brown, black or bay preferred; grey allowable; other colours objectionable.' Well, what do we make of that? Evading the question or a nice exercise of restrained (but not restraining) guidance? Our answer depends, of course, on our school of thought on judging – on judging anything, if it comes to that. Should as much as possible be decided by factual observation rather than on opinion, thus lightening the load on the judge's overtaxed shoulders and

---

[3] *Dartmoor, Exmoor, Fell (Brough Hill), New Forest, North Wales, South Wales, Scotch. The Connemaras first appeared in Volume VI; the two Welsh divisions were amalgamated from Volume VII onwards. The Dales completed the line-up in Volume XV, soon after the end of the First World War.*

[4] *His brother, Lord Arthur, is commemorated by the cup bearing his name, awarded every year to the Champion Mountain and Moorland Broodmare at the NPS Show.*

freeing him to use his famous judgement where it really matters? Alternatively, should he be given a free hand to judge the animal *in toto*, as a single entity, taking note of its colour, to be sure, accepting guidance, but not orders? It is evident that the local committee belonged to the latter. They phrased their instructions with care. Is not 'allowable' slightly less welcoming than 'allowed'? And, as for 'objectionable', does not this suggest that the skewbald *could* win, but it would have to be first rate in every other way (admittedly an unlikely occurrence).

Height is a horse of a different colour. It is entirely factual, or should be, measured by a competent official with a metal-shod stick, with the horse standing naturally on level ground. A hand is 4 inches (or 101.6 of those alien millimetres) and that is all there is to it. Nothing to argue about, or so you'd think.

Well, 'hands' are not easily tampered with, but why in 1899 fourteen of them for a Dartmoor stallion and thirteen and a half for a mare? It seems odd at first sight (and with considerable hindsight), with those actually running on the moor seldom going over 12 hh and the limit for mares at the society's own show in 1896 set at 12.2 hh. The local committee, charged with deciding such matters, gives no reason. All that can be produced here are, therefore, some possibilities for the reader to test against his or her own knowledge or theory.

First, Dartmoor-pony owners may have been irked that the polo pony was taking more than its share of the manger; at that time they had to admit that the best market lay nearer to Hurlingham than to Chagford. And the breeders of those highly prized – and highly priced – 'playing ponies' were all the while on the look-out for top-quality mountain and moorland mares; small, but since their own size-limit had been raised (1895) to 14.2 hh was there not an excellent reason for breeding and registering to suit?

Second, there was what we might term the 'Hackney connection'. The breeding of these attractive animals, half-horse and half-pony, is too large a subject even to touch on here, but it is fair to say that the Hackney was at that time at the peak of its favour and fame, much boosted by Kit Wilson's foundation of the Hackney pony, a breed, according to Roy Charlton, that will go down in pony history.[5]

Then there was the 'Call to the Colours'. Around that time the army was becoming more interested in pack animals. And what could be better than the tough but amenable little Dartmoor?

Only not too little. Another reason for setting that limit considerably higher than Nature had evolved over the centuries.

Some or all of these factors may have prompted the initial decision to put the limit for stallions at 14 hh and that for mares at 13.2 hh. It seems likely, too, that the local committee soon changed its mind, for only five years after the first registrations both were reduced by 2 inches, to 13.2 and 13 hh, where they remained for over two decades. One cannot but wonder why.

It was, of course, symptomatic of the age that authority did not feel obliged to give *reasons*. It just went ahead and did what it thought best. However, to give them (in this case the Council of the Polo Pony Society and the local committees) their due, more often than not their actions were directed to the common good rather than their own. Their duty was clear (to them) and they did it. In this case those concerned felt strongly that the native breeds must not be deprived of their character and hardiness; as might happen if they were to be out-crossed to infuse too great a proportion of non-native blood. Thus we find the NPS ruling in May 1901 that foundation stock of mountain and moorland ponies should contain at least three-quarters pony blood. In September of the following year the Dartmoor local committee directed its inspectors to reject any pony with more than one-quarter Thoroughbred or Arab blood (which is the same thing but the other way round), adding that they should not accept any with more than *one-eighth* Hackney (i.e. nothing nearer than a Hackney great-grandparent).

A change of heart? At any rate, suggesting an adjustment of policy within three years of accepting as 'true to type', a pony that was pure and registered Hackney on both sides (Volume V). However, before criticizing our great-grandfathers, we should remind ourselves that they were starting from scratch and in a business about which very much less was known than it is today. One tenet they held staunchly: keeping the breed 'moorland'.

So the Dartmoor entered the twentieth century with a most encouraging prospect: a stud book (if not yet a society) to look after him, well-wishers with both the knowledge and the time to 'encourage' him. (Wasn't that the very word selected for prominence in the 'Objects' of the Polo Pony Society?) He was (and is) a staunch little animal. All he needed was that encouragement – to include understanding and only the least bit of help – to allow him to evolve into the splendid individual we have with us at the end of this century.

---

[5] A Lifetime with Ponies, *p.10.*

4 FOUNDATION STONES

So far we have concerned ourselves mostly with abstractions: societies, committees, resolutions and the like; desirable, of course, if we are to have our picture in proper perspective, but not to be too long drawn out. In short, it is time that we 'cut the cackle and got to the 'osses'. After all, they are what this book should be about: not abstractions at all, but very real, alive and frequently beautiful for good measure. Very well then, what sort of animals were those first registered Dartmoors? Who were their immediate forebears? And from the information thus obtained, can we determine what qualities were being sought: by judges, inspectors, owners, breeders? What part did the parent organization, then the Polo Pony Society, play in their development? How did interested parties think at the time and what legacy have they passed on?

First, however, the briefest of scene-setting. If we are to achieve any worthwhile understanding, it is important that we should see the moor and its denizens as they were in the days of our great-grandparents. In addition to being aware of the revolution in transport (almost complete in the case of the railways, but with the long-distance roads still awaiting the full flowering of the powered vehicle) we should bear in mind that, in the countryside at least, the great social revolution was still to come.

In the deep country – and where deeper than the moor? – life was static. All but the most exalted spent their lives in small local communities, to a great extent isolated from other communities. They were only able to communicate over any appreciable distance slowly and by rumour or possibly by the written word. Anywhere beyond the parish boundary was 'abroad', those living there 'foreigners'. The parish was the unit: close-knit,

independent and largely self-sufficient; the whole countryside a patchwork of these little kingdoms ruled – autocratically, casually or not at all – by the squire in undefined concert with the parson (whose living, as often as not, lay in the gift of that same squire). Benignly paternal or deplorably feudal? Most likely a bit of both. However it strikes us today, that was the way around 1900; hierarchic, but in the main accepted in the same way as the weather; a way of life very soon to be bulldozed into oblivion, good and bad alike. For just a few more years, however, Society in rural England was to remain, without any great change, more or less as it had been ever since the Norman Conquest.

Thus, at the time when the Dartmoor pony was achieving official recognition, the country was still very much the country; several centuries behind the times; unaware of its coming translation into a Rural Recreation Area; accepting as quite proper that 'the inspectors appointed by the local committee' (itself appointed by whom?) should turn out to be those members of that same body living within riding distance of the moor, (apart from Lord Lionel in far-off Lymington). They knew the moor, its inhabitants and the ponies on it. They could (and did) speak with authority. Could anyone ask for more? Was there, for that matter, any practicable alternative? Anyway, there was the local committee with its built-in team of inspectors. The important question for us is not how they got there, but what they did with their authority; for the breed then and later.

On this, contemporary opinion is hard to come by. The *Annual Report of the Polo Pony Society* dated 1899 describes the inspection scheme as 'an undoubted success', but this only related to it being 'on a satisfactory basis'. In other words, the vehicle was running nicely, but was it being driven in the right direction?

Which *was* the right direction? For anything like a realistic answer we should, once more, send our minds back across those ninety-odd years. How did the breeders see the situation? After all, in the final analysis they were the ones that mattered. And they were, almost exclusively, upland farmers hard put to wrench a livelihood from a tough, ungenerous environment. To them, ponies were simply stock. They had to be. Times were hard and animals had to be raised as cheaply as possible to be sold at a narrow profit. Thus the first question would have been: what sort of pony was saleable?

The pre-eminence of polo in the pony world has already been noted. Polo's powerful voice made it clear that ponies – of the better sort – were for polo: directly as players or indirectly as breeding stock. And, since polo gave its name to the society and the society ran the stud book to which, in turn, those willing and able to pay top prices for what they wanted would look for information, that was about all there was to it.

Well, not quite all. That voice was still powerful, but no longer did it drown all others in the market-place. Other outlets were there and expanding; not so rewarding perhaps, but less exacting in their requirements. For pack animals for a start. These have already been mentioned. Out of date? Generally becoming so, but there were special cases. Recent exertions in building and maintaining the Empire had persuaded the War Office to look again to the horse – and more particularly the pony – as a means of carrying its ever-increasing load of material around those far-off, roadless, out-of-the-way battlefields. There was, indeed, much to commend the pack pony. Even by military standards it could be said to have been adequately tested, over four millenia at least. It was undaunted by rugged terrain, anywhere a soldier could go on his two feet the pony could follow on four. Its abilities, upkeep and idiosyncrasies were understood; to say nothing of usually possessing personal attractions quite absent from the internal-combustion engine. All in all, the pack pony offered an excellent deal all round: to the breeder a small but dependable return, subject only to his satisfying the War Office's modest requirements; to the soldier some reassurance that all was not lost.

Parallel with this there was still some demand from coal pits and for transport on the less-accessible parts of the moor itself. Not much of either, for in the pits the smaller Shetland enjoyed the advantage of what might be termed a better power-to-height ratio, while on the moor the steady spread of roads – rough but passable – allowed the cart to take over most of the work. Still, openings, although diminishing.

Then there was The One in The Middle, neither supporting The Game at the top of the market nor relegated to humdrum load-toting at the bottom: the pony for riding or driving. The Long-sighted had already seen that this must be the future *métier* of the Dartmoor – though the object of the PPS was carefully open on priorities. One fact, however, could not be ignored: the arrival of the iron road. This helped the pony.

Horses had, of course, been ridden and driven for many centuries. Now, however, the emphasis was shifting. Journeys were shorter and loads, in the main, lighter. The doctor's spanking dog-cart, the short-haul delivery vans of the butcher and the baker had taken over the roads from the lumbering, long-distance wagons. When men rode it was mostly over a few miles within the parish (still the parish) on their own affairs; or, more likely, for sport, recreation or simply for pleasure. If they needed to travel further, they took the train. No longer would a successor to Trollope be found holding *ennui* at bay over the long weary miles to some isolated post office by recounting to himself the plot of his latest story, to be set down on paper that evening when he at last reached shelter.[1] Riding, in short, had ceased to be the means of making any journey, short or long, when a good, large animal would make better time than a small one. So the pony was coming into its own, to meet a clear and growing requirement in what would nowadays be called the leisure industry; one, moreover, clearly here to stay.

How did this affect the Dartmoor? If we set aside the business of the pack animals (though, as related, they continued to find buyers), we become aware of greater emphasis on 'quality'. Does not the object of the PPS itself stress it? Quality not just for polo ponies, but all along the line. Naturally, 'quality', then as now, meant different things to different people. However, we should not be too far out if we classify the Dartmoor breeders of the Edwardian age under three headings, as demonstrated by how they bred their ponies. First, there were those who, for one reason or another, kept their breeding within the existing ponies running on the moor. Possibly they were swayed by the addition in 1903 of an injunction added to the object of the society (now 'Polo *and* Riding Pony') to 'encourage the native breeds'. Wasn't the emphasis here on 'native'. Very well, they would use what was at hand. Were there not 'Dartmoor' stallions – of a sort – and to spare? They would stick to these and so keep the breed pure. Keep it pure? The claim surely begged the question. How pure was it in the first place?

Next came the slightly more venturesome (or, some said,

---

[1] *Trollope's* Autobiography *(1883).*

risky). They were willing – indeed, eager – to try mating Dartmoor mares with hand-picked stallions of one of the other related breeds, arguing that, since all (or most) native ponies were cousins (and in many cases not very distant), there would be no danger of losing the toughness that was so highly prized. At the same time such modest out-crosses would give more scope for general improvement.

Finally, there were those prepared to look further afield – anywhere, it might be said – for that elusive 'quality'. So why not a dash of blood entirely alien to the moor – to any moor? Polo/Riding Pony, Arab, Hackney, even Thoroughbred? Just a dash; not much, but enough. But how much would be 'enough'? There was only one way to find out ...

Thus the categories of breeders; admittedly conjecture, but a reasonable generalization. How did the society itself feel about the matter? The council was made up of practical men. They realized that a 'breed' could not be expected to spring up out of the heather at their behest, pure bred and with origins (if not precise lineage) fully accounted for. They had, in effect, to produce order out of, if not chaos, at least anarchy in its true sense. Arbitrary setting of standards coupled with expert and responsible officially sponsored inspection was the only practical way of getting things moving; this inspection would be indpendent of any day-to-day interference by council but, as events were to show, under the critical eye of those finally responsible for policy.

Matters jogged along thus on a loose rein for a couple of years. There was an encouraging response from breeders: 10 stallions and 102 mares. But were sheer numbers enough? In short, were the right animals being registered? Or, the real question, were those being registered the right ones; those likely 'to improve the breeding of high-class riding ponies' (in the words of the society's object)? Perhaps authority was being too free and easy and some guidance was needed?

Accordingly, on 9 May 1901 council 'desired' committees to 'register only ponies that are of riding type, and that, on the dam's side, are of pure pony blood', backing this with a general rule that 'foundation stock of mountain and moorland breeds should not be registered unless they contain three-quarters pony blood.'

So far pretty restrained, to be seen as practical steering in the right pony-oriented direction. Now it was up to the local committees, so, after a brief interval of sixteen months, the Dartmoor committee produced its 'resolution' (9 September 1902). And now there was no more 'desiring', the business was spelt out, the order nailed to the mast.

No pony (it said) was to be passed that had 'more than one-quarter Thoroughbred or Arab blood or one-eighth Hackney blood.' It added that they (the inspectors, presumably) 'should, as far as possible, adhere to the pure Dartmoor and ponies of the riding type'. The bit about Thoroughbred and Arab blood was, of course, no more than expressing council's rule in terms of arithmetic, for if the dam had to be 'pure pony' and the pony to be registered had to be at least 'three-quarters pony' *(see above)*, that left a maximum of one-quarter for any non-pony out-cross. Then there was the doubly severe restriction on Hackney blood. Not more than an eighth! That meant no Hackney forebears nearer than a solitary great-grandparent. Very well, one is inclined to say; if that was the way the local committee felt, no doubt they had good reason and so be it.

But it wasn't quite as simple as that. There had arisen an anomaly in the rules they had made for themselves. When the stud book was first thrown open to the native ponies, it seems that the local committee encouraged considerable out-crossing, especially from Hackneys, then at the height of their well-deserved popularity. Indeed, thanks to the efforts of Christopher Wilson,[2] many Hackneys were ponies in the broader sense. At all events, the figures tell their own story. Of the ten Dartmoor stallions in Volumes V and VI, four were by Hackneys and one was itself a full-blooded (and registered) Hackney in its own right. Among the hundred-odd mares we can identify nine first-cross Hackneys, four with one-quarter Hackney blood and, topping the bill, one by a Thoroughbred out of a half-Hackney mare. How much native in this last? Under the new resolution of 1902 none of them would, themselves, have been eligible, while of their progeny only that from the quarter-Hackneys could now reach the pages of future volumes.

Let us first, however, have a look at how the show judges treated these official Ishmaelites. The eight of them that appear in the results over the seven pre-registration seasons collected in all 13 firsts, 7 seconds and 6 thirds either at Brentor & Lydford or Okehampton; a total that might arouse the scorn of today's highly mobile pot-hunter but was not at all bad for 'outcasts' in 1890s. Whatever the merits of this performance, the general intention of council, backed by the local committee, was clear: to ensure that the process of 'improvement' did not swamp the 'native' characteristics they were – and rightly – so keen to foster. Had they, in modern parlance, over-reacted to the threat, real or

---

[2] See Ponies Past and Present, by Sir Walter Gilbey, p.55 *et seq.*

Brandsby Cyclone (1978) (*left*) **and Shilstone Rocks Cloudburst (1970)**

imaginary, of the non-pony out-cross? Was the added generation of restriction on Hackney blood really necessary? This last was a matter of judgement at the time and it is not easy to offer any evidence of what people thought. What can be said, however, is that, in so doing, the committee had made for itself a nicely balanced dilemma.

This arose from its use of the word 'blood'; an unalterable essence bred into any animal (just as it is into *homo sapiens*, so called), a heritage that no amount of paperwork (or elevation to the peerage) can alter or ameliorate. By thus imposing precise limits on proportions of various bloodstreams the committee had not only closed the gates against those, previously welcome, who wished to enter the fold and be registered, but had also illegitimized the progeny of a number of those already within; that is, already inspected, passed and duly registered in the happy carefree unconfined days before September 1902, especially as applied to the once-applauded Hackneys.

As can easily be imagined, none of this actually happened.

Those already registered stayed registered and their progeny (as far as they themselves were concerned) were all eligible. The committee, having been the least bit careless in its rule-drafting, demonstrated the validity of the propostion that a dilemma can safely be ignored, provided no one waves it around.

As far as we can tell from the stud book, no new Hackney blood above the prescribed eighth was introduced after 1902. In Volume X we find three daughters of sires admitted to the first list (Volume V). The fillies 1810 Dolly and 1812 Maggie were both by Brentor Confidence 149 (himself a first cross, so they were quarter-Hackneys and hence outside the new limit) and 1816 Twinkle was by Hotspur 152 (the full-blooded Hackney referred to above). Both were slipped in and justified their inclusion by collecting between them half a dozen firsts at Brentor, South Brent and Cornwood – as Dartmoors, naturally.

We cannot escape the conclusion that Dartmoors with Hackney blood won a disproportionate number of prizes in the years immediately prior to and after the introduction of registration. Why, then, did the local committee turn its face against out-crosses and especially Hackneys? Or should the question be put the other way round: why were Hackneys ever favoured? Perhaps it was something to do with height in the progeny? In those days Dartmoor (in common with other native) mares were much in demand for breeding ponies for polo. Crossed with TB or Arab they would throw foals to grow nicely to just within the then limit of 14.2. No less an authority than Sir Walter Gilbey strongly favoured crossing 'a small and compact Thoroughbred or Arab' with 'the best of our forest or moorland ponies'.[3] From the pont of view of the immediate needs of the game he was no doubt correct, but it was soon realized that such matings were tending to undermine native toughness and blur other valuable characteristics, causing the breeders on the moor to ask themselves whether their priorities were right.

An evergreen subject for debate, with or without acrimony, was – and still is – height. Just because it can be measured, it is sometimes thought that it can also be accurately planned. Not so, though general trends have been noted. Admiral Rous, 'Dictator of The Turf' in late-Victorian times, declared that since 1700 the Thoroughbred had on *average* added 1 inch to its height every twenty-five years. This he put down to more care and better feeding. Also, he might have added, to hindsight.

As for the racehorse, so with the Dartmoor. Around 1900, as now, Dartmoor breeders broadly agreed that the maximum height *in the natural state* seldom went above 12.2 hh. Bring them in and feed them up ·and they grew – eventually. Cross a Dartmoor mare with a bigger animal and it produced a bigger foal, at least this would be likely but by no means assured. And, as always, there would be a price to pay: the loss of those admirable moorland qualities, not least adaptability and ability to survive. So could this giant be called a Dartmoor? Evidently council thought not, said so in general terms, and passed it on to the local committee to be put into a precise directive.

In this matter of actual measurement, it is interesting to discover that the average height of 'pure' Dartmoors (i.e. from those parents known or presumed to live rough on the moor) entered in Volume V is between 12.1½ hh and 12.2 hh; that of the Hackney out-crosses almost exactly 13 hh. Just over 2 inches difference. That's not much – or is it? All in all, therefore, it would seem that the present limit of 12.2 hh is about right; right, that is, if we want a real moorland pony.

This is, of course, the nub of the matter. What *do* we want? If

we are looking for a tough, weatherproof pony to ride, drive or carry things, then the true Dartmoor is the answer – or, at any rate, one very good answer. If, on the other hand, we want a mount for the polo field, then we must find something bigger (at the turn of the century it was only a little bigger, now it's quite a lot, but that is by the way); a bigger animal than the moorland pony, but to which the Dartmoor can serve as a stepping stone. If that's what we want, we cross her with a small horse and hope. If we're lucky, by all accounts we're likely to have a cracking good polo-pony; a mount with 'blood, speed and courage' (as Sir Walter puts it). But it's not a Dartmoor and has no place in the Dartmoor section of the stud book.

Almost a century later we can do no more than speculate about what might be termed 'the polo pressure'. What we do know, beyond all doubt, is that the height limit as initially laid down (by the local committee) was several inches above the tallest of the genuine moorland ponies. Was it a kind of licence to 'grow tall'? At all events, it was not long after registration had been brought in that authority, in the shape of the council of the Polo Pony Society, saw that the tendency to out-cross so as to 'breed to the limit of the measuring-stick' would, if not checked, pose a very real danger to many of the characteristics of the breed. The results, which are indicative of an admirably broad outlook, can be seen in the rule and regulation mentioned above and, in addition, the progressive reduction in the height limit.

This two-way pull on the Dartmoor – for such it surely was – probably explains why it took authority so long to come within shouting distance of reality. Let us follow their leisurely progress. The first official mention of height was, of course, in Volume V, when the native pony sections were introduced: 14 hh for stallions, 13.2 hh for mares, as recommended by the local committee. Some time between 1903–4 the stallions were put on par with the mares at 13.2 hh, with the differential restored in September 1905 when the mares went down to 13 hh. The official height limits remained thus until well after the First World War; odd, in view of the society's own stipulation of 12.2 hh for Dartmoor broodmares as long ago as its 1896 Hurlingham Show. Unfortunately, not a single entry was forthcoming, so it is not possible to record its effect. The limit was 12.2 at other, lesser, shows too.

Nor has the date of the final acceptance of 12.2 come to hand. Volume XVIII (1924) still has the 13.2/13 hh rule; the first definite mention of 12.2 hh in the stud book being in Volume XXV (1948), when it says briskly that 'the maximum height is 12.2 for both mares and stallions'. And there, for the moment, the matter rests.

---

[3] *His summing up (p.112) in* Ponies Past and Present *(Vinton & Co, 1900).*

BELLEVER TOR

5 INTO THE SHOW-RING

Before the year 1899 there were, of course, no classes for registered Dartmoors, but there were a large number of shows on and around the moor at which those subsequently registered won prizes, as recorded in the stud book. In Volumes V and VI we find that thirty-four Dartmoors had won, between them, close on a hundred awards over the previous decade. But in what kind of classes? The record is tantalizingly curt. '1895 1st Lydford' (for instance) offers no clue whether it was in a moorland, riding pony or even a polo pony class, in hand or ridden. Brent is slightly more explicit, being shown as holding a 'Dartmoor Pony Show' in 1897, 1898 and 1899, but the whole period is shrouded in the mists of long ago, so that no analysis of the fate of this or that individual or line is possible.

The list of prizes won by Dartmoors tells us that there were shows at Brentor, Lydford (these two later amalgamated), Okehampton, Tavistock, South Brent, Holsworthy and South Zeal. Not bad for the days before Rice, Bedford *et al*. Perhaps a whiff of this enthusiasm wafted as far as Hurlingham, reminding the pundits of the potential of the little breeds, unregistered and, indeed, scarcely recognized?

What else can we learn or surmise from these Victorian outings? Those busily searching for a statistic may have discovered that, of the thirty-four winners, the stud book records the heights of all but two — at an *average* of 12.3 hh. A knock for the theory that Dartmoors stayed *under* 12.2 hh in their natural state? Not really, for a second look will reveal nine of those thirty-two to be part-Hackney and a further two part-Thoroughbred. It would seem that, even in 1890s, the cry of 'bigger must be better' was on some lips. These out-crosses were certainly bigger, but were they still truly 'mountain or moorland'?

With the introduction of registration, we are at once on firmer ground; not rock solid, to be sure, for details are often sketchy, with parentage of many of those in the early volumes given simply as 'Dartmoor Pony' on one or both sides. We should not cavil at this apparent vagueness, for these pioneers had to start somewhere. Where better than with 'Dartmoor ponies'? The inspectors knew the moor and the ponies on it. To a large extent the whole affair was autonomous, in that the Polo Pony Society had invited the local committee to lay down the description of points, to appoint inspectors (themselves) and get on with finding ponies 'typical of the breed' and 'with the unmistakable appearance of hardiness peculiar to mountain ponies'.

To meet this, the breeders had the choice of three courses, as already outlined: from 'Dartmoor and nothing but that', through judicious use of the blood of other *suitable* native breeds, to the bold out-cross to non-native ponies or even horses. What then was the effect of introducing registration? For the majority of the breeders and owners of the 10 000 ponies on the moor,[1] life went on very much as before. In this pamphlet she comments that 'it cannot be emphasised too often that the intention was never to register all ponies running on the moor, but to select ponies of the right Dartmoor riding type likely to improve the breed and as foundation stock for registration ....'

Today such a policy would, no doubt, be dismissed as élitism, but in those happier times the word did not exist and, if it had, would have been bestowed and received as a compliment. Elitism or not, this search for quality runs all the way through her words and actions. She speaks highly here, as elsewhere, of

---

[1] *Sylvia Calmady-Hamlyn's estimate in her pamphlet 'Short History of the Dartmoor Pony' (ST Elson, Ashburton, 1953).*

the moormen: of Edmund P. Northey, a member of the original local committee, who (together with his father before him) had for a century kept a herd of ponies on the highest moorland under Yes Tor (2030 feet) from which came Judy V, a winner over seventeen years and the direct ancestor of Jude, Jenny, Janus and most of her own Vean Stud.

Of another moorman, Herbert J. Madders of South Zeal, she writes: 'He knew all there was to know about the small pony breeds, and insisted on the true pony type, but knew well that fresh blood, carefully selected, was at times necessary, and used Welsh Mountain of riding type himself.' She also mentions Mr Whitley of Widecombe, who 'ran a pedigree Welsh stallion *on the open moor*' (her italics) and, like Mr Madders, believed that the Welsh was the best cross for Dartmoors.

Here is not the place to try to weigh the success of these various ventures, but simply to record that they happened. As previously mentioned, Sylvia Calmady-Hamlyn was seeking that elusive 'quality'. Often she travelled a long way from Dartmoor, even from moorland of any kind, but always with this firm purpose in mind. More than half a century after the time of which we are writing, she produced a leaflet entitled 'A List of Stallions ... authorized to initiate the *Dartmoor Pony Stud Book* in 1899 and subsequent years ... and a short history of development until today 1958'. Her list differs in detail from the stud book, but presents a useful broad picture. In addition to the names and 'history' she adds a considerable amount of comment, including the following:

It is interesting to see the selection of 'pure ponies' made by two leading Moormen ... evidently the small pack-pony type was still in their minds. About 1906 it was realized that other blood was more suitable to breed the type of Dartmoor pony required and a beautiful 13.2 TB pony, Lord Polo, by Rosewater, was introduced in the Tavistock area. Extensively used, he left plenty of invaluable stock, with small pretty heads, quality and plenty of substance.

At this distance it is not possible to say whether she was justified in her accusation of undue interest in pack ponies, so let us instead concentrate on Lord Polo: on his parentage, himself and his foals. The evidence is far from complete, but such as it is gives an interesting glimpse of the result of crossing a moorland mare towards the Thoroughbred. Towards, but not with, for in cold fact Lord Polo was not TB. His sire, Rosewater, certainly was, but the stud book dismisses his dam, Lady Florence, with 'pedigree unknown'. Unknown, but not necessarily ignoble. The

story, as told by Wynne Davies in his *Welsh Ponies and Cobs*, is that Sir Humphrey de Trafford bought her 'on the Welsh Border' and that she was 'thought to be Welsh'. If this supposition is correct, it makes Lord Polo himself Welsh x TB, thus his progeny from a Dartmoor would have the required three-quarters pony blood, as laid down in the society's rule of 1901.

Sir Humphrey knew a good pony when he saw one. Lady Flo's descent may have been misty, but her achievements are clear enough. At all events, at nine years old (1887) she carried off the Trent Steeplechase, the Ladies Plate at Southport (carrying 12 st over 2 miles on the flat) and 'many other races at Manchester and Southport'. Then, just to demonstrate that speed wasn't the whole story, she came south to try her hand in the jumping event at Ranelagh. She won, of course. Just thirteen hands and three inches 'competing against horses', as the stud book points out; a Victorian 'super-Stroller'.

It is a pity that we have no portrait of Lady Florence, but there is some compensation in the very clear picture of Rosewater in Volume I. It shows a most handsome animal and there need be no surprise that he did so well in the showing classes: thirteen wins at major shows in the decade 1892–1902, a most creditable achievement when we call to mind the small number of such events in those days and the complications of getting to them. Nor was that all, for the note under his entry in Volume I remarks casually that he was 'a winner of many races as a two-year-old under Jockey Club Rules and also under National Pony and Galloway Racing Club Rules'. Dam and sire, two splendid life-members of the 'Try-Anything Club'.

And so to Lord Polo himself. He was not the all-rounder to match either of his parents, for he confined his competitive efforts to the show-ring. There, however, he was almost unbeaten: a first at Birmingham (when he was five), three more firsts in the next two seasons (good wins too: the Royal at Maidstone, at Crystal Palace and the Polo Pony Society's Show at London). Then came his only recorded seconds: PPS London and Cambridge & Ely 1901; on each occasion being beaten by Hermit (by the Monk, ex Sybil, the latter by a coincidence also of unknown breeding). The next year at London he reversed the placing. Apparently the judge, Sir Richard Green-Price, had been in two minds, duly reporting that there was 'nothing much to choose between Lord Polo and Hermit'. Later he adds: 'Rosewater, although nineteen years old, still easily held his own against all competitors.' A pleasant double for the pair.

It is as a sire, of course, that we should judge Lord Polo. How did his stock do? Unfortunately, we have very little to go on, despite the comment of Sylvia Calmady-Hamlyn that he left 'plenty' of foals. No doubt she was perfectly correct, but once again we are up against the reluctance of the Dartmoor breeders to go to all the trouble and expense of registration. One can see their point of view. What was the purpose? There was no time-limit, so why all the rush? Hadn't Zeppa been born in 1896 and not registered until 1916? A world record for apathy? Anyway, weren't prize-winners in properly constituted Dartmoor classes automatically considered as 'inspected and passed'? Time enough to do the paper work when you collected your prize money.

Sylvia Calmady-Hamlyn's attitude, as quoted above, was firmly realistic. There is much to commend it. Although there are wide gaps in our factual information, some of these can be filled from old mens' memories, others from verbal tradition handed down in the family. Memories may be weak on facts and figures (even Miss Calmady-Hamlyn, like Homer, nodded at times) but they recapture the essential flavour. The width of these gaps can be judged by comparing two figures: on the one hand the Calmady-Hamlyn estimate of 10 000 ponies on the moor; on the other the number actually registered before the First World War: 272 ponies (40 stallions, 232 mares); 3 per cent registered, 97 per cent unaccounted for.

We should not therefore be surprised at being unable to discover more than eight of Lord Polo's 'plentiful' progeny in the Dartmoor section of the stud book. So be it. Let us see how that sample pans out. The first to be registered were Rose-Marie and Marie-Rose, foaled in 1905 and 1906 respectively, full sisters out of Dartmoor Queen and bred by Frederick Ball of Lydford. They were registered by Imogen Collier in Volume XI (1911). And that is the last we hear of them. Did Miss Collier ever show them? Perhaps not, for they only stood 11.1 hh and she may well not have fancied her chances against animals anything up to three *hands* taller. Another gap in our knowledge. However, there is no doubt on one point: Imogen Collier did not allow this presumed failure to put her off Lord Polo, for a year later she bought another of his foals. Diana II was bred by Moses Bawden of Tavistock, out of Queenie and standing at exactly 13 hh. She did Miss Collier proud, as will be told later.

Sylvia Calmady-Hamlyn bought Diana II as a five-year-old, but (sadly for the Dartmoor breed) sent her to Thoroughbreds over the next four years. In 1913 she had Janus (not to be confused with his later Dartmoor namesake) by Cruickshank, in 1914 Dynamite by Percussion, in 1915 Tertius and 1916 Tyra both by Tyranny. Why this switch back to the larger sires? The answer is probably because at that time Miss Calmady-Hamlyn had not yet started to breed Dartmoors, but to use Dartmoor mares as one step in the process of breeding polo ponies. Although she owned several Dartmoors before the First World War, it was not until 1922 that she appears in the stud book (Volume XVI) as an actual breeder.

Later we find one of Diana's foals in the Dartmoor section, the circumstances of which are, to say the least, murky. She was sold to the Tor Royal Stud about 1918, covered by Dwarka and in 1919 duly produced Dwarka's Beauty, to be registered as a Dartmoor. A Dartmoor? Not if one takes into account the mixture of blood that council was going on about at the turn of the century, the rules on which had never been modified, still less cancelled. In the royally sponsored veins of Dwarka's Beauty there ran the following: one-quarter Dartmoor (from Diana's long-forgotten dam), one-eighth Thoroughbred (from Rose-water), one-eighth Query-Welsh (from Lady Florence) and one-half Arab (from Dwarka, see Chapter 8). Nor was Dwarka's Beauty the only one to break that rule. But was it still in force? Available records are reticent. It would be interesting to know the answer to that one.

Turning tactfully away from that question, we ask what happened to the 'invaluable' stock referred to earlier. Of the remaining seven after Diana it cannot be said that their performance was scintillating. Two, as we have already heard, sank without trace (Miss Collier's Rose-Marie and Marie-Rose). In 1912 White Star (ex Smallspur, unregistered) was second at

Diana II (1907), 13.0 hh., by Lord Polo

Brentor & Lydford. In 1913 Lady John (ex Violet, also unregistered) won at Cornwood. In 1914 Heather Mixture (ex 1659 Queen of the Moor, herself winner of the class for Dartmoor broodmares in London in 1904 – and, one feels, the reason for her belated registration) was third at the NPS London. In 1917 Cup Moss (ex another Violet, unregistered) was also third at London. Of the eighth, Sunbeam III (ex 'Dartmoor Pony'), we know nothing apart from two (unnamed) foals by threequarterbred polo ponies.

Through the records of such breeding we discover a strong tendency to use a Dartmoor mare as just one step towards breeding the end-object: a tough polo pony within the height limit. This makes sense of sending the next generation back to the larger sires. Thus we should assess Lord Polo's influence during his sojourn on the moor as being directed to one or other of two widely divergent ends; either to providing a once-only, single-generation infusion of moorland blood into breeding polo ponies or, contrariwise, to infusing a single generation of half-Thoroughbred blood as a means of improving the general quality of the Dartmoor – *as a moorland pony*. The alternative purposes were by no means incompatible. Indeed, the same sire and dam could be used at the first step in either. It was in the next generation that the divergence would usually occur.

However, it is wise to bear two important facts in mind. In the early days of this century the physical height of the polo pony, limited to 14.2 hh by the rules, was little different from that of the moorland pony, whether at its official 13 hh or its natural 12.2 hh. When later the two sizes drew apart – the polo limit being removed entirely, the moorland average to something around 12 hh – this proximity also disappeared, thus closing the door on one option.

The second fact, though not so clear cut, is that no one, not even the most expert, can precisely forecast how a foal will turn out; probabilities yes, certainties no. Thus in the manner of out-crossing to, say, a Thoroughbred or an Arab, there can be no saying how much 'fineness' from the one side or 'toughness' from the other will appear in the result. A classic example of this unpredictability was seen in The Leat: by a pure Arab bred in the desert and standing 14.1 hh, out of a 13-hand Dartmoor; himself standing 12.2 hh and 'every inch a moorland pony'. More about The Leat later.

In this matter of out-crossing two leading figures were Imogen Collier and Sylvia Calmady-Hamlyn. They would have been well aware of these simple facts (though not at the time being able to foresee the 'bigger-is-better' change in the rules of polo). From their actions it is evident that their interest, at the time, lay in breeding ponies for polo and that, for them, Dartmoor mares were no more than a means to this end.

Perhaps this was the way they saw it; a perfectly legitimate viewpoint for breeders of polo ponies, though it does leave the official record sadly short on the Dartmoor side. Are we, then, devoting too much attention to a sire that, while admirable in himself, has not left an identifiable mark on the breed in the form of registered progeny? In individual terms the answer is, of course, yes; but taking the Dartmoor breed as a whole it is a decided no. It must be remembered that Lord Polo was actually 'on the moor'; his control, even his surveillance, at the best sketchy; his whole life a world away from the strictly regimented, closely fenced existence of his fellow-sires at Lambourne and Newmarket. *He ran on the moor.* It cannot be said too often. True, he would have had his own herd of mares, but this would have spelt no more than probability. All in all, then as now, it was a brave owner who could state with confidence which foal was by whom.

Anyway, how about those percentages already quoted (see p.19)? How many of those mares and their foals driven into the pound would form part of the registered 3 per cent? All the same, as she says, 'his stock from Dartmoor mares ... were easily recognizable for generations for type, constitution and quality.' Lord Polo contributed to the achievement of the quality that Sylvia Calmady-Hamlyn was after. There was no doubt in the breeders' minds about that, even if it didn't appear in any stud book.

Other beneficial outside influences were also at work in that decade and a half. Captain Muntz was an ardent experimenter, sometimes happily as with the Welsh Mountain Punchinello, sometimes apparently not so well as with a Fell called The Mikado. Punchinello? Wasn't that a 13.2 hh polo pony? Well, yes, he was, in that there is a pony so called on page 26 of Volume VIII under Muntz's name; by an Arab ex a 13.3 hh polo mare. Hardly a Welsh. Just to make things easier, this Punchinello started life as Polo King. Were there two Punchinellos?

Let us turn to The Mikado. Surely he will present no problem. Not of identity, but of performance in the opinion of Sylvia Calmady-Hamlyn. In her short history she describes him as a 'useful pony, but without the Dartmoor quality [who] left much hardy stock and some prize winners.' Five years later she records in her 'List of Stallions' that he was 'not a good cross, and left little stock'. Some confusion? Calmady-Hamlyn against the stud book on whether Punchinello was polo or Welsh; Calmady even against Hamlyn on the merits of The Mikado. The detail may be blurred, but the main outline is clear: a number of non-Dartmoor sires were used; the Welsh were highly thought of. Reasonable; after all, for were they not close cousins?

That there was a large amount of out-crossing can be established by even the most cursory glance down the Dartmoor section in those early volumes; a wide − could it be called reckless? − use of Hackneys until this was chopped in 1902; not so much of Thoroughbred or Arab at the start, but more as the years went by (as epitomized by Lord Polo); finally there was that 'other native blood'. To this last the Polo Pony Society had never raised any objection. The Dartmoor resolution of 1902 called for a general minimum of three-quarters pure *pony* blood, hedging it with the exhortation to 'adhere to the pure Dartmoor and ponies of the riding type'. The resolution placed exact maxima on Thoroughbred, Arab and (even more so) Hackney blood, but none at all on what kind of pony or even requiring that the pony blood should be native. Of course, there was the inspection. The inspectors had to satisfy themselves that the animal before them conformed to true moorland type, 'with the unmistakable appearance of hardiness peculiar to mountain ponies'.

They made mistakes, of course, individually and collectively. Nowadays we can see that the height limit was set much too high, but we should, at the same time, remember the market forces at work. Their business called for knowledge, integrity and firmness. That they had these qualities the results of their judgements must surely bear out, as instanced by the many championships won by Dartmoors against other native breeds and even against their distant cousins the 'riding ponies'. Most of this interbreed activity lay far in the future at the time we are considering. Let us instead see how the Dartmoor breeders managed their own assessment of quality in the years before the First World War.

Factual and objective information on those days is far from plentiful. However, we are fortunate in having one excellent source that not only meets these two requirements but also covers the field of our search, albeit thinly. The stud book of the National Pony Society in the days when it was the *Polo Pony Stud Book* contained a great deal more than its modern counterpart: not only the results of sponsored shows but also the comments of judges and others connected with them. Volumes III−XIII, those covering the pre-First World War shows, are indeed eleven little goldmines. To them we can turn in confidence to give us a pretty clear picture of which ponies were put 'on the right of the line';[2] where, by whom and against what opposition. And not only the placings, but what the judges thought about the various animals brought before them. Add to that lot the reports (without comment) from 'Associated Shows' (soon to include news of local Mountain and Moorland classes) and the reader should feel that he has a broad and balanced picture; at least of what the pundits *thought*, which after all is the best to be expected from any matter of visual selection; be it of horse, pony, dog or bathing belle.

The society staged its first show in June 1895 at Ranelagh, just two years after its formation. It was called the Polo Pony Show and that was what it was; no classes for anything else. Still, it was a start.

Next year the venue was shifted to Hurlingham and the programme extended to include four classes for the native breeds. These were for Exmoor, Dartmoor, New Forest and Welsh Mountain broodmares, to be judged as 'typical of (their respective) breeds and suitable foundation for the breeding of polo and riding ponies'. Two Exmoor, 14 New Forest and 7 Welsh were entered (all but 2 forward, present-day absentees please note). But not a single Dartmoor − disappointing.

Not surprisingly there was no class for Dartmoors the following year when the Polo Pony Society's classes formed part of the Royal at Manchester. The interesting point about that year's show was that there were *two* classes for each breed (stallions and mares); a tacit admission that the natives existed in their own right. Another comment of general interest appeared in the report compiled by William Scarth Dixon and, in view of its evergreen interest, is quoted in full. Dixon wrote:

> It is at the Royal Show contrary to rule for the judges to have a catalogue; but it may reasonably be urged that it is impossible to judge young polo ponies or even polo pony stallions and mares satisfactorily unless the pedigrees of the animals are in the hands of the judges. It is one of the first requirements for a polo pony that he should gallop fast and a pony sired by a trotting horse is scarcely likely to take his part in a fast game.

Strange reading to those brought up on the principle that 'the judge judges as he sees, on the day and in the ring, guided only by the schedule'. We include it for historic interest only; characteristic of those less formal (less serious?) days. Nor is our current 'sight-only' rule universal by any means. We've all heard

---

[2] *Except, of course, at Richmond. Richmond was unique, glorious − and different. There the winner stood on the left, opposite the Royal Box; surely as fine a touch of oneupmanship as you'd meet in a season's showing.*

of shows – quite respectable ones too – where the judge is handed his programme on entering the ring. Abroad, of course. Dixon's point is that the judge should be able to judge the complete pony. But is this ever possible in an in-hand class? Good material here for argument by the fireside.

In 1898 the Royal Show was at Birmingham and again it included the Polo Pony Society's classes as an integral part. These were for mountain pony stallions and mountain pony mares; all breeds together, but limited to 12.2 hh; in fact, just as they had been in the original Exmoor, Dartmoor and Welsh classes in 1896; that is to say, some way below the current limits (except for the Welsh). There were twenty-three entries all told, but no mention of any Dartmoors among the winners. Pride of breed suggests they did not compete.

In general, the stud book is unforthcoming about the events of 1899. It mentions that the Royal staged a 'meeting' at Maidstone, but there is no word of any national show of its own. In that year, however, it initiated a scheme of offering gold and silver medals to 'Associated Country Shows', initially for 'polo ponies'. One of these shows was Brentor & Lydford and it is gratifying to see that both classes were won by registered Dartmoors: Brentor Confidence and Miss May – both by Hackneys.

The year is important in the history of the Dartmoor, of course, as it marks the breed's arrival on the pages of the stud book. Nor was this merely a formality, for the very next year the PPS announced that the medal scheme would be extended to include the native breeds and invited the local committees to nominate the shows at which they would be awarded. This would be in addition to any mountain and moorland classes at the national show. The results are recorded in the stud book, which means that from then on we have a record of achievement; nationally and (to some extent) locally.

In 1900 the half-Hackney Miss May won at Okehampton and the half-Thoroughbred stallion Fetler at South Brent. The honour of the true-blue moorland was saved by Black Bess's win at South Brent. There were, indeed, some curious anomalies, in ambush for the unwary researcher. For instance, the open broodmare class at Brentor was won by Sunbeam (out of the Dartmoor Biddy). A Dartmoor? No, a polo pony. No mystery really: she stood some 13.3½ hh and even our forefathers at their most casual could not wink at an inch and a half over height. Such turmoil was all part of the breed's 'growing pains'. Some breeders were, perhaps, trying to move too fast in the search for 'improvement'; others would have none of it. In short, the situation was slightly unstable. Indeed, it remained so for some years; disconcerting to some at the time but in the long run to the benefit of the breed. It is against this turbulent background that we have to view the events of the first years of the new century. Let us, then, take them in turn in the next chapter.

River Dart

6 EDWARDIAN ADVANCE
A Review of the Results at the Pre-First World War Shows

1901

The Polo Pony Society had come back to London in 1900, holding its show jointly with that of the Hunters Improvement Society on the latter's spare day; a useful money-saver but at another kind of price – a date early in March. Even though it was all under cover, participation must have demanded some hardiness; to say nothing of the sheer slog of grooming out winter coats. Luckily in those days there was plenty of help on call. Anyway, our great-grandparents were tough and in March the show stayed until some years after the First World War – when not in February.

The first year of the new century (1901) saw the start of the Dartmoor classes officially sponsored by the Polo Pony Society, when the local committees of native breeds were invited to nominate shows at which the society's silver medals would be awarded. Thus at Brentor & Lydford the aptly named Brentor Confidence (by the Hackney Stratford Confidence and bred by John Symons of Lewdown) won his class, though this time as a Dartmoor. Best mare was Queenie; even less of a native, being by a Thoroughbred out of a half-Hackney mare. She too had been a consistent winner, having won at Lydford in 1896, 1897 and 1898.

The winners at Okehampton were Patter (by the polo stallion Pat by the Barb Zouave) and Dainty. The latter very soon changed her name, moved to Monmouthshire, shifted to the polo pony section of the stud book and won an immense number of prizes for the Keynsham Stud (twenty-six entries in Volume IX alone: under saddle, in harness, jumping ....). She was 'pure' Dartmoor too, bred by F. Norrish of Ashburton. At South Brent moorland-bred Blackbird shared the honours with Bessie (by the Hackney Triumph).

Deductions on the merits of out-crossing? All that can safely be said is that there does seem to be more than a dash of non-native – even non-pony – blood in those selected for the blue (West Country) rosette.

1902

There were two classes for mountain and moorland mares and fillies combined at the spring show in 1902: for '13 hands and over' and 'under 13 hands'. In the latter, Dainty (the winner at Okehampton the previous year) was 'Highly Commended', which in fact meant that she was fourth out of five. Pixie, a seven-year-old of unstated breeding, was second in a class described (apart from the winner, a Welsh four-year-old of which the judge approved) as 'of mixed character, with nothing specially to recommend them.' Dainty also went in for the open broodmare class where she was 'Commended' (i.e. seventh). A half-Dart (by a Hackney) stood fourth. Not a very successful show for the breed.

For 1902 the local committee nominated Brentor & Lydford, Okehampton and South Brent for the society's silver medals. Patter (winner in 1901 at Okehampton) was successful at Brentor, with Rosebud the best mare. The latter, then fourteen, had been a big winner in the 1890s, but three of her four foals in that period had been by Hackneys, the most interesting of these four being Brentor Confidence. By all accounts she was a good mare and produced winning foals, so it is sad – for the breed – that she went so often to Hackneys, by whom even second-generation progeny would no longer be eligible for Dartmoor registry.

At Okehampton, Brentor Confidence won the stallion class. All fair and square this, but how did Lady Gay come to collect the

Dartmoor mare title? She herself is shown in Volume VI as a polo pony mare (number 969). Her dam, Rose of Devon (which sounds very Dartish but isn't) is not only in the polo pony section but by a Thoroughbred out of an Exmoor. Lady Gay had won many a rosette in the 1890s, but she should not have been allowed to add this one to her legitimate tally.

The third PPS nomination was for South Brent. There the stallion class went to Lord Bobs, of unknown (but clearly patriotic) breeding, and the mare class to Stella, a dyed-in-the-wool Dart. There is an interesting detail to be dug out from the note on her own and her dam's achievements: that, from 1896 onwards, these prizes had been awarded by 'The South Brent *Dartmoor* Pony Society', an association antedating the official DPS by some thirty years. One up for South Brent.

In July 1902 the Polo Pony Society changed its title to 'The Polo & Riding Pony Society' and stated its object as 'promoting the breeding of ponies for polo, riding and military purposes and for the encouragement of the native breeds'.[1] We should not read too much into putting polo first; for the senior member of the alliance this is no more than courtesy. But how about this 'encouragement' of the native breeds? A bit patronizing? What of it, for was not encouragement just what they needed? And, incidentally, what they have received in generous measure ever since. Rather we should look on 1902 as the year in which the natives emerged as breeds in their own right, standing on their own sturdy four feet.

1903

The Polo & Riding Pony Society's 1903 show was once again held in the Royal Agricultural Hall. It was now a two-day affair, following that of the Hunters Improvement Society. In case this sounds simple and easy, it should be added that the hunters left at 5 p.m. on the Thursday evening (all 330 of them) and the 200-odd ponies had been 'comfortably boxed by 7.30'; with not a powered horsebox or trailer in sight. A swap-over at the rate of four a minute isn't bad by any standard; they could smack it about in those days when they had to.

The mountain and moorland classes more or less repeated those of 1902, except that the heights were 'over 12.2' and '12.2 and under', which put those measuring exactly 12.2 hh where they belonged – in the class for smaller ponies. Whatever the break-point, Dartmoors would be entered according to their registered heights, their own limits still being 13.2 for both

stallions and mares. Large or small, however, the breed could not be said to have left its mark on either section, with no better than 'Commended' for any of the three mentioned. All three were of 'pure' moorland descent (in that they laid no claim to outside blood and listed parents as 'Dartmoor'). If we are to deduce anything from all this we might say that the tendency was back towards the 'pure' breed. And, it might be added, down towards the bottom of the line.

No success against the other breeds that year, with the Welsh having things almost all their own way: first, second and fourth in the large section; a straight first-to-sixth in the small. Modern exhibitors in similar classes might care to note that this was for broodmares of *three* years and over, presumably to allow for the likelihood that two-year-olds running on the moor would be put in foal, applicable to all breeds then and for the remaining two years before the broodmare classes were transferred to the local shows. Height limits 1904–5 were: Dartmoor and New Forest 13.2, Exmoor 13, Highland 14.2, Welsh 12.2.

As regards the nominated shows, the local committee once again chose Brentor & Lydford, where the winners were Little Star and Rosebud (repeating her 1902 success); Okehampton, with Patter (last year's winner at Brentor) and Duchess (presumed Dartmoor born and bred); South Brent, where Dart was best stallion and Stella repeated her several previous wins. Both were pure Dartmoors, the former by Cliquot one of the original five registered stallions in 1899. Something here to cheer the Pure Moor School: hardly a drop of TB, Arab or Hackney in the lot of them – just a touch in Patter. Otherwise, apparently, 'pure' Dartmoor. Mind you, one has to dig around to make sure – or sure enough. Stella's sire was King of the Forest. A popular name. Was this the New Forest (dark brown, 13.1 hh)? No, ours was chestnut, 14 hh, won at Devon County in 1898 and 1900 and almost certainly also sired Okement Queen. (There was a third King (black, luckily) which we need not worry about.) We are, therefore, pretty safe in describing this one as 'unregistered Dartmoor'.

1904

The P & RPS (to give it its newly coined initials) revised its programme for 1904 by putting on classes for individual breeds: Dartmoor, Exmoor, New Forest, Highland and Welsh; together with a single class for mountain and moorland stallions. Eleven Dartmoors were entered, but their judge, Edmund Northey of the Dartmoor Local Committee, was 'somewhat disappointed' in them (apart from the top three). His suggestion: 'If the prizes could be made higher ... it would be the means of a far better

---

[1] *Stud Book, Volume VII, page clvii.*

animal being exhibited. The distance is so great that it does not pay to send the animals for the present prizes.' This suggests that at that time pony-breeding was much more of a business than a pastime.

The winner of the Dartmoor class, Queen of the Moor (a nine-year-old 'by a stallion on the moor' and bred by John Daw of Mary Tavy), was Reserve Mountain and Moorland Broodmare Champion; this in contrast to the stallion class, where Judge Northey dismissed Dartmoors and Highlands as 'the weakest breeds'. From all of which it is evident that Edmund Northey was not one to favour his own.

The locally nominated shows were, as for the previous years, Brentor & Lydford, Okehampton and South Brent. At the first the presence of outside blood was much in evidence, with Patter continuing his winning career (Brentor in 1901, Okehampton 1902), accompanied by Daisy Bell (by the Hackney Prince George 2nd). There was only one class for Dartmoors at Okehampton and it was won by Okement Queen, a five-year-old by King of the Forest.[2]

At South Brent Tin-Tack won the stallion class. He was moorland-bred on both sides (by Cliquot, out of Norma a 'winner of many prizes for Dartmoors at South Brent'). The class for mares went to Lady Bampton, bred by John Edmonds and almost certainly a 'pure' Dartmoor.

1905

The society's event for 1905, now called the London Spring Show, was held on 10–11 March and followed the lines of the previous year. Once again the Dartmoors failed to impress their judge and once again he told them so with that refreshing Edwardian frankness: 'A very poor class', wrote W. Pearse. The three-year-old Flirt won (all Dartmoor, bred by J. W. Westaway of Mary Tavy), followed by Miss Scrimgeour's Gunhilda and Swallow. These two had been described as 'aged' five years before when they were registered. In view of the Judge's unflattering comment, perhaps it would have been kinder to have left them at home.

Brentor & Lydford, Okehampton and South Brent as before around the moor. Little Star repeated his 1903 win at Brentor, alongside Moor Maid, 'purchased at a moorland sale'; a good buy for A. R. Bray of Okehampton, for Moor Maid won prizes galore for him in 1905 and 1906. In 1905 she went to Oscar Muntz's

Mikado (Fell). The result, Moor Maid II, was bought by Sylvia Calmady-Hamlyn, for whom she won at Brentor in 1908 – though not as a Dartmoor, so presumably she grew out.

At Okehampton the three-year-old Sambo (by Patter, see above) was best stallion, with Okement Queen successfully defending her previous year's title. She too went to Mikado and produced a filly called – guess what – Okement Queen II. At South Brent Tin-Tack was again best stallion, with a newcomer, Why Not, best mare.

Milestone: 23 September 1905, height for mares down to 13 hh.

1906

The year 1906 saw major changes in the society's programme for its London spring show. The classes for individual breeds were scrapped and in their place were two open broodmare classes: for 12.2 and 13.2 hh. Back to 1903? Not quite, for these were *open* classes, so that native ponies having the temerity to enter would have to take on polo, riding, Arab, Thoroughbred ... anything that could pass under the stick. Not that Okement Queen was daunted. She made the long journey and won the 12.2 class for Mr. Bray, beating Y Ffran D Du, – now there's a name to floor any non-Welsh announcer – the previous year's champion mare. Predictably, the competition in the 13.2 class was even hotter, with a win for the polo-pony mare Greek Lady (by Sandiway, by Rosewater, out of a Zenophon mare). However, Okement's stable-mate Morella stood second, so the journey was well worth while for Bray of Okehampton.

The mountain and moorland stallion class was retained. There were four entries, with Welsh first, second and third followed by an Exmoor. To compensate for this cut-down, the society transferred the mountain and moorland prize money to the various districts, to be allocated by the local committees, hoping to make life easier for exhibitors from the far-flung moorlands – one kind of answer to Edmund Northey's suggestion of two years before. A bonus for the researcher too, more information on those local shows, names of all prize winners, numbers entered, judges' names, even the names of some sires (when known). For some reason Brentor & Lydford was the only local show to be nominated. There the thirteen-year-old half-Hackney Daisy Bell (the winner in 1904) beat the 'pure' Dartmoor Moor Maid (the winner in 1905), with Okement Queen in third place. No mention of a stallion class. Presumably it was thought they had been catered for in London.

---

[2] *One of several, possibly seven, of that name; only one registered – and that a New Forest.*

1907

In 1907 a Dartmoor again won the 12.2 hh open broodmare class at London: the one-time Dainty bred by F. Norrish, now named Little Wonder and owned by Mrs Pillers of Monmouth; presumed in foal to His Lordship (Welsh and by Lord Polo ex a Welsh Mountain pony). Alas, another good line lost to the breed.

South Brent was the nominated show this year. And with only one class: won by Maggie, a Brentor Confidence seven-year-old; with Twinkle, by Hotspur, a nine-year-old, in second place. The latter a winner in her time – first at Cornwood in 1898 and 1901, second in 1900.

1908

The broodmare classes at the 1908 London show were for 14 hh and 14.2 hh – open, of course, so they did not attract any identifiable native entries. Once again only one local show – and one class at it – was sponsored by the society. At Brentor & Lydford Daisy Bell won for the second time with Dolly second. Thus we have a half-Hackney followed by a quarter-Hackney. In contrast, Imogen Collier's Sea Pink, in third place, was bred on the moor – and picked up at Princetown Fair.

Looking over these two years, we cannot but be struck by the way the Hackney crosses were consistently chosen. How does one reconcile this preference on the part of several judges with the official turning-away from this breeding? And why were there only two classes sponsored by the society where a few years before there had been six (three each year)? Was the poor entry the result of the withdrawal of inducement or was it the other way round?

1909

Nothing to lure Dartmoors to London for the 1909 show, but slightly better prospects down west, with three shows nominated, though only for the broodmare classes. Three classes and seven entries all told. Daisy Bell won once again at Brentor & Lydford, making it three in a row. The 'pure-bred' Flossy was second (bred by W. L. Palmer of Milton Abbot). At Okehampton Cudliptown Queen had a walk-over. At South Brent Bluebell II (moorland bred) beat Princess May I. Small entries all round. From this angle 1909 can be acclaimed as 'Rock-bottom year'.

1910

Things did begin to look up in 1910. Perhaps council felt that the natives were being neglected. At all events, at London that year there was a mountain and moorland broodmare class. It allowed in ponies up to 14.2 hh, but as it was not open to all this did not

matter. Best of all, it was won by a Dartmoor: Sylvia Calmady-Hamlyn's Junket (*ci-devant* Dot), an eleven-year-old bred by Edmund Northey of Okehampton; 12.3 hh by the roadster Young Belthorpe Venture out of Spec. Second was Mrs Philip Hunloke's Princess of Wales; third Little Wonder (previously Dainty), winner of the open 12.2 class in 1907. A win for maturity too, for these three knocked up thirty-nine years between them. Twelve entries, all very encouraging. (It is only fair to the Welsh, however, to add that they had their own classes, for both stallions and mares, which must have reduced the competition in Junket's class.)

Three local shows were again nominated to receive the broodmare sponsorship. New ground was broken this year, with Cornwood joining the regular trio and for the next two years the form was to nominate three of these four in rotation.

At Cornwood Judy II, a four-year-old, 12.3 hh by Punchinello, Captain Muntz's polo-pony stallion, and out of Spec, beat Peggy II, a previous winner at Cornwood. At Okehampton the winner was Black Bess II, with Rosebud II in second place. Black Bess is recorded as winning the previous year at Okehampton, though this could not have been as a Dartmoor, as Cudliptown Queen had a walk-over. One cannot escape the deduction that some of the so-called 'firsts' may not have been very arduous.

Finally that year, at South Brent, Indian Queen was placed

Sylvia Calmady-Hamlyn with Junket at Islington 1910

above the curiously named Soap (possibly for her previous owner, Mr Soper?). She was by King of the Forest. Which one? Well, he is described as 'chestnut, 14.2'. Unregistered, of course, but almost certainly the sire of Princess Olga and probably of Okement Queen. Indeed, if we can overlook a discrepancy of a couple of inches, he could also have sired Stella and Ruby; or, a whole hand away, Venus III and an unnamed mare. More to the point, the numbers of entries were well up on the previous abysmal year – eighteen all told.

1911

Possibly reassured by having had twelve entries for the mountain and moorland broodmares in 1910, the society repeated the class the next year. And once again it was won by a Calmady-Hamlyn Dartmoor, Black Jeanie, five-year-old, bred on Princetown Prison Farm, beating her stable-mate Junket (last year's winner), Mrs Philip Hunloke's Welsh Princess of Wales and Little Wonder (alias Dainty). These first four ran up a total of some forty-seven years. The judge, Norris Midwood, described them as 'quite a nice class', take that as you may. Again the Welsh received special treatment – two classes all to themselves. Why? Two reasons can be paraded straight away: their height limit was 12 hh, exactly suited to the mountain breed; there were lots of

Black Jeanie, Jack Partridge Jr up

them; consequently, there was always a good entry (14 in 1910, 12 in 1911). Fair enough?

In 1911 the local committee nominated Cornwood, Okehampton and South Brent. At the first, Little Sister and Peggy II offer no clue on their breeding apart from being good, run-of-the-mill moorland. At Okehampton Sylvia Calmady-Hamlyn's Junket (second at London) beat George Glanfield's Queen of the Lakes (Dartmoor on both sides and a previous winner at that show).

Edwin Sampson's Black Bess III won at South Brent. Her breeding is described as by an 'improved Dartmoor'. It has not been possible to discover a precise definition of this term as understood at the time, but it is thought to indicate that the pony in question is the result of a first cross of Dartmoor with non-native pony. Bess was out of a Dartmoor by an Exmoor. Second was John Kingwell's Lily of the Valley, 'bred on Dartmoor'.

1912

Another London win for the Dartmoors in 1912; better than that: first second, third and reserve in a general 14.2 class for mountain and moorland mares. The winner was Imogen Collier's Diana II, the Lord Polo filly she bought from Moses Bawden as mentioned earlier. At that time she had also bought another filly from the same mare, Queenie. This was Lucky Star II and now in second place. By the Dartmoor stallion Little Star, she was as pure moorland as anyone could wish. Third was Miss Calmady-Hamlyn's Black Jeanie (no more than a dash of Hackney).

Very nice for the Lord Polo connection, but it is worth nothing what the judge, Oscar Muntz, had to say in his official comment on the class:

> The first and second ... both bred by Moses Bawden of Tavistock, were daughters of the same Dartmoor pony. The second is particularly interesting as an instance of true riding type being bred from Moorland blood solely by careful selection and without a cross of Thoroughbred, Arab or Polo blood.

This, it should be noted, from not only an expert but also one by no means averse to experiment. Incidentally, it must have been an especially good day for Miss Collier, for not only did she collect £11 – and in real gold – but received her rosettes from the hands of the man she was very shortly to marry. Alas, the Western Front claimed Captain Muntz.

It was Cornwood's turn to stand down from the local circuit. The season opened at South Brent, with a win for Peggy II, bred by S. J. Wonnacott and as far as one can tell straight moorland. She had been a winner there in 1907 and 1908, though the classes are not specified. Second was Venus III, yet another product of a King of the Forest (this one chestnut, like Stella's sire, though shown as 2 inches smaller). Venus also went to a Thoroughbred that year, though the name of her foal is not given.

Brentor & Lydford came next. And there the judges favoured the out-crosses. John Symons' Daisy Bell (by Prince George 2nd, Hackney) won, with John Maunder's six-year-old White Star (by Lord Polo, out of Smallspur by Hotspur, Hackney) second. Third was Junket, bred by Edmund Northey, now owned by Sylvia Calmady-Hamlyn, and moving pretty steadily upwards in the line-up. She was by the roadster Young Belthorpe Venture.

Junket won at Okehampton a month later, beating Polly V, C. H. Vinson's 'pure' Dartmoor bred by J. Hopper of Tavistock. Polly had been to Little Star in 1911. Their foal was called Lucky Star; not to be confused with Lucky Star II, also by Little Star, which was second to Diana at the 1912 London show.

1913

The class for mountain and moorland mares at the London show was won by Lizzie II. She was a twelve-year-old Exmoor, stood a mere 12 hh and was bred by Mr Williams of Exford. And that is about all we can find out about her apart from the fact that the judges thought her 'a real good sort', only conceding that Diana II, who stood second, was 'much stronger and bigger', though without 'the quality and character of the winner'.

Diana was back at the right of the line at Brentor & Lydford, beating Polly V (second at Okehampton the previous year). At Cornwood Lady John (by Lord Polo out of Violet and by one of the numerous Kings of the Forest) beat Ruby V and Dot (nothing known of these two). At Okehampton H. Down's Morning Star II beat George Glanfield's Star Face, both home bred and probably 'pure' moorland. Finally, at South Brent Soap beat Gipsy, both apparently moorland-bred.

1914

In the last season before the First World War, Junket scored her second win at the London show, now officially that of the National Pony Society. She was also successful at Brentor & Lydford, in each case nosing out Diana, now her stable-mate. At London too another first: winning the recently presented Lord Arthur Cecil Memorial Challenge Cup.[3] With Dartmoors first, second and third (Imogen Collier's Heather Mixture, by Lord Polo) it was a good day for the breed.

The class at Cornwood was won by Miss Collier's Pink May (Dartmoor on both sides). Bit of Fashion was second. Her owner's comment in the stud book runs: 'Has won Prizes at Blackwater, Brent, Cornwood, Ivybridge, Brentor and Lydford, Plympton and Tavistock'. Okehampton was 'abandoned'. Why, one wonders? Rumour of invasion? Fratricidal murder in committee? Or, more prosaically, the normal Dartmoor downpour? At all events, this decision set the pattern for the next four years, the first mention of renewed Dartmoor activity being in the stud book covering the years 1919–21.

However, is it not opportune to pause at this point so that we can take stock of the years roughly corresponding with the reign of King Edward VII? Four years after he had gone, the First World War, rightly called 'the Great', burst over Europe, very soon to extend over what had until then been looked on as the civilized world. So that, when the business was over and apparently done with, nothing was quite the same as it had been in those halcyon years between 1899 and 1914.

By Imogen Muntz

---

[3] *Subscribed for by members of the society in memory of Lord Arthur who had died a few months before. Still awarded at the NPS Show (now at Malvern) for the Champion Mountain and Moorland Broodmare.*

7 STATE OF PLAY 1914

That the start of the First World War meant the end of an era was not readily apparent at the time. The army had gone off to the continent to sort out those quarrelsome continental potentates; just as it had done, off and on, over the last six centuries. While it was seeing to this, the navy would take care that the conflict did not overflow in our direction. It would all be over by Christmas, when the heroes would return to a suitably heroic welcome. In the meanwhile the rest of us would 'carry on'. Wars were the business of the professional fighters; let them get on with it. So thought our grandparents.

But, as they found out, it wasn't like that at all. This new kind of war was not over by Christmas – nor the next, nor the next, nor the next – and when, eventually, we had won there were precious few of those original heroes to come back to a welcome of any kind. And, as for wars being the business of soldiers and sailors, this one had touched every man, woman and child; some permanently, some more or less closely, all to some extent.

Everyone and everything had changed; even the meanings of words. Thus, if we are to assess how things stood on the moor immediately before this general upheaval, we should take cognizance of these changes. Such assessment should, as far as possible be based on authority. But what constituted 'authority' in, say, 1912, the year we have chosen? Of all such abstractions, it is possible that this one's meaning has altered most since the days of King George V's Delhi Durbar.

To his granddaughter's subjects authority is all too familiar, for it is ever-present, ruling our lives; telling us what we may do, more often what we may not. Authority today is the person (not to be mistaken for anything so human as a man or a woman) on the far (or official) side of the desk or, even further aloof, behind the little rabbit-hole marked Enquiries (closed 12.30–2.30). Authority is well versed in the rules, but cares not a jot for the purpose – if, indeed, there is one, other than yet another statistic. Authority is … But there's no need to go on. Authority today is built into existence. If we're very nimble we may now and then bend it to our advantage; if we're wise we placate it; but we cannot ignore it. So much, then, for authority 1990-style

But what of authority in 1912, the kind we are seeking? He – and feminists must accept the sad fact that it was almost invariably some man, at least outwardly – was something quite different, almost another species. And authority meant exactly that: one accepted as knowing what he was talking about; knew it and was willing to say it. Over the years he would have devoted his time (of which he had plenty to spare) to studying this or that subject congenial to him. He was his own master and gave his opinion without any fear of losing his job (anyway, he didn't have one). He was, needless to say, pragmatic, arrogant, casual. But he did know his stuff. Nor was he to be cowed or browbeaten; not even to be swayed by argument, still less by theory (he simply didn't listen). In short, he was the very antithesis of the modern Corporation Man; he wouldn't have survived five minutes at Group Headquarters. But in 1912 he served the excellent purpose of helping to formulate a common-sense, practical, unbiased answer to questions such as that posed by the President of The Board of Agriculture and Fisheries. 'What can we do for the mountain and moorland ponies?' he asked. And he set up a five-man committee under Lord Arthur Cecil to suggest a solution.

Authoritative? For a start, Lord Arthur was enough for two; literally, for not only was he Convener of the New Forest

Divisional Committee but also a member of its sister committee for the Highlands. Nor were his four colleagues far behind. The Dartmoor interest was admirably represented by Edmund Northey, no stranger to our readers: judge, critic, breeder, owner, divisional committee member. The others were cast in similar moulds. Between them they certainly amounted to authority in the world of the mountain and moorland breeds.

Five is a good number for a committee; that is, if it is for business rather than show. This one was set up in February 1912 and six months later its report was on the president's desk – or at any rate in his in-tray. It was published in Volume XII of the stud book (1913) and revealed itself as an admirable combination of comprehensiveness, absence of waffle, common sense – and, of course, authority. It is well worth reading in its entirety (by those having a complete set of the *NPS Stud Book*). Here, however, there is room for no more than a summary of the main conclusion and, in particular, those especially touching the Dartmoors.

The five good men and true kick off with a brave try at defining 'a mountain and moorland pony'. It is, they declare: '... one whose ancestors have lived on the mountain, moor or common for the last three generations in a semi-feral condition.'

Given the vagueness usually surrounding those three generations, this is probably as close as we can get; a picture, as it were, rather than a photograph, and pretty much in line with what we have been calling 'pure' in the previous chapter; something to be taken as a guide. A guide, maybe, but also an important reminder of the question mark hovering over those animals already in the stud book. How much moorland blood in their veins; how much living on the moor? Yet these had been inspected and accepted as 'typical of the breed'.

On selection (or acceptance) of sires the committee saw the need to differentiate between 'the mountain and moorland stallion pure and simple' and 'the developed sire bred on polo-bred or other registered lines'. In other words, the continuing process must be directed in one way or the other: either breeding *towards* the polo pony with some (but not too much) tough native blood or *back* to the mountain and moorland with some (but not too much) improving outside influence.

The committee also accepts the fact that market value increases with sheer size; also that out-crosses do stand a reasonable chance on the moor, as argument to the contrary fails to take any account of the tendency for the best of such crosses to be sold off (and therefore away from the moor), leaving only 'the inferior and weakly'. Cross-breds, the committee maintains, might look 'light and poor', but in say, three or four generations

they are 'assimilated to the local type, yet retaining some of the characteristics of the finer breeds'.

Predictably, the committee is strong on self-help, expanding the foregoing with an injunction to breeders to make up their own minds on the sort of end-product they want, after those three or four generations. They should not look for results too soon: Nature is not to be hustled. Closely connected with out-crossing is its view on the interchange of stallions between mountain and moorland breeds. This is seen as 'the truer and better line ... introducing the qualities and improvement desired from those herds which have already shown their ability to stand the hardships inseparable from the life of a mountain and moorland pony; this life being the most valuable agent in making ponies a useful factor in national horse-breeding.' A most interesting comment coming, as it does, in 1912. Do we here discern a foretaste of the crosses with Welsh Mountain ponies in the years between the two world wars?

The function of the native pony is concisely stated: to form 'the natural reservoir from which all our national breeds of light horses derive ... and as the means of re-invigorating many of their characteristics of temperament, courage, intelligence and resource.'

Fine – as far as it goes. The inference is clear: the job of the mountain and moorland pony is to improve other, larger breeds. No more than that? Apparently not; a deduction borne out by the actions of the top-flight breeders. Having won at, say, the London show, where do the Dartmoors go to stud? Off to some Thoroughbred, seldom to a Dartmoor, as clearly shown in the notes in the stud book. Not that there is anything reprehensible in this, for there lies the demand for the best ponies. All the same, it is a pity that no role has yet been seen for the Dartmoor – the quality Dartmoor – in its own right, under saddle or between the shafts save in the most utilitarian style. No way to 'encourage' the breed, surely?

From the general to the particular. The committee had some hard things to say about the native pony: 'coarse head, badly set-on neck, low withers, drooping quarters, badly laid shoulder and absence of bone (of which, however, the quality is close and well knit), qualities to be found in almost all the mountain and moorland breeds'. This dolorous catalogue it ascribes to 'immature, unsound or aged breeding stock; too close inbreeding; curtailment and deterioration of range and pasture'; the story, it declares, of 'man's neglect and interference with their freedom'. Later in the report the committee suggests three ways of 'preserving the purity of the breeds and improving and maintaining their admirable qualities':

1. Compulsory registration
2. Institution and encouragement of a pony association in each district
3. Exercise of the Commons Act, 1908

Registration, in operation for some thirteen years at the time, 'had resulted in a marked improvement'. It had indeed, but compulsory registration would be something altogether different. It would certainly be most unpopular with the breeders not interested in showing (i.e. the majority). The committee (guided by Edmund Northey so far as the Dartmoors were concerned) would be aware of this. It mentions premiums, already proving beneficial at Burley and Church Stretton. One cannot but wonder whether 'compulsory registration' would ever have been enforceable on the moor without an effort out of all proportion.

The idea of 'district' (by which one presumes is meant 'breed') associations is new. The Welsh had had their own stud book since the turn of the century, having founded their Pony and Cob Society in 1901. The New Forest also already had a stud book and a society at Burley. The Shetlands had formed their society in 1890, but none of the rest had anything beyond the district committees formed in or soon after 1899.

We should not be too ready to upbraid our predecessors for their apparent slothfulness, for the tide was not yet favourable on a number of counts. First, in their reluctance to register, the bulk of the breeders had shown that, at the best, they would give any such body no more than luke-warm support. As has been mentioned in an earlier chapter, they produced their ponies as stock to be sold; not for much, but then they had cost practically nothing in the first place. And to their buyers a pony was a pony; a basic unit of – literally – horsepower.

Naturally, this state of affairs was not in the interest of the breed as a whole; especially it disregarded the idea of the 'reservoir' mentioned above; a pity, but that was the way things were at the time of which we are writing – and, indeed, for some years more. Small wonder then that the Committee selected the Dartmoor as the breed requiring 'most assistance'. This took the practical form of recommending 'thirty premiums of £7 10s each to be given annually for stallions ... selected by the District Committee'. Six for fillies as well.

Of course, it was not only West Country conservatism/ indolence/stubbornness (take your pick) that put the brake on the chariot of progress. Conditioned as we are to the availability of road transport since the Second World War, it is hard to appreciate the difficulties simply of moving around. A pony –

any stock for that matter – either went by train or it walked. Thus we find our two shortages: interest and transport. Activities had to be local, if they were to achieve any worthwhile support. And so it remained, waiting for something or someone to come along and shake all concerned into action. This came about, but not for some years.

The committee looked at transport, by which was meant transport by rail. It produced a number of useful, practical suggestions, mostly involving some agreement with the railway companies (rates for ponies to be on a par with those for cattle, ponies to travel by passenger train (separately), special rates to and from well-known fairs etc.). Of course, none of this touched the real business: that of carting the animal from its stable to the actual showground and back again; a luxury not yet dreamt of.

It should not surprise us, therefore, to find most of the breeds taking some time to bring themselves into corporate existence. From the stud book it would appear that the Dales Pony Improvement Society, formed in 1916, showed the way, followed across a decade by the Fells, Exmoors, Highlands, Connemaras,[1] New Forest, Welsh and Dartmoors, so that Volume XIX of the stud book (1927) was able to announce that each native breed had its pony society (adding, slightly illogically, that this 'ensured that every pony entered (was) of the desired type') However, we are getting a little ahead of our story, so let us return to 1912.

The third suggestion, to invoke the Commons Act (1908), did not at the time affect Dartmoor. Broadly, this Act empowers the Board of Agriculture to bar certain stallions from open ground, undoubtedly a good thing. As it was, any commoner with grazing rights could turn out whatever he fancied, a process only too liable to muddy the waters of the aforesaid 'reservoir'.

The committee summarized its recommendations as follows:

1. Registration of *suitable* sires and mares.
2. Premiums to mountain and moorland stallions to roam at large.
3. Premiums to young mares.
4. Use of the Commons Act to eliminate the unfit (by barring poor stallions).
5. Interchange of registered stallions to combat the effects of too-close inbreeding.
6. To seek better terms from the railway companies.
7. To eliminate abuses and encroachments injurious to pasture.

---

[1] There was also an English *Connemara Society, formed in 1947.*

There they are, copied out neatly from the pages of Volume XII. But what actually happened? Well, for a start there was that war referred to at the start of the chapter. This tended to ensure the pending-tray for all but the most urgent matters pleading for official interest. Still, the National Pony Society (as it had become) did take notice, if only obliquely, by forming a Mountain and Moorland Committee to match those for Show, Finance, Editing and Judges' Selection. The Dartmoor representative? Edmund Northey.

We should not leave our scrutiny of this quintet without noting a remark of Northey's – almost an aside, but important – a reference to the newly aroused interest in Dartmoor ponies on the part of the Duchy of Cornwall. He outlined wide-ranging plans to be 'applied to the encouragement of Dartmoor ponies'. What these were and what they achieved can best be left to following chapters.

The Cecil Committee was undoubtedly beneficial. It was sheer bad luck that the First World War intervened so soon after the publication of its findings. If it achieved nothing else, it did remind the horse world that it needed the native breeds. That it ignored the uses of the native pony as an end in itself is understandable, in view of the times, especially the lack of transport; not just across the country, but from stable or moor to show or meet. All that was to come, but Lord Arthur and his colleagues brought it that much nearer.

Dartmoor mare with Alona Newbolt-Young

8 PRINCELY VENTURE

In the year 1785 young Thomas Tyrwhitt, of Wickham Bishops in Essex, arrived on the moor; surprisingly to seek fame and fortune. Such hopes were not ill-founded, the reason for this uprooting from his native county being traceable to his close friendship with George, Prince of Wales, his exact contemporary whom he had met while up at Christ Church, Oxford. Thus, after the manner of the age, he soon found himself established as Secretary to His Highness and, better still, the owner (or, at any rate, the occupier) of 2300 acres of moorland to the south of Two Bridges on the West Dart. Over the next thirteen years he transformed this empty landscape into a useful estate, building several houses and naming it Tor Royal in honour of his patron.

Nor did he stop there, for he was above all an ardent 'improver'. Not content with snatching Tor Royal from the surrounding wilderness, he cast about for the means of bringing prosperity to the whole area. He had lots of land, but it was not very productive, save in one direction. Several of his tors, as usual of solid rock, offered what was reputedly the hardest and best granite in the kingdom; there for the taking and only waiting for the muscular quarrymen to prise it loose and the means of carting it away to where it was needed.

Tyrwhitt set about the business with characteristic impetuosity. And, it must be added, a happy insouciance regarding the practical obstacles. His quarrymen would need houses. Very well, he would build them. The result was 'Prince's Town' (later contracted to Princetown), set on a dismal site some 1600 feet above sea-level; cold, wet and wind-swept; a chilling catalogue which hardy folk who have been there, even in high summer, cannot but endorse. But build it he did, topping off with an inn loyally named The Plume of Feathers.

Next he set about finding a buyer for his product. And, in view of its weight, the nearer home the better. On the other hand, selling granite on the moor might be likened to carrying coals to Newcastle. Not a bit of it! In no time this energetic entrepreneur had clinched a deal with, of all unlikely customers, the Admiralty. It happened this way. At the time the Napoleonic Wars were yielding a steady crop of prisoners, so that Their Lordships, though not notably prone to pampering their own folk, let alone captives, had to face the fact of severe overcrowding in the hulks at Millbay in Plymouth. They thus swallowed the Tyrwhitt scheme: a fine, new prison up on healthy Dartmoor, built to last from local material; a nice, neat, well-rounded arrangement appealing to all concerned – except possibly the 2500 Frenchmen who had, in due course, to tramp the 15 miles uphill to their new home-from-home.

But even the best of wars has to end some time. By 1816 the last of the inmates had left and once again Sir Thomas (as he had become in 1812) was at his wit's end over how to realize his vision of a moor of lush pasture and waving corn. He needed transport. Very well, he would build a railway. And so he did; all the 25 miles from his quarries to salt water at Sutton Pool; horse-drawn, to be sure, but no mean feat in 1823. It is sad to record that, despite all his efforts, the venture slid steadily downhill. Finally, in 1828 even he lost heart, sold all his interest and retired to die abroad at the early age of seventy.

Had he failed? It depends on how one assesses much matters. In immediate material terms, the answer must be yes. He had overreached himself in attempting the impossible. It is true that local advice tends to be gloomy, especially from farmers, but perhaps he should have listened to these apparent pessimists. For

Dartmoor Pony Society Show, Prince Hall 1949: Brood mares (*left to right***) Jim Holman, John Coaker's Heatherbelle VI, Pat Hyett's Cater's Beam, Jean Palmer's Yeoland Lady Hamilton.**

all that, let us at least give some honour to a gallant effort. And he did create Tor Royal. Thus, when a little over a century and three Dukes of Cornwall later the holder of the title had a fancy to try his hand at pony breeding, there it was, all ready for him. The stud book records the facts of germination, blossoming and, alas, the withering of this project, like its predecessor over-ambitious. The tale starts in Volume XIV (published 1917). Bowing deeply from the ankles, 'The Editing Committee have *(sic)* the honour to announce that His Royal Highness the Prince of Wales has graciously permitted his name to be associated with the present volume … by a representative entry of an Eastern Sire … and of Dartmoor Pony Stallions and Mares.'

And there they all are, each under its heading: 1 Eastern sire, (of which more anon), 3 polo pony mares, 1 New Forest mare, 3 Dartmoor stallions and no fewer than 26 Dartmoor mares. Let us inspect those that concern our story.

First the Dartmoors. The three stallions were: Master Forester (aged, bred by Reddaway of Belstone, Okehampton) and his two sons, Tinner (1912, from an anonymous mare) and Abbot of Buckfast (1913, from a 'Dartmoor'). The last two are shown as having been bred at Tor Royal.

The 26 Dartmoor mares of this original registration comprised the following: 6 home bred by H.R.H., 1 from William Worth of Princetown, 1 from Mead of South Brent, 2 from Cornwall, 1

Two examples of stallions used on Dartmoors at Tor Royal: Black Shales and Grey Shales; a type, now extinct, originating in Norfolk.

incognito, fifteen from A. E. Barrington whose address is given as Tor Royal. Of the 2 colts and 6 fillies shown as bred by H.R.H. (between 1911 and 1914), the 2 colts and 4 of the fillies are by Master Forester, 1 is by a 'Dartmoor' and the sire of 1 is not given. The record of their dams is even vaguer: 3 'Dartmoor', 5 anonymous. The breeding of those from Worth and Mead is given as 'Dartmoor'; that of the two from Cornwall as 'probably Goonhilly'. In short, apart from the six mentions of Master Forester, not a single name of a sire or dam.

There were no entries for Tor Royal in Volume XV, but in volumes XVI and XVII (published together in 1922) there are 9: 8 foals and 1 new arrival (a mare foaled in 1907). The foals (all born between 1917-19) are all given sires and dams, the latter being seven of the original purchase, plus Diana II, acquired from Sylvia Calmady-Hamlyn about 1918 (though her registration is not transferred until Volume XIX, published in 1927).

Diana was clearly a cut above all the other mares at Tor Royal, none of which seems to have won any prize in any ring. Nor did any of them produce any known winners — with one notable exception of whom more shortly. Nor were Diana's own winning days over. In 1921, when she was fourteen, she won at NPS London, Devon County and Brentor & Lydford.

It is disappointing that the stud book should contain so little information about this royal venture apart from the two batches of registrations. This has, in later years, given rise to some criticism; especially that it did not 'do enough' for the indigenous breed. Let us, therefore, consider the basic question: what was the business (or, if you like, the purpose) of Tor Royal and thence to see how this impinges on our subject, the Dartmoor pony.

The present-day popularity of mountain and moorland ponies for riding and driving can blind us to the fact that in the years shortly after the First World War the Dartmoor was far from being valued as a superior animal in its own right. Rather it was seen, if at all, as no more than a (humble) step in the production of something else. Its usefulness lay in one or other of three directions: first and most highly rewarded, it could be put to a larger, high-quality stallion — usually a Thoroughbred, an Arab or perhaps a Hackney — to achieve a polo pony, either straight away or after two or three generations. Lower down the scale — quite a long way — it could likewise be crossed, but this time with something hefty and without worrying too much about quality (a cob, for instance), to produce a good, strong carrier or hauler. Finally, it could be itself, fulfilling its centuries-old task of carrying the moorland farmer and his loads about his roadless domain. And that was about all. Nothing yet, even in the offing, about 'private' driving or riding. The Dartmoor was a working pony — in its most basic sense.

The activities at Tor Royal — and those of others making breeding their *business* — endorse this generalization. In the case of Tor Royal the Dartmoor mares were seen as no more than the means of meeting the demands of the first two categories, the produce that did not being sold off as Category Three. Thus, for the polo field there was the Eastern sire already referred to, whose progeny out of the Dartmoors would, it was hoped, combine his quality and pace with the toughness and stamina of the moorland breed. And, with any luck, their height would remain below the then prescribed 14.2 hh. For the load-carriers and haulers (for which the army was still a good customer, especially after the losses suffered in the First World War) the stud invested in Welsh cobs. Finally, to maintain the supply of Dartmoor breeding stock, it had Master Forester and his two sons. In addition, there would have been found at Tor Royal a wide variety of horses and ponies from, literally, all over the world; presents to Edward P during one or other of his tours; not strictly relevant to the Dartmoor story.

The overall purpose of Tor Royal was never actually spelt out, but its actions speak. It was set up to breed for the polo field and for the army. The Dartmoors were all part of that purpose. Despite their numerical preponderance and the fact that it was on the moor, Tor Royal was *not* a Dartmoor stud; certainly not as we understand the term today. Not everyone agreed; if not at the time, then later; notably Sylvia Calmady-Hamlyn who had some hard things to say about it in her otherwise excellent and informative pamphlet produced in 1958 when she was nearing the end of her long reign as secretary-plus of the DPS. 'Then [she wrote] came a period when the Duchy of Cornwall Stud bought up *all* the cream of the mares and crossed them in every imaginable way, and when the stud was suddenly dissolved it was too late and the few good ones had vanished.'[1]

Clearly, Miss Calmady-Hamlyn is far from pleased with Tor Royal's record so far as the native breed is concerned. Do the facts she quotes justify these assertions?

We have already quoted from the NPS Stud Book, our only contemporary authority, let us recapitulate.

During the decade and a half of its existence Tor Royal acquired and registered twenty-eight mares, all but one previously unregistered, all but two of unknown breeding. The cream? As for *all* the cream .... Let us, however, keep the matter in perspective. We should bear in mind that Miss Calmady-Hamlyn was writing some thirty-five years after the event, when a fire had destroyed many of her records. She thus had little more than her memory to rely on, plus what others had said.

It is possible, for instance, that she remembered what Edmund Northey had told the Cecil Committee shortly before the First World War.[2] He had then laid before his colleagues 'the schemes which the Duchy of Cornwall [was] applying to the encouragement of Dartmoor Ponies'. These included 'the purchase of twenty of the best typical Dartmoor mares and two of the best stallions'. But, as later stud books reveal, the Duchy did no such thing, contenting itself with scraping together what can only be described as a job lot. Northey was, of course, quoting an *intention*. It would seem that, forty-six years later, this was assumed to have actually taken place.

Perhaps the Duchy did miss an opportunity of doing a bit of good for the indigenous breed. On the other hand, it cannot be upbraided for aiming at the two markets open at the time. A matter for regret, but not for censure. Anyway, not every one of the descendants of the Tor Royal Dartmoors 'vanished'. Several went to neighbouring studs, such as that at Sherberton. And one left an indelible mark on the breed. How then did this come about?

If we are to do justice to what can only be described as equine high romance – except that it is all true – we must first translate ourselves through time and space: back twenty-two years before the First World War, south and east some 3000 miles away from cold, foggy, snowbound Princetown. Then and there – that is, a scant five years since the Empire had gathered from all over the world to celebrate the Golden Jubilee of the Great White Queen and somewhere in the unmapped land between the Red Sea and the Persian Gulf – an Arabian mare dropped a bay colt-foal. Nor was this any ordinary colt, for his dam was of the Anazeh tribe and 'of the highest caste'. He must have been an eye-catching youngster, because it was not long before he was picked out by Major Broome, Remount Agent for the Government of Bombay, shipped off to India and introduced to the track. There he fully confirmed Broome's judgement: first past the post a dozen times out of fifteen starts, including (as his new owner proclaims in the stud book) the Hurricane Stakes at Rawal Pindi 'where he did the mile in 1 53 4/5 – easily'. He also won 'numerous gymkhana events' and even a class for ladies' hacks.

Anyway, when he was about twelve years old this versatile performer arrived in England under the care of Captain McDougall of the Army Veterinary Department who registered him as a polo pony stallion. Finally, around 1914 he appeared at Tor Royal. He was the 'Eastern sire' referred to above. Volume XIV (published in 1917) shows him as belonging to the Prince of

Wales. His name was Dwarka. He measured 14 hands 1⅛ inches. There is a picture of him at the front of Volume XIV. Handsome and, more important, very much a pony type.

In sharp contrast to this august lineage and sparkling record were the forebears and early activities of a Dartmoor filly born at Princetown some fifteen years after the lordly Arabian. Blackdown was bred by Mrs Crocker, wife of the landlord of that same Plume of Feathers built a century before by the optimistic Sir Thomas. She was by the roadster Confident George out of an unnamed 'Dartmoor pony' and stood the full 13 hh. Known as Kitty, she earned her keep between the shafts of the cart that delivered the fish in and around the little town. There is a picture of her doing it (see p.38). It would be pleasant to be able to depict a Cinderella-like progress: seen in her humble calling by Edward P himself, recognized at her true worth, whisked off to a place of honour in the royal stable. There is, alas, no evidence to support this fairy tale. For all that, the end result was just as dramatic. There is, indeed, no need to stray from the well-attested facts as given in the stud book.

She must have arrived at Tor Royal in about 1914, for she had foals for her new owner in 1915 (by a 'Moor Stallion') and in 1918 and 1919 (by Dwarka). It is the one born in 1918 that

Kohailan Arab Stallion Dwarka (1892)

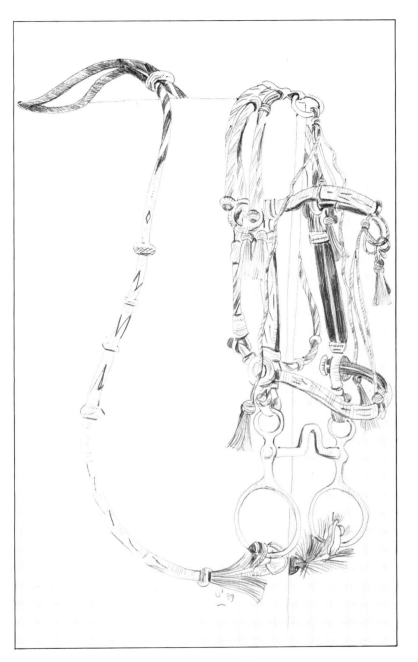

Dwarka's Arab bridle

Blackdown (1097) 13.0 hh., dam of The Leat

concerns us. He was a bay colt. No doubt this was a disappointment at the time. At all events, his arrival did not arouse enough interest to do more than note it below the name of his dam. Indeed, it was not until he was four years old that he achieved his place in the Dartmoor section. By then however, he had come into the keeping of Sylvia Calmady-Hamlyn, who, whatever her subsequent views of the goings-on at Tor Royal, knew a good pony when she saw one. They named him The Leat. And, if ever there was an appropriate name, this was it, for from his veins flowed the blood of virtually every single successful Dartmoor in the years to come – right up to the present day.

He was, of course, the supreme example of the uncertainty of breeding. First, in the matter of height. Dwarka stood 14.1 hh and Blackdown 13 hh, as already mentioned. Should not their offspring, with a half-Arab, a quarter-roadster and only a quarter-Dartmoor blood, have topped 13, even 14 hh? He came nowhere near it. The moorland blood on his dam's side must have been strong (like, perhaps, her merchandise in those days before universal refrigeration), for at maturity he measured exactly 12.2 hands; thus not merely complying with the existing rule (with a hand to spare) but apparently foreseeing that of the years to come. Nor was this all. Despite his scant quarter-share of true Dartmoor blood, his numerous photographs show that in

The Leat (1918), 12.2 hh.

every one of those 50 inches he presented the quintessence of what might be termed the 'New Model Dartmoor', that elusive combination of toughness and quality. At any rate so thought a wide spectrum of eminent judges over several years; of him and of his progeny; the latter even to the present day.

After all this, it might appear unseemly, even profane, to cast any shadow across his memory. However, this must be done, for one doubt remains, one basic question to be faced and, if possible, answered. Was The Leat eligible for registration? That is to say, did his entry in the stud book comply with the rules then in force? At that time, shortly after the First World War, the registration of Dartmoors was still governed by two official utterances of nearly twenty years' standing: broadly, by the 'desire' expressed by the Polo Pony Society in 1901 that registration of mountain and moorland ponies should be confined to the progeny of 'pure pony mares' and those actually registered should have at least three-quarters 'pony blood' over all. This was followed a year later by the Dartmoor local committee's 'resolution' forbidding judges to pass any ponies known to have more than a quarter Arab/Thoroughbred or an eighth Hackney blood. Nor should these be seen as passing thoughts, for both were reprinted over the years. How did The Leat contrive to surmount (or skirt round) these formidable obstacles?

A determined breeder is, of course, seldom put off by anything as low key as a 'desire'. On the other hand, a 'resolution' is, or should be, quite another matter. There, apparently, was the rule, clear and unequivocal, repeated in every volume from VIII (1905) to XVII. Then, in Volume XVIII, came the surprise; the dog that didn't bark: after iteration through ten volumes covering almost twenty years – silence in the mountain and moorland section of the stud book. Where at the head of Dartmoor entries the excluding resolution had been quoted and re-quoted there was now no more than an invitation to refer back to the original 'description and characteristics' in Volume V (1899). The resolution had simply vanished. Did this imply that it was by now 'sufficiently promulgated'? Or, contrariwise, was it stage one in the process of sweeping an inconvenient (and self-inflicted) restriction under the carpet? Of course, it may well have been properly and officially rescinded, but it's odd that the stud book says not a word. The modern reader is left guessing. Guessing, but, if of a practical turn of mind, surely not unduly disturbed about the long-term effect of any irregularity. Correctly or otherwise, The Leat was registered as a Dartmoor. He certainly looked the part, for it was not long before he was collecting firsts at the the hands of competent and respected judges at major

shows: Bath & West and Brentor & Lydford 1922-3, Devon County, Cornwood and Plympton in 1923. Perhaps he should not have been let into the ring – or the stud book for that matter – but he was. And he won, resoundingly.

Nor are his own wins in Dartmoor classes the end of the story. His progeny won too. And have kept on winning to this day. And the point is that these descendants did qualify under the rule known or surmised to be in force at the time. In short, if The Leat did beat the gun, he only did so by one generation. Let us not then begrudge him his triumphs, piratical though they may seem to some, but instead applaud his lasting contribution to the making of the modern, high-quality Dartmoor. Let us also remember with gratitude his singular forebears: the anonymous Arabian mare 'of the highest caste'; Dwarka, the aristocrat of the desert; never forgetting Kitty, the fish-cart Cinderella who introduced the vital moorland blood. And on the human side: Broome of the Bombay service who spotted Dwarka's merit, McDougall who brought him home from India, Hurn who bought Kitty for the Tor Royal stud, Sylvia Calmady-Hamlyn who saw, acquired *and registered* The Leat himself.

The interwoven stories of Tor Royal Stud and The Leat have been related at some length, for together they can stand for that part of the history of the Dartmoor breed when interest was shifting away from the larger pony suitable for polo or load carrying to something smaller and finer, essentially a pony rather than a small horse. The transition occupied roughly the period between the end of the First World War and the formal foundation of the Dartmoor Pony Society in 1925.

Before we leave Tor Royal, however, it is interesting to review its activities as those of one of the last of the polo-and-pack-oriented studs. Nor should we forget that, apart from this business side, it was also the stable of its ducal owner. Edward P was a keen rider, though on his own admission a little accident-prone. He enjoyed riding across country, either to hounds (usually in the Shires, but occasionally in the West Country) or in point-to-points (until stopped by his father, who objected that he was jeopardizing the succession). For these amusements he needed plenty of hunters. It is reported that, at one time in the mid-twenties, there were sixteen of these passing the summer at Tor Royal, plus three belonging to his brother Prince Henry; further, that there were at times more than a hundred horses of all kinds at Tor Royal in its heyday, engaging the attention of over a score of stable-hands.

Presumably the reference to the hundred horses includes everything on four legs, but, however it was, there is a fine Edwardian lavishness in the casual mention of 'twenty to thirty' on the pay-roll. Nor was this all. At Tor Royal House itself, a mansion of ample size, there was a housekeeper permanently 'in residence'; a sinecure if ever there was one, for on his infrequent visits H.R.H. and his friends put up at the nearby Duchy Hotel. There was also a chauffeur and, naturally, a car for him to drive.

But even royalty has to take some notice of where the money goes. Thus, as early as 1923 we find the Duchy Secretary, Sir Walter Peacock, complaining to the Stud Manager, Arthur Hurn. He notes with distress that the previous year's 'expenses' had run up to £2,258, against which he could set only some £1,700 of 'receipts', with the prospect of less than £1,000 in the current year. They must, wrote Peacock (and one can see his point), get the 'costs' down to £1,400 if possible. There is no reason to believe that Hurn was not doing his best, but it does seem that the enterprise was carrying far too many passengers, human as well as equine; that is, if it was expected to come within shouting distance of paying for itself. Hindsight suggests that it never had a hope. The quality of the ponies for sale was too low, the numbers insufficient, the overheads too high.

The stud book endorses this sad conclusion. The spate of registrations in volumes XVI-XVII, already referred to, fell to a trickle. In later volumes, right up to the mid-thirties, the Dartmoor section lists exactly three ponies bred at Tor Royal. And of these three two are registered by later owners. There is only one possible conclusion: Tor Royal was not interested in breeding Dartmoors.

Luckily others were. Tor-Royal-bred Heatherbelle VI went to John Coaker of Sherberton near Princetown. Her breeding is not recorded. This is a pity, for she did very well in the ring: three wins at the Dartmoor Pony Show at Brimpts, three at the Devon County. And, of course, there was The Leat, safely in the discriminating hands of Sylvia Calmady-Hamlyn. Which suggests that, cream or not, she herself had skimmed to excellent effect and to the great benefit of the whole breed in later years.

The stud itself remained in being for a further eight years after Sir Walter's warning. Finally, in 1931, the shutters went up, the ponies were sold for what they would fetch and that was that.

And what of Tor Royal in the nineties? Gone are the hundred horses, along with the 'twenty to thirty men' to look after them. Gone too are the housekeeper and the chauffeur, the horse-boxes waiting in a siding at Princetown station. Gone, for that matter, is Princetown Railway. Instead, the visitor will find the Tor Royal land once more being farmed, with the house leased to the farmer. And how about the famous stables? Here is the most remarkable transformation of all. No longer do they produce ponies for pit, platoon or polo field, but dresses for women. The buildings, built to last, had suffered some neglect, but over the last decade have been repaired, refurbished and reorientated into an outpost of the rag trade. One wonders what Tom Tyrwhitt would have made of it.

Dwarka by Peter Upton

Postbridge

9 FOUNDING THE SOCIETY
(AND FUNDING IT TOO)

The story of the Dartmoor pony during the first quarter of the twentieth century is essentially that of individuals, owners as well as ponies. It is true that, ever since its inception in 1899, registration had been overseen by the Polo/National Pony Society and kept within its not too stringent rules, but it all remained markedly personal: qualifications for inclusion very much a matter of opinion, criteria minimal, the decision of the inspectors paramount, the voice of the people unheard. There were benefits too: a number of local shows received 'official' – that is, the society's – recognition; more to the point, such recognition meant better prize-money, adding welcome substance to the kudos of a society-sponsored award. All in all, then, the pony business (if business it could be called) on and around the moor was run on lines which, even in contemporary Ireland, would have been seen as 'aisy'.

At the time 'aisy' served well enough. But times were changing. Slowly the breeders were becoming aware that the potential of the Dartmoor – at the top end of its scale – need not begin and end with the polo-ground. For the best – and even for the not-quite-top class – there were other outlets, profitable or enjoyable, sometimes both. And not just for the Arab or TB cross but for the pure native.

Thus the area of activity to be encouraged, and hence organized and regulated, could no longer be confined to the simple informality of inspection and the subsequent registration of those deemed worthy of the Dartmoor imprimatur, most of which had been covered by three or four inspectors acting more or less independently and only slightly constrained by guidelines. Gradually over the quarter-century the ground was being prepared for the formation of a duly constituted and elected body to take care of these widening interests.

Whoever brought the matter to fruition is not evident. In 1923, however, Sir Walter Peacock (whom we have already met in his office of Duchy Secretary) remarks in a letter to R. B. Phillpotts of Ilsington that he is 'glad to hear there is a chance of a Dartmoor Pony Society being formed'. Finally Volume XIX of the *NPS Stud Book* (published 1927, covering the years 1925–27) presents the DPS to the pony world. This initial line-up is impressive: three vice-presidents (none below the rank of baronet), sixteen lesser mortals on the council. The list includes the hon treasurer and the secretary, so presumably these are also voting members. Rather dashingly for those days, the sixteen includes some ladies; only four of them (chivalrously put at the top of the list) but all what would today be called high-powered: Mrs Vinson-Thomas, Mrs Muntz, Miss Calmady-Hamlyn, Miss Cave-Penny; none likely to allow herself to be thrust aside in debate, all pony breeders of standing. Possibly the most interesting point of all is that, of these nineteen, all but one live in Devon.

The new society seizes the opportunity to report 'activities and progress': notably 'membership increased considerably during the last year' (presumably 1927), 'purity of ponies well maintained… number of ponies registered far in excess of previous years.'[1]

---

[1] *Trumpet-blowing, but muted and surely to be forgiven. The 'increase' in membership is not surprising, as the society had only been going for a couple of years. In the matter of 'purity' (presumably of native breeding) opinion even then was divided. However, there is no doubt about the increase in registrations, for this is established in the stud book: in Volumes XVI–XVII (1919–21) 3 stallions, 34 mares; in Volume XVIII (1922–4) 7 stallions, 18 mares, but in Volume XIX (1925–7, i.e. unde the aegis of the DPS) 23 stallions, 79 mares. The report also announces that 'the War Office has recognized the purpose of this society', without actually letting on exactly what this is.*

The Dartmoor entry for the next volume (Number XX, published in 1930) is disappointing, as there is no report and therefore little news on how things are going. However, we see that the society has now elected a president. This is Sir Alfred Goodson of Brixham who, most commendably, has acquired and registered two 1928 filly-foals from John Lentern of South Zeal. To back him up there are now no fewer than 11 vice-presidents, bringing to 25 those entitled (we surmise) to put their feet under the council table (21 indigenous, 4 'foreigners').

Volume XXI (published in 1935) reveals a number of significant changes. Sylvia Calmady-Hamlyn is now Hon. Secretary, though still firmly ensconced in her place (head of the list) on the council. The treasurership (apparently vacant over the last few years, leading the modern reader to wonder who, if anyone, totted up the accounts) has been taken over by Nora Dawson of Holne Park, also honorary. She too remains on the council. The society now has a chairman as well as a president, but only a single vice-president. However, if we are to follow the fortunes – or, initially, the misfortunes – of the DPS, it is not at the exalted personages, doubtless as public-spirited as they are distinguished, that we should be looking, but at the new holders of the offices of treasurer and secretary, now honorary and therefore powerful; especially the secretary.

At the heart of the society's affairs lay the inconvenient truth that it was spending more than it was raking in; a situation by no means outside the experience of virtuous endeavours. Everyone was giving of his or her best, but the books simply did not balance. It was intolerable that the society should wind up its existence after less than a decade. But what else could it do in those days before sponsorship and nationalization? The predicament must have seemed insoluble to the president, all those ex-vice-presidents and eminent members of council. Not quite all. The line-up in Volume XXI, already outlined, reveals the presence of the two stalwarts mentioned above. They brought to their offices – and onto the council – knowledge, enthusiasm and, not to beat about the financial bush, the requisite backing in hard cash. They could see what was happening and with no great difficulty could extrapolate where the society was going to end up – and sooner rather than later.

They got to work; their plan was quite simple. In effect, in return for a tacit free hand the two of them would take the weight; that is to say, they would pay off the debts (including ex-Secretary Yeo's modest salary), see that future costs were met and, in general, keep the society going. This was never stated in so many words, but it is how it worked out. In addition, from then onwards the subscriptions (five bob (25p) per annum) went straight into a deposit account, to build up what Sylvia Calmady-Hamlyn referred to later as 'a nest egg'. So how *did* the society keep going and do what it wanted? Easily. The whole net costs of shows, rosettes, prizes, office and all the rest came out of the pockets of the secretary and treasurer. Nor were administration and finance the end of the matter. Again in partnership, they set about breeding Dartmoor ponies; the very best, as might be imagined. And this they achieved, if show results, inter-breed and up and down the country, are anything to go by; all of which is touched on elsewhere in this story.

It is no kind of exaggeration to say that the combination of Dawson and Calmady-Hamlyn brought the Dartmoor breed right to the forefront of the world of native ponies. And the price? The hon. secretary did not so much ask for a free hand; she took it. And, it must at once be added, to the immense and long-term benefit of the society, the breed and, indeed, all the native breeds. In this *coup d'état* she was fully (and financially) abetted by the hon. treasurer's playing the Great Agrippa to a resolute, intelligent and long-sighted Octavian Caesar. It was a great achievement, the benefits of which the breed still enjoys. It is relevant, therefore, to turn aside for a short while to take a more detailed look at a remarkable personality.

Sylvia Calmady-Hamlyn was born in 1881 to a family long established in the West Country. Thus she set out in life with what were then considerable advantages (and even a century later are far from inconvenient): she knew the countryside, was known and (one surmises) quietly aware of her own assured position. In her early teens she was packed off to Wycombe Abbey School, then recently opened; a rare concession to a female in the nineteenth century and an opportunity of which she made good use; advantages, admittedly, but none too much for one set on elbowing her way to the fore in a man's world; even when allied to a sharp intelligence and enough fortune to allow her to take her own line. Finally, she had strength of purpose.

It was, of course, this last that made all the difference. She had character. Even those critical of her arbitrary methods (or possibly jealous of her many successes in the show-ring) had to concede that. She had strength, to be sure, but to *what* purpose? In other words, what did she want to do with all those advantages and abilities? The answer was by no means clear at the start, possibly not even to herself. Indeed, she was in her forties before it became evident that she knew exactly what she wanted. Then that purpose set rock-hard. From then on she would devote her talents, her time, her fortune, her life to the Dartmoor pony. And for another forty years she did so.

We should not be surprised that she apparently took so long to find her *métier*. Circumstances were against her. Up to the First World War hunters, hacks and polo ponies were the fashion. She rode hacks in the ring and bred polo ponies with considerable success. To the fashionable breeders the native pony, on the other hand, meant no more than a useful out-cross. Thus, when she came by some Dartmoor mares it was natural that she should cross them with thoroughbreds or Arabs. Her purpose was to breed polo ponies, not more Dartmoors; as is borne out by her registrations in the pre-First-World-War stud books.

Volume X (1907–8) records her first batch: 6 mares, 1 foal bred by herself; among the 6 a filly by a Fell out of a Dartmoor which might, at a stretch, be called her first Dartmoor.[2] The other five in this volume are, of course, polo ponies; notably, all but one are by Thoroughbreds. And so it goes on. In Volume XI (1909–10) there are 5 mares (all by Thoroughbreds), 3 home-bred foals (by Thoroughbreds), 2 Dartmoor mares. But with these two, Black Jeanie and Junket, it can be said that the Dartmoor eased its way into what became the Vean Stud. Well, yes and no. They were Dartmoors and they were there, but if we are to see the picture clearly we must admit that they had no real connection with their successors, in that neither had any further part to play in breeding *Dartmoors*. All the same, they did very well in the ring, despite antecedents far from impressive; Black Jeanie, 12.2 hh, bred at Princetown Prison Farm, by 'pony' ex Jeanie II (herself unremarkable apart from a dash of Hackney through Hotspur four generations back); Junket (late Dot), 12.3 hh, bay, by Young Belthorpe Venture (roadster), ex Dartmoor Spec bred by Edmund Northey. Nevertheless, their new owner must have chosen with her usual skill: 27 firsts for Black Jeanie, 8 for Junket (plus a 2nd to Jeanie at NPS London), all in the seasons 1911–14.

The next two volumes tell a similar story: lots of polo ponies arriving, a slight increase in the number of new Dartmoors – five in Volume XII (1911–12) and five again in Volume XIII (1913–14). However, from the point of view of the Dartmoor *breed* the important point is not that the Dartmoors arrived, and in some strength, but what use was made of them. There is a two-part answer: to most of them nothing happened so far as the stud

book reveals; to a select pair, Junket and Diana, a succession of GSB matings (Descender, Harvest Money, Percussion, Cruikshanks, Tyranny, Tyrant) nine foals in the years 1911–16, all for polo. Then, some years later, she bought Thyrza from Edmund Northey (about 1919) and from her (by 'Dartmoor pony') bred her first (official) Dartmoor. This was Kezia, who was good enough to win her classes at Devon County and Brentor & Lydford. Again, was this the dawn? Not if we are to go by what happened to Thyrza the next year – she went to the Arab Chandi.

All the same, within the world of horse breeding, interest and emphasis were moving, as it were, towards the native pony. In the case of Sylvia Calmady-Hamlyn other factors were also at work, all pulling in the same direction. Not that she was on any kind of equine Road to Damascus with a blinding flash of realization; rather she was more and more feeling the lure of the Dartmoor – and its improvement.

First, there was the shift of emphasis *away* from the polo field already referred to. Even a Calmady-Hamlyn follows fashion or at least takes note of it. Next there was her move from Bridestowe to near Buckfast; from just off the north-western edge of the moor to very much onto it, thus bringing the Dartmoor into the foreground of her vision. Third, there was the

Jolly Jankin (1921), 11.3 hh.

---

[2] *Moor Maid II was by The Mikado (Fell) out of Moor Maid, bred by A. R. Bray of Okehampton, as were many of her other earlier ponies. She appears just the once in the two-entry mountain and moorland section of the 1908 supplement, together with the note that she was second at Okehampton and won at Brentor & Lydford. Hardly a start; more like a flash in the pan.*

Judy V (1915), 12.0 hh.

news of quickening enthusiasm for founding a society to take care of the pony's interests. Finally – and could it have been the most important? – there was The Leat. We have already met this splendid little pony in Chapter 8, so all we need do here is to remind the reader of the basic facts about him: that Sylvia Calmady-Hamlyn bought him from Tor Royal in 1921 and immediately started to mate him with her growing herd of Dartmoor mares. So much the stud book tells us: Volume XVIII (1922–4) includes The Leat himself, four bought-in mares, a colt and three filly foals by The Leat, plus a foal by Edmund Northey's Copper King. Volume XIX (1925–7) follows more or less the same pattern: three stallions/colts (from John Lentern of South Zeal, H. J. Madders also of South Zeal and George Mortimore of Chagford), a mare from Madders and two home-bred filly foals by The Leat. Although only one foaling is recorded in Volume XX (1928–30), the pattern is becoming clear: breeding *Dartmoors*. This volume is of especial interest in containing a second-generation foal by a Leat mare (Water Wagtail).

Thus by 1930 Sylvia Calmady-Hamlyn had registered half a dozen Dartmoors by The Leat, had acquired four more Dartmoor stallions and herself bred a fifth (by The Leat). On the female side she had acquired 22 mares and bred 6 (4 by The Leat). On the other side of the coin, she was no longer breeding polo ponies (i.e. crossing Dartmoors with larger animals, mostly TB), the last having been the First World War foals from Diana and Junket. The shift of interest was not absolute – the partners still had some polo ponies – but the emphasis was now very much on native breeds. So says the stud book, our only authoritative source.

So far so good, but discord was already poised to heave its golden apple into the ring. It is true that The Leat's descent was far from 'pure Dartmoor' (as already mentioned), but he had been out of a registered Dartmoor, had been inspected and all that. Anyway, whatever people thought of him, his progeny were in the clear by any reckoning. But how about using a pure registered Welsh Mountain stallion? Wasn't that, almost literally, a horse of a different colour? For use a Welshman she did – and a very fine one too. Dinarth Spark was Welsh from his small, elegant little muzzle to the end of his admirably flowing tail. Bred by John Jones & Son of Colwyn Bay, he arrived at the Vean Stud around 1935, when he was put to a handcount of Dartmoor mares. Forthwith there was trouble; not because of these matings, but arising out of the fact that pretty soon ponies from Vean Stud started to scoop up all the prizes at the better shows; first in the Dartmoor classes, then in the inter-breed championships. In short, those less successful were hollering copper on Sylvia Calmady-Hamlyn, charging her with showing ponies in Dartmoor classes that weren't Dartmoors at all. To which her answer might have been (had she bothered to give one) that one and all had been inspected whenever the rules so required, that the judges had judged them as Dartmoors and that was that.

It is not seen as any business of this chronicle even to comment on this question, let alone find an authoritative answer. It confines itself to recording that a five-star row did brew up and kept going, off and on, for some twenty years, even surviving the Second World War. Dinarth Spark was, indeed, the spark that set if off, but the trouble, as ever, lay deeper. Looking back from the calm of half a century on, it all stemmed from the way in which Sylvia Calmady-Hamlyn ran the society. Nora Dawson and herself had saved it, kept it alive and, few would deny, steered it on an excellent course. (In this connection, although Nora Dawson supported her friend splendidly until the day of her death during the war years, it was of course the Calmady-Hamlyn knowledge and drive that counted all along. The Great Agrippa was a superb Number Two, but it was Octavian Caesar that ruled the Roman Empire.) Sylvia was at the helm, she knew the best course to steer, and she was going to steer it; best for the breed; her transcendental purpose to a truly remarkable degree.

It is undeniable that, in following her star, she rode pretty roughshod over opposition, ignoring criticism and not unduly fussed about any tedious formality standing in her path. Now this would have been fine in her grandfather's day in the High Victorian Age, but in the new world of 'duly elected councils', minutes, points of order, quorums and all 'that tribe' her high-handed activities tended to ruffle some feathers. Her friends and admirers – and she had many – saw all this as the price to be paid for a thriving (and winning) breed. Others, while glad to benefit from her (and Nora's) deep, but not bottomless, pockets, saw the situation – well, differently.

Now it must be admitted that the running of the Dartmoor Pony Society was both personal and casual. Records were scanty and, after such as there were had gone up in the flames of a major fire at Bridestowe, virtually non-existent, proceedings informal, finances off-hand. Or so the critics would have the world believe. On the other hand, we can set against these shortcomings (or at any rate the large question mark) the fact that the secretary could not be making off with the funds, for the plain reason that, ever since she had taken over, *all* subscriptions had gone straight into the bank. Likewise the costs to the society of its annual show were nil, these being met by Treasurer Dawson. And, most important of all, had she not raised the standard of the ponies themselves to heights never thought

Juliet IV (1923)

Scintilla (1914), 11.3 hh.

Water Wagtail (1924)

attainable when the Dartmoor was a humble first-cross? What else really mattered? Ah, said the critics, did you say 'Dartmoor'? What about that Welsh blood? Here the issue is not so clear-cut. The Vean ponies (or some of the best) were half-Welsh. Was it legitimate to cross with another *suitable* native breed and still call the product a Dartmoor? And here let us hearken to an acknowledged and respected authority.

If there were such a thing as an elder statesman in the pony world, then surely one qualifier would be E. G. E. ('Eddie') Griffiths, judge of both Welsh and Dartmoors of long standing, a man of considerable erudition and one whose claim in this instance to be 'an unbiased observer' can be carried by acclamation. His 1500-word article in the January 1959 News Summary of the NPS should be required reading for all those interested in breeding policy. Here are some extracts.

> I make no apology for referring to the controversy which has arisen amongst supporters of the Dartmoor breed over the introduction, some time ago, of a single strain of Welsh Mountain blood. I can at least claim to be an unbiased observer, who has spent a lifetime amongst ponies and most other varieties of pedigree stock, and who has been fortunate in having had wide opportunites of studying both breeds concerned.
>
> There is no doubt in my mind that the Dartmoor and Welsh Mountain ponies are closely akin, that before the 'pedigree era' there must have been much interchange of blood, and that it is probably a mere geographical accident that, today, they are separate breeds. These two breeds, then, are probably the only native breeds which can draw on one another for an out-cross. It is my considered opinion that both breeds could do this to their mutual advantage, without any loss of type, character or hardiness.

Warning against 'uncontrolled introduction of outside blood', he ends this section of his article with what can only be seen as unqualified praise for Sylvia Calmady-Hamlyn:

> Most fortunately, this planned improvement of the Dartmoor pony has been in the skilful hands of one of the master breeders of our time. You may criticize the principle: I defy anyone to criticize the ponies. Judged by results – and what other criterion can one use? – this is a brilliantly successful essay in livestock improvement.[3]

---

[3] *Taken (verbatim where shown) from the NPS News Summary, January 1959.*

Thus an acknowledged authority. Of course, the same freedom is not available to the breeder today. 'Inspection' is no longer just one of several ways onto the pages of the stud book. It has not been entirely excluded, but has become part of a more protracted process involving the supplementary register, dealt with in Chapter 14.

The introduction of Dinarth Spark (and The Leat, for that matter) well illustrates the skilful way in which Sylvia Calmady-Hamlyn went about what can be termed, without exaggeration, her later-life's work. She was fortunate, in that the circumstances were all propitious. She knew exactly what she wanted to

Juniper (1950), presented by Sylvia Calmady-Hamlyn to the Queen at the 1954 Royal Show, to be ridden by Prince Charles, after training by the Bullen Family, Mrs Bullen on the right.

achieve and how to set about achieving it. She was, and always had been, in an established position (most useful for independents, say what you like). She had fortune (greatly diminished on behalf of her work), the drive and, above all, the knowledge and skill.

The many owners of ponies descended from hers have every reason to be grateful. It is true that she ignored the rules whenever they got in her way, but didn't the end-results justify such irregularity? Anyway, there stands Sylvia Calmady-Hamlyn, Secretary of the Dartmoor Pony Society and *de facto* co-patron from 1931 until 1959, two years before she died. As today we stand in or alongside the show-ring during a Dartmoor class, we should think of those bloodlines she established and allow her to share the epitaph accorded to Sir Christopher Wren in St Paul's Cathedral: *Si monumentum requiris, circumspice.*

So much for her achievement in the world of the Dartmoor, considerable by any reckoning. There was, however, a great deal more to her than the dictatorship of the society. It might be misleading if we were to describe her as a 'character', with its current connotation of television 'personalities' and similar cardboard products of showbiz. Yet character she was, in the true sense of the word. She didn't act the part – didn't act any part, if it comes to that – just was herself. She certainly didn't dress up; from the crown of her pork-pie hat (rumoured to have set her back five bob (25p) around the time of the Diamond Jubilee), via her mackintosh to the soles of her serviceable boots, she was unfailingly herself: single-minded, forceful, generous.

Inevitably her strongly voiced views and independent decisive action earned her some hostility; but, friend or foe, high or low, every one respected her. She reckoned she was right and events proved that this was so. An opinion? Then, if she wasn't right, how is it that over the decades her ponies and their descendants have continued to stand 'on the right of the Line'?

Nor should it ever be thought that here was some bucolic pony breeder, but rather someone extremely well educated, well read to back it up, quick witted and highly intelligent; equally at home when telling royalty a thing or two as when gossiping with fellow-moormen in Tavistock Market.

Probably the highlight of the Calmady-Hamlyn-Dartmoor partnership came in 1954 when on behalf of the DPS she presented her four-year-old Dartmoor gelding Juniper (by Jude out of Wild Rose IV) to the Queen for Prince Charles, then aged six. Juniper had been trained by the Bullen family and, at the presentation at the Royal Show, Jennie Bullen and her sister Jane were able to demonstrate his impeccable manners. Indeed, when he went on in due course to Sybil Smith the latter is

Juniper with Jennie (now Loriston-Clarke) at his head and rider Jane (now Holderness-Rodham).

reported as telling a DPS council member that 'he was one of the best ponies she had ever had for teaching small children to ride'. A Prince-of-Wales feather in the cap of the breed and yet another generous gesture on the part of Juniper's breeder.

Dictatorial though she may have been, even dictators warm to praise, especially from high and independent authority. Thus the award of the British Horse Society's Meal in 1960, in the last year of her life must have given her great pleasure, it was for 'outstanding services'. And who would say that, arrogant and fond of glory though she undoubtedly was, she did not fully deserve it? We must remember, too, that she was a woman of her times, brought up in a very different climate to that of today. She was paying the piper, so why shouldn't she take on herself to vary the tune? And, after all, if the society of her day didn't like her variations, the members (even then) always had the option of finding another piper – or trying their own hands at composition. Mind you, it would have called for some nerve.

Jenson (1954)

10 ENTR'ACTE:
A WORD ON PREFIXES
(and a little about suffixes too)

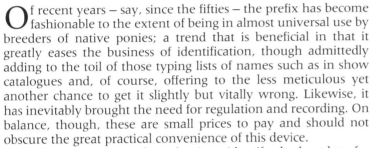

Of recent years – say, since the fifties – the prefix has become fashionable to the extent of being in almost universal use by breeders of native ponies; a trend that is beneficial in that it greatly eases the business of identification, though admittedly adding to the toil of those typing lists of names such as in show catalogues and, of course, offering to the less meticulous yet another chance to get it slightly but vitally wrong. Likewise, it has inevitably brought the need for regulation and recording. On balance, though, these are small prices to pay and should not obscure the great practical convenience of this device.

The function of a prefix today is to identify the breeder of a pony carrying that prefix rather than its own lineage; no more and no less. But it hasn't always been so. Let us therefore briefly trace 'prefix's progress'; with, of course, especial note of its relevance to Dartmoors.

Dartmoor owners did not invent the prefix, which had been in use for many years in the New Forest, Wales, the Highlands and, no doubt, elsewhere before Imogen Muntz introduced it into the West Country soon after the First World War. She lived then – as indeed she did virtually all her long life – at Foxhams in Horrabridge, so 'Foxhams' it was. Thus, in Volume XVIII (1922–24) we find Foxhams Mundic and Foxhams Waif (both bred by herself), together with Foxhams Dot ('bred on the moor'). The prefix had arrived and it signified ownership.

In stretching it to cover Dot, she was not breaking any rules – there weren't any – but was merely following the fashion set by Welsh owners as far back as the turn of the century.[1] Anyway, she started it. The habit spread; not very fast, but steadily. In the following volume (XIX for 1925–7) it received a boost when Joan Vinson-Thomas of Little Lyndridge, Okehampton,

signalized her arrival in the world of the Dartmoor pony by registering no fewer than twenty-one 'Lyndridges': twelve home bred, nine from elsewhere. However, a more significant first in this issue was Henry Scott's registration of a stallion and six mares, all prefixed 'Hole' and all bred on Hole Farm, Chagford; followed in Volume XX (1928–30) by a second stallion and eight more mares; all prefixed 'Hole' and all likewise home bred.

We note that Scott did not automatically bestow the Hole prefix on all the stock he registered, even some born at Hole Farm. On the other hand, those prefixed 'Hole' were invariably of his own breeding. So, as we should accord to Mrs Muntz the distinction of introducing a recognizable prefix into the Dartmoor section of the stud book, we must credit Farmer Scott with being the first to apply to his own registrations the 'breeder only' discipline, now universally recognized.

To judge from the record in the stud book, Mrs Vinson-Thomas was coming round to this stricter point of view. In the meanwhile, however, her registrations occupy the blurred borderland between ownership and actual breeding. In Volume XIX she registered five stallions with the Lyndridge prefix: four home bred, the fifth from Jordan of Redstone Farm, Clovelly (but out of a Lyndridge mare, Lydridge Tinsell *(sic)* herself bred by Baldwin of Beaworthy – are you still with us?). Yet, in contrast to this slightly casual approach, at more or less the same time she registered her stallion His Knibs (bred by Albert Hodge of Higher

---

[1] *For instance, volumes VI and VII (1900–02) show J. Marshall Dugdale of Llwyn, Oswestry, as using 'Llwyn' for all his stock, bred or bought.*

Vean Dorabella II (1984) ridden by Katie Tyler

But back to the main trail. In Volume XX, as well as the Scott prefix we can identify eight newcomers: Beacon, Cheston, Collie Hill, Cornwood, Frenchbeer, Jordan, Park and Shapley; all except Beacon and Cheston plainly based on the breeders' properties, their use mostly confined to home-bred animals. We might call eight an encouraging number, but it still leaves us a long way to go before we can claim that the merits of prefixes – and to a general rule of 'breeders only' – are anywhere near universal acceptance. A closer look at those registering will, moreover, reveal that many breeders, and by no reckoning the most lowly or humble, continue to eschew prefixes in any guise. Sylvia Calmady-Hamlyn for one. By then she was well on her way to dominating the Dartmoor world by a combination of sound knowledge, excellent judgement, singleness of purpose and good plain clout, as recounted elsewhere in this story. She had registered Welsh ponies with the Vean prefix as long ago as 1930, but for some reason she withheld it from her Dartmoors. In 1953 she gave in.[3] It would seem, however, that her conversion, though belated, was complete, for within a couple of years all her ponies carried the Vean prefix.

So this was the way it went. By the mid-fifties prefixes were springing up like toadstools all over the moor and even in the outer lands nearer sea-level; a forest of new names, many still going strong.

Per contra, it is sad to have to record the demise of almost all the earlier herds. Foxhams died with Mrs Muntz in the fifties; there is no sign in later volumes of Henry Scott or his eight near-contemporaries. In short, there is almost a clean sweep and a fresh start. If we look back to the first post-War (Volume XXV, 1945–7) we will find but one prefix in it that is still running around on four legs today under the original ownership. Only one, for it is not until the next volume that Sherberton makes its debut with 16 mares (13 bred by the Coaker family, 2 from nearby, 1 from 'the moor'). The Coakers have, of course, bred Dartmoors at Sherberton for generations, but their actual prefix does not appear as such until Volume XXVI (1948–52), being joined within a couple of years by the new generation: Leighton (for Bulteel), Jurston (Mollie Croft), Hele (Stephens of Cornwood), Oatlands (Jane Durrant, later Dod) and a lot more, even

Halstock) most punctiliously as 'of Lyndridge'.[2] She also registered at that time sixteen mares, half and half home bred and from elsewhere. However, in the next volume (XX, covering 1928–30) the balance swings towards 'breeder only', with 8 Lyndridge stallions all home bred and 10 mares of which 5 are home bred, 2 from other breeders and 3 from anonymous 'Dartmoors'. Finally, in volume XXI (1931–33) all 4 Lyndridge stallions are home bred, as are the 6 mares.

And then? Not another word; just silence. Why? So far the entries in the stud book have suggested a thriving and growing establishment, yet after Volume XXI there is not a single new entry for Little Lyndridge Stud (as it has now become). It is as though the moor has swallowed it. What *has* happened? Has the stud been dispersed, the ponies exported? Or sold to those that either didn't know or didn't care? So far all efforts to solve this one have failed, even though directed by highly competent experts on the Dartmoor pony. And what has happened to His Knibs; a big winner and sire of many Lyndridge foals? Let us hope for some eventual light. Mrs Vinson-Thomas and her stud deserve better than oblivion. And she did much to popularize the prefix.

---

[2] *His Knibs did well in the ring, notably in thrice winning the Linnel Cup (1925–7) for the Best Mountain and Moorland Stallion; not at all bad for a pony of unknown – or at any rate unnamed – parentage, for breeder Hodge does not commit himself beyond 'Dartmoor pony' for either sire or dam.*

[3] *Vean Wayzgoose: a filly foaled in 1953, by Pipit ex Zigzag (both bred by herself); class winner and reserve for the Lord Arthur Cup at NPS 1957. But what, we may ask in passing, is a wayzgoose? An incautious pedestrian? Not at all. The dictionary enlightens us: it is an annual festivity especially for [of all unlikely people on the moor] printers. Anyway, there she is, in Volume XXVII (1953–4), the very first Dartmoor Vean.*

Whitestone Bayard (1973)

Shilstone Rocks Cloudburst (1970)

Boveycombe Redwing (1976)

one (Weald's Gate) as far away as Sussex, probably the first non-West Country Dartmoor prefix; new, that is, so far as prefixes are concerned.

So it came about, over the post-War decade, that the prefix took root in the West Country. To start with, owners and breeders used it pretty casually, but gradually they came to accept it as a breeder's mark, eased in that direction by the societies, breed and national. Eased? What were the societies actually doing about regulating the whole business?

For many years, of course, the answer would have been nothing. This does not reflect indolence on the part of authority, but the fact that for all that time no action was needed. Perhaps we can take Volume XXVI as the watershed between the old *laissez-faire* and the eventual regulation of the prefix. The simple fact was that there were too many ponies and, in the nature of language, not enough names. Glancing down the Dartmoor entries we find Lassie 11th, Queenie 23rd and Peggy 28th among a herd of Betties, Sallies and Judies. In this same volume, however, we find an encouraging sign – at least one to appeal to those preferring order to chaos however amiable – a 'List of Prefixes and Suffixes'. There are only 120 of them country-wide and the stud book commits itself no further than printing the list without comment. Still, it's a start. It gradually builds up in subsequent volumes, until in Volume XXX (1959–60) the number has doubled. Better still, the names of the editing committee are shown (with Mrs Yeomans in the chair) and, best of all, the Preface stresses the importance and 'great interest' of prefixes. These, it goes on to state flatly, 'are issued only to *breeders*'; a clear-cut ruling, duly passed on by the DPS to its members.

By the end of the next decade the list had stretched to some 2400. Of course, this number included all breeds and a few surviving suffixes as well, but it was certainly a far cry from Henry Scott and his eight pioneers. It is reliably reported that there now are some 15 000 prefixes 'on file' at the British Central Prefix Register (BCPR). Prefixes have been defined, tamed, tabulated and regimented. The BCPR was set up in 1978 with a founder membership of half a dozen pony societies, of which the Dartmoor Pony Society was one. Today it comprises fifteen members; that is to say, all the breed societies, together with the NPS and similar organizations. Which is another way of saying that, so far as registration in a stud book is concerned, what it says goes. It has its rules, not too stringent. They are the price to pay for acquiring nationwide exclusive rights over one's prefix; if not always the prefix of one's choice then as near to it as avoiding duplication allows.

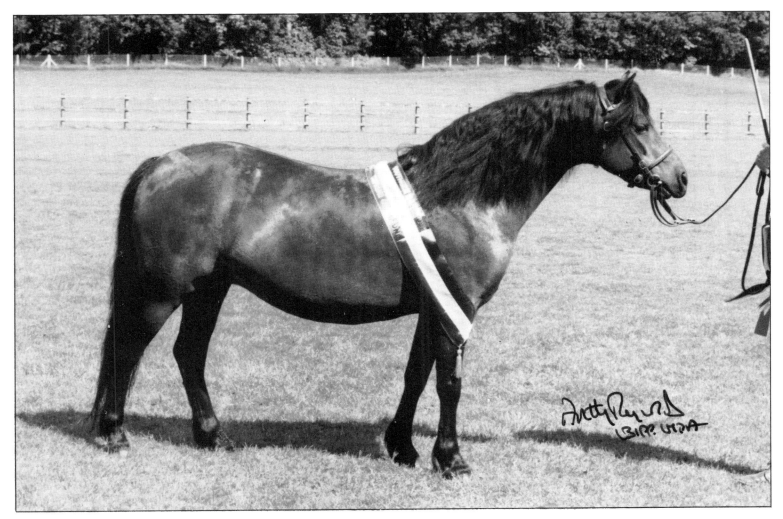

Shilstone Rocks Another Bunch (1976) a Supreme Champion at the Dartmoor Pony Society Show, and Wembley prizewinner

But what about suffixes? They are, without doubt, the poor relation and, like their human counterpart, used for the odd job. Anyone can register a suffix (provided, again, it isn't a duplicate) and then only he can tack it onto the name of any pony on registration or at any time (on notification). A few Dartmoor owners used suffixes (notably Nora Dawson with '... of Holne'), some still do, though the prefix has largely taken over. The BCPR 'discourages' them. Authority is even sterner on prefixes: two-word prefixes 'not accepted' according to the official notes on registration.[4]

---

[4] *There are extant several two-word prefixes, but presumably these were registered before the ban, which dates more or less from BCPR's foundation. Anyway, no new two-worders. Or, one presumes, no three- or four-worders either. It seems that the computer – which has, of course, like Moloch to be placated – won't wear 'em. So that's that, isn't it?*

Haytor Rocks

U'85

11 THE TWENTIES AND THIRTIES

For the first half dozen years of its life the Dartmoor Pony Society was largely preoccupied in finding its feet; or, more precisely, in discovering some firm financial ground on which to plant them before being swept away on a rising tide of insolvency. Happily, by 1930 it was safely on dry land, as narrated in Chapter 9, so could turn its attention more confidently to its prime purpose: the ponies themselves.

Despite this overshadowing distraction, as soon as it had been constituted, the society did get to work in two important fields: registration and competition; the latter only in a small way, to be sure, but a start. All the same, it was not until it had put the six lean years safely behind it that the DPS could start to get into its stride. We could, indeed, divide those fourteen pre-Second World War years into 'BC' (or 'Before Calmady') and 'AD' ('Anno Dawson').

In the matter of registration, the society had first to overcome the inertia built into all West Countrymen (and especially the farmers who, taking their cue from Nature with whom their lives were passed, were not to be hustled); allied to scepticism on its advantages, if any. It was, indeed, uphill work all the way; convincing them that such registration was in their own interest, to say nothing of being to the benefit of the breed as a whole. How? Well, for a start, registered ponies could be seen to have reached at least some standard and also, by being in the stud book, would be brought to the notice of a wider circle of possible buyers. And (said the society in effect) registration was so easy! First, any offspring of parents already registered would automatically be eligible without more ado, apart from filling in the form. And, even if they weren't, it really wasn't very difficult. Any moorland-type pony deemed suitable by its owner could be 'inspected' by persons appointed by the society. Finally, any pony winning a first, second, third or fourth prize in a Dartmoor class at a recognized show and under a Dartmoor panel judge was accepted as having been 'inspected and approved'. And, as for deadlines on age – there weren't any. For guidance the inspectors had their experience, their good sense and not much else. There was, of course, an official description, but this had not been amended since its publication in 1899; save in the still-vexed matter of height. Opinion on this was, as ever, divided.

The earlier battle of the heights has already been reviewed. It will be remembered that Volume IX (1905–6) had eventually anchored the Dartmoor limits at 13.2 hh for stallions and 13 hh for mares. These figures remained in force for almost twenty years, being reprinted in each volume up to Number XVIII (1922–4) at the start of the mountain and moorland section, after which there is silence for a further two decades. Finally, in Volume XXV (1945–7) there is the flat statement (shifted to the Dartmoor section, we note) that 'the maximum height is 12.2 hh for both mares and stallions'. And that, at the moment, is that.

But what were the *actual* limits during the period we are looking at: between the foundation of the society and that crisp post-war directive? There is nothing to be found on the 'official' pages of the stud book, but we can pick up some actualities from its reports on shows. These, as might be expected, are somewhat conflicting. As late as 1928 Cornwood accepted Dartmoor mares up to 13 hh, whereas from two years earlier Okehampton had set its limit at 12.2 hh – and kept it there. Also in 1928 Devon County said 12.3 hh for stallions and 12.2 hh for mares. In other words, a slow, general trend down towards 12.2 hh.

So much for official rules and guidance – or lack of them. Then what height did the actual *ponies* run to? Again, using the stud book, we find that the last pony to be registered at over 12.2 hh appears in Volume XVIII, which was, of course, the last volume to offer the 13.2/13 hh limits. From this it is reasonable to deduce that the 1945 announcement did no more than recognize reality.

Finally, what height *should* a Dartmoor be? If by this we mean 'what is its natural height?', then we cannot do better than quote the voice of experience: that of the moormen themselves. Is it a matter of taste or even of the mysteries of market forces? Neither, they say, but of observable fact. They maintain that, if a larger 'improved' Dartmoor (at around 13 hh) is put out to run on the moor – the proper moor, mind you, nothing below 1000 feet – within two or three generations its progeny will be down to 'below eleven-three'.

A maximum height is, of course, important when setting standards for a breed. As it is factual (well, almost) and can be easily (well, fairly easily) ascertained, there is much to be said for having it laid down – and at the figure that Nature intended. There are, however, many other details to be assessed; the recognizable but unquantifiable qualities that make the pony what it is; qualities that cannot be measured, but must be looked at. And, of these, the one that is largely not even amenable to visual inspection is the intangible quality of toughness. Many would hold that this is the most important of all, the prerequisite. A true moorland pony – anywhere – must be tough enough to fend for itself on its moor all the year round; a way of life that is by no means an ordeal to a *real* Dartmoor. At the same time, such toughness need not exclude quality – an intangible if ever there was one – and it was here that skilful breeders could play their part; none with greater effect or benefit than Sylvia Calmady-Hamlyn in those formative years before the Second World War.

So the society set about its business, gathering momentum as it moved into the thirties. It cannot be said that the breeders (in those days almost entirely local and farmers at that) flocked to register their herds. Society or not, they were only slightly more forthcoming than before the First World War. And for similar reasons. A handsome certificate might look very well hanging on the wall, but as farmers they were in business; to make a living if not much profit. They had to stick to essentials, which in this case

meant crops that brought in some return. Yes, they would think about it. There were local shows with money prizes? They just might have a go. They'd see …

The entries did trickle in; not very many, but steadily and faster than in pre-DPS days. Over the years the stud book reveals the extent of that increase. Annual averages for the years 1919–24 (i.e. between the First World War and the society's birth) were 1–2 stallions and 8–9 mares; for 1925-39 (i.e. thence to the start of the Second World War) they rose to 6–7 stallions and 16–17 mares. Not many really when one thinks of the thousands of ponies (of one kind or another) out on the moor and presumably belonging to someone.[1] All the same, it was a start.

Registration first, then competition – the shows.

In the earlier years (the 'BC' era) the society did not venture to run its own show, but from the start it sponsored Dartmoor classes at the Bath & West and Devon County. These, together with the mountain and moorland classes sponsored by the NPS and other Dartmoor classes on and around the moor, did mean that there was reasonable scope for those wishing to take their animals into the ring, though nothing to compare with the pot-hunters' delight of the seventies and eighties.

And then there was the National Pony Society's annual show in London. At that time there were no actual Dartmoor classes, but several for small mountain and moorland (i.e. 'with the exception of Dales, Fells, Highland and Welsh' – the Welsh having their own classes) and overall mountain and moorland championships for both stallions and mares. It was a long way to go, and by rail at that, but it is heartening to find the Dartmoors well represented.

The results at NPS London give an excellent (and encouraging) idea of how the Dartmoors fared against other breeds; in particular those of Little Lyndridge Stud, the herd owned by Mrs Vinson-Thomas of Okehampton; wins not merely against other Dartmoors but over other (and sometimes all) the natives. His Knibs (see p.53) won the Linnel Cup (for all mountain and moorland stallions) in 1925, 1926, 1927 and 1930; having had to be content with only the small mountain and moorland stallion class in 1928, 1929 and 1931; as near a clean sweep as makes no difference. In addition, his stable-mate Lyndridge Sally won the

---

[1] *Compare these figures with those in the latest published volume of the society's own stud book (volume 8 – for 1988 only): an increase to 48 colts and 119 fillies; all but one dutifully wearing their prefixes, these latter now very much* de rigueur; *addresses all over the country, a few even on Dartmoor.*

small mountain and moorland mares' class in 1929 and the overall mares' title (the Lord Arthur Cecil Cup) in 1930.[2]

There is a portrait of His Knibs in Volume XIX. He was bred by Albert Hodge of Higher Halstock; 'by Dartmoor, ex Dartmoor', which, alas, tells us little beyond the claim that he is 'pure' Dartmoor. He was foaled in 1921, measured 12.1 hh at three (so must have been well up to height) and actually registered at four. Oddly enough, although he himself won prizes far and wide, as well as siring a lot of Lyndridge foals, there is no sign of a champion among his progeny.

A large number of mares were bought in to the Lyndridge Stud, but very seldom is their breeding given beyond 'Dartmoor' on both sides. An exception is Lyndridge Tinkle, who won the NPS Silver Medal at Okehampton in 1927. But then he was by The Leat. Not that anonymity connoted lack of quality in those days; quite possibly only lack of registration. Anyway, with or without noble quarterings, in the late twenties the Lyndridge ponies were hard to beat. For instance, they had a straight run of wins in the small mountain and moorland group class from 1926–1930.

The year 1930 marked the apogee of the Little Lyndridge Stud: the two most important championships at the national show, backed (as usual) by a win in the group class. And then, without warning or explanation (at least as far as can be made out half a century later) silence, as recounted in the previous chapter. Little Lyndridge vanished from the Dartmoor scene, leaving not a wrack behind. This was a great pity, for the Lyndridge ponies had certainly kept the Dartmoor banner flying during some lean years.

On the subject of local shows in the late twenties, these followed their pre-First-World-War traditions, as already re-counted. Transport was still scarce, expensive and far from salubrious for exhibitors and their helpers (being largely shared with other more profitable livestock and redolent of their occupation past or current). Though few were put off by this last, the combination did prune the number of entries at West Country shows where the distances made transport essential.

Half-a-dozen was the normal average per class even at such important events as Devon County (which in 1928 attracted no more than sixteen entries all told for three classes).[3] Still, they kept going.

Up to 1930 support for the local Dartmoor classes may have disappointed the enthusiasts, but this did not mean that time was standing still for the society as a whole. By the following year the reorganization was complete, at least far enough advanced to make it possible to hold the first of the society's annual shows, and continued ever since except during the period so tediously deranged by the Second World War. For seven years these took place at Brimpts, on Mr H. Down's farm high up above Dartmeet; central but draughty; a moorland venue for moorland ponies. And, for those willing to look around, what a splendid prospect!

The DPS's own show catered for all sorts of Dartmoors. It was, on the other hand, exclusive. 'Only Dartmoor ponies eligible for any event' said the schedule, though in 1932 it relented to the extent of adding a couple of classes for the Advanced Register (up to 13 hh). More to its advantage, it was given a right royal send-off by Edward P, who presented a 50-Guinea Challenge cup for the broodmares, which encouraged numerous donations to the prize fund (all from individuals, apart from the War Office). There were ten classes (plus gymkhana): young stock, stallions, broodmares, barren mares and geldings, colt premiums, groups; an ambitious programme amply justified by encouragingly large entries. In 1931 the Prince of Wales's Cup went to Jim Glover's Cornwood Winnie and the stallion class to E. W. White & Son's Punch. The same pair won again in 1932.

So the society's own show had been well and truly launched. It was certainly well supported, but had it paid its way? Or, more likely, had Nora Dawson any need to dig into her reticule? Whichever way it was, the society had no call to worry, with the firm of Dawson & Hamlyn meeting all outstanding charges; a help to say the least, over those early years.

Once again, it is interesting to trace the height limits at these shows, when these can be found. The schedule for the initial show gave them as 12.3 hh for stallions and 12.2 hh for mares (which some might see as a slightly retrogressive step or, if not a whole step, then a shuffling of the feet). In 1932 it clipped 2

---

[2] *Another headache for the researcher here. The stud book says the 1930 Lord Arthur winner was a Fell, though the cup itself is engraved with Sally's name. Our money is on Sally; not on account of any partisan feeling, but it seems unlikely that anyone, even from the warm-hearted North, would pay to have someone else's name cut into a cup he himself had won. Assuming, then, that the cup has it right, we can record a pleasant left-and-right for Mrs Vinson-Thomas.*

---

[3] *Compare these meagre figures with those for the geographically more compact New Forest. In 1925 there were 46 brood mares entered for the Burley Show; 37 the following year. In 1930 at Lyndhurst the catalogue contained 63 stallions; backed by 30 three-year-olds, 25 two-year-olds and 21 yearlings.*

At the first Summer Show and Sale of Dartmoor Ponies, Brimpts 1931. Front row, from left: H Kingwell (judge), Glover (with Cornwood Winnie), E. W. White (with Sparklet II), Tom Holman (with Queenie VII), G. Scott (with Hole Fancy), Mr White Jnr (with Daisy). In the background facing camera: Mr Madders, another judge.

Also at the 1931 show *(left to right):* **Sylvia Calmady-Hamlyn, Nora dawson, H. Kingswell (judge), Joan Cave-Penny, Captain Jack Lethbridge (Master of the Eggesford), Edmund Northey (dark glasses), John Wakeham (auctioneer).**

inches off on both sides: 12.1 hh for stallions, 12 hh for mares: why is not evident. This was maintained for 1933, but in 1934 the heights for both were set at 12.2 hh. And there they have remained ever since.

There were one or two classes at each show for what were variously called 'improved' or 'Devon riding' ponies or, later, 'of riding type'. These were allowed to run up to 14 hh; excellent mounts no doubt, but not by any stretch moorland so must fall outside this survey. Needless to say, cups and trophies were presented to this invasion, including the right to compete for 'best in show'.[4]

[4] *Progress from winning a class to taking part in a championship should be simple but often is not, being fraught with snares, surprises and, worst of all, anomalies. An example of the last: a pony may have been placed, say, fifth, in what might be termed the basic class. However, it happens to be able to compete in another, quite different class which it wins. It then proceeds to a championship where it beats the four ponies previously placed above it. No reflection on the judging, but how about the organization? This chronicle may not go further than remind the reader that such situations do arise and can lead to tears, tantrums or even to a rise in the insurance rates on judges. In this case the possibilities were not too dangerous, although it is open to Dartmoor owners to suggest that 'best at show' at a breed show should be confined to the breed in question. (In 1936 it went to a 'riding pony'.)*

After seven shows at Brimpts the society moved its venue north-west to Lydford for those last two years of peacetime. The numbers of entries were well maintained – perhaps because the ground was right alongside the railway station. Unfortunately, the records for these shows are scanty, though we do at least know the names of the winners of the two chief classes, the stallions and the broodmares, so can include them to complete our very sketchy survey of the pre-war breed shows.

After the first two years (already reported) the stallion class was monopolized by E. W. White & Son's Boxer. He was by Punch and thus ensured that the stallion prize came to the White stable every single year throughout that period. (Until he was old enough to compete Boxer had had to make do with winning as a yearling in 1931 and a two-year-old in 1932). The only measurement we have of him is at 10.0½ hh as a yearling, so he must have been pretty small. He was out of Sparklet II who was by The Leat. Boxer sired a number of prize winners, including Tawton Dart, the 2–3-year-old winner at Brimpts in 1936.

The competition for the broodmare prize was slightly more open. Winnie won it for the first three years, thus carrying off Edward P's 50 Guinea Cup for good ('not re-presented' the record notes), so that John Coaker's three-year sequence with Heatherbelle brought him no more than some rosettes (plus the prize money given by the NPS). Heatherbelle was bred at Tor Royal (she had the plume-of-feathers brand on her shoulder) and, as well as her Brimpts wins, was first at Widecombe in 1933 and 1936, first at Devon County in 1934, 1935 and 1936, first at the Royal (at Bristol) in 1936. After Heatherbelle's run there were three individual winners of her class. In 1937 Syd Horrell's Virtuous Lady beat a strong class (including Heatherbelle) despite her reputed eighteen years.[5] Next year's winner was F.H. Caunter's Wonder Why, a steady performer with a third in 1936 and a second in 1937 at the DPS, first and champion at Okehampton in 1938. Finally, J. Maunder & Son's Fearless won in 1939. We can discover no more about her, apart from the statements that she was a bay and eight years old. She was never registered, then or later; a pity for she beat a strong class.

From this brief glance – not to be dignified with the title of analysis – one thing stands out: it was a cracking good time for the White Stud at South Zeal, with Punch and his son Boxer clean-sweeping the stallion classes. Among the mares some good sequences for Glover and John Coaker, followed by three singletons. And there for the moment we must leave them. Later we will see how their progeny fared.

It is disappointing to find this continuing reluctance to register, for as often as not such neglect leaves us little more than the owner's and pony's names to go on. It might have been a deal worse, had not at that time Sylvia Calmady-Hamlyn been snapping up any winners that took her fancy in her search for quality foundation stock. As soon as she had them, she registered them, with or without forebears. Not all *their* progeny were winners, but some were…

The nine pre-war breed shows lit the way for those that came after. To modern eyes they may look pretty casual, even rough and ready, as pioneers often do. It is true that the organization was sketchy (but sound), the amenities now taken for granted either rudimentary or non-existent. For a start, the showground itself; that is to say, the field in which it took place; cleared of the stock that could politely be described as *hors concours*, if not freed of the hazard of stepping into evidence of their recent occupation; the ground itself not really steep, bearing in mind that moorland seldom is flat (and even less often level). The essentials were there and that was all that mattered. There were separate gaps in the stone wall for coming in and going out, with plenty of good Devon muscle-power on hand to clear any stoppages. Above all, the classes were consistently well filled and every year the quality was going up – or so it was said. What more could anyone desire?

There were just four weeks left of the fragile twenty-year peace when the last lorry bumped out onto Station Road at Lydford on that Saturday evening in August 1939. How many imagined that it would be ten whole years before they would be driving in again, probably in the same transport, to pick up the threads? There was, however, a small ray of light: thanks to the devotion of their predecessors (and their own when ten years younger) those threads would be there.

---

[5] *Not to be confused with Sylvia Calmady-Hamlyn's Virtuous Lady. Horrell's was by Little Star (sire of Lucky Star II) ex Polly V.*

_U'86_   HOUND TOR

12 THE YEARS OF AUSTERITY

The climactic events that engulfed us in the autumn of 1939 brought to an abrupt halt virtually every activity not concerned, in one way or another, with putting the upstart dictators where those nearer, if not dearer, to them should have consigned them several years before. So, as with many another pleasant and innocuous occupation, the Dartmoor Pony Society went into hibernation for what was then called 'the duration'; an elastic term suggesting an indeterminate time to be endured. In effect, it curled up, having cut its commitments to what was necessary to keep it just alive; specifically by ruthlessly culling all but its very best animals. This done, it settled down to await the springtime of eventual, never-doubted victory.

The DPS was hibernating, but it was not dead. Far from it. Happily, there had been time in that vital pre-war decade for the breeders, led, goaded and helped by Sylvia Calmady-Hamlyn (herself unfailingly backed by Nora Dawson), to establish those bloodlines she had been seeking over a considerable period; the lines that were eventually to make so great an improvement in the quality of the Dartmoor breed.

So when the time came to revitalize the society the ponies were there; not many of them, but enough to make a second start. Nor should we forget that £95 nest-egg at the bank, the unspent five-bob subscriptions collected ever since the Dawson-Hamlyn take-over. All the same, there was much leeway to be made up. Dartmoors live a long time, but they do not live for ever. The pre-war winners were in their teens at least; the wartime stud book (Volume XXIV, 1940–44) recorded no more than two stallions and ten new mares, only one of which was in the name of an identifiable farmer. Indeed, writing of these times some years later, Sylvia Calmady-Hamlyn goes so far as to state that 'no moorman offered any pony for registration'.

She may have overlooked one or two, but to all intents she was correct, for the previous commercial incentive no longer applied and, in any case, few farmers had any time to spare for ponies. Nevertheless, the stud book bears out that her idea of the new, high-quality moorland pony had taken firm root. There may have been only a dozen new registrations, but they were good ponies every one, among them her own Jude, Judith III, Peewit III and Zigzag; all by Dinarth Spark and each destined to leave its mark on the breed.

There was new blood too, accepted after inspection. According to her, this too was of the right sort. In a pamphlet on Dartmoor breeding[1] she commends 'the wisdom of the Inspectors and Judges, especially that of Messrs. F. Coaker (John's father) and M. Madders.' Their good judgement, she wrote, 'was amply proved by the number of prizes won in open competition [i.e. against ponies of other native breeds] at the leading shows.' Nor have the further thirty years since she published her leaflet produced anything to refute her contention, though her claim that 'the public widely appreciated ... the recognizable type' is perhaps imputing to that amorphous mass more knowledge (and interest) than in reality it possessed.

At any rate, the society had survived. It shook itself and set about resuming an active life; not with a rush, for that was impossible, but steadily. For a start, it encouraged registration. This is reflected in Volume XXV (1945–7): nine stallions and thirty-two mares. (Incidentally, this volume includes an interesting revival: the use of the prefix, which had fallen into disuse

---

[1] _'A list of stallions ... and ... a short history ... of development until today'_ 1958.

Dora IV (1938)

Jenny VII (1945) at two years

ever since the demise of Little Lyndridge, (see Chapter 10). There had been one or two casual uses – for instance, Syd Horrell of Bucktor had called a 1935 foal Bucktor Lass – but no general use since Lyndridge. Now they were beginning to come back.

Then, just as soon as such activities became practicable, it put on its first post-war show. This was in August 1947. Two whole years after VJ Day! Before we pitch into the society for its West Country sloth, we should remind ourselves of the circumstances of the aftermath of 'The War to End Peace'. In the late forties things didn't just happen at the time of one's choosing. These were the years of austerity, when food was still rationed, petrol initially unobtainable and later tightly controlled, when livestock transport (mostly dating from the thirties and even then often elderly) had to be coaxed to spin out its precarious existence for those few more months (which somehow stretched to years); in short, when almost every kind of enjoyable activity was closely circumscribed, if not forbidden. Small wonder, then, that it took all that while to stage what was, at the time, a major undertaking.

But they managed. To Princetown, therefore, near enough on the second anniversary of final victory, so called. By today's luxurious standards of stabling, public address and all the rest it would no doubt be rated on a par with a (small) village fete, but it was a start; the first of an annual series still going well. And this first show was a test, to say the least: real Princetown midsummer weather, driving rain (known locally as mist) and visibility fading beyond the pony standing fifth. At least, so said the survivors.

Information on this first post-war show comes entirely from memory, for no records have been discovered. From the stud book, however, it is surmised that E.W. White & Son retained the male championship with Punch II (by 'Dartmoor Pony', possibly the pre-war Punch, ex Julia ex Daisy XVI) and probably the female championship as well with Fairy X (by Boxer, also ex Julia). Both were big winners soon after the war.

There is no record of a show in 1948. For the next year, though, the society (that is, Sylvia Calmady-Hamlyn) staged its breed show at Prince Hall, a Duchy farm just south of the Two Bridges–Dartmeet road, repeating it on that site every year until 1963. Before reporting on these, however, let us look at the society in general.

Students of the stud book will no doubt have noted an innovation in Volume XXV, its first to be published after the war. Each mountain and moorland section carries what can be likened to a magazine's masthead: officers of the respective societies and a lot more; useful as back-ups for shaky memories

Jenny VII (1945), on the hill above Buckfast Abbey. The old wool-mill is on the right.

Jude (1941), twice a winner of the Shalbourne Cup

and also, when studied over the years, helping to provide revealing glimpses of the progress of the society's ideas forty years ago.

First there are the names of the Chairman (Mrs Marwood-Tucker of Horrabridge, a pre-war Dartmoor owner and currently a judge) and of the hon. secretary (with whom the reader is already acquainted). These are followed by the official description, the first time it has been reprinted *in toto* since its appearance in 1899, largely unaltered but with some additional discursive description. There is also the question of body colour. And, of course, height.

The original rule on colour had been 'black, brown or bay preferred; grey allowable, other colours objectionable'. Volume XXV said: 'the colours preferred are bay, brown and black; grey is rare.' The society must have realized that this left one or two stray ends, for in Volume XXVI (1948–52) it says: 'the colours preferred are bay, brown, black and grey; piebald and skewbald are debarred.' Grey is in and on level terms with the others; 'paints' are out. All right so far, but what of the other colours, chestnut (or, as *Horse and Hound* would have it whatever the *Oxford English Dictionary* says, chesnut) for instance? Ponies of this colour had been registered since before the First World War.[2] Those preferring the rules neat and tidy have to wait until Volume XXIX (1957) when 'chestnut' is slipped in at the end of 'Colours'. This volume adds that there is 'no colour bar except piebald and skewbald.'. And there, so far as official utterances in the stud book go, the matter rests.

With regard to height, the matter is simple. The first 'masthead' in Volume XXV says: 'the maximum height is 12.2 hh both for mares and stallions'. And has gone on saying so. One hears talk of altering this, though it would seem that proponents are far from agreement on whether this move should be up or down – a fairly basic requirement. Up, say some; that'll boost the exports, for do not foreigners believe that 'Big is Best'? Down, say others; let's get back to the natural height of a moorland pony. 12.2 hh looks pretty safe for some time to come.

Three lists are included, amended up to date in each volume. First there are the principal shows. In Volume XXV these are: Bath & West, Devon County, Okehampton, NPS London. It is odd that there is no mention of the society's own show. Perhaps at the time of going to press it was not entirely clear whether the 1947 show would or would not presage the revival of the annual event. Anyway, there they were: four shows; hardly a crowded programme. Searching around, one can see there were also quite

[2] *E.g. 2353 Heather Mixture (by Lord Polo, no less; himself a chestnut).*

Punch (1925), 12.0 hh.

Boxer (1930), with E. W. White and trophy

a number of local events, many of which had kept going through the war years. Not counted as 'principal' apparently.

The 'principal sales' are given as Princetown, Tavistock, Chagford and Ashburton (autumn). Judging from what is published, this would seem to be a wasting asset; the next volume does not mention Tavistock; by Volume XXVIII they are down to Chagford and Ashburton and by XXIX they have disappeared altogether. A pointer that the breed is becoming less confined to the moor?

More interesting is the list of judges. In Volume XXV these number 12: 9 men, 3 women, Devon folk one and all, only 1 actually living off the moor. However, by the next Volume this is no longer true. And, to emphasize it, the 16 members of the panel are divided under the headings of 'Living in Devon' (5) and 'Living outside Devon' (11). By Volume XXVII (1953–4) the Devon contingent has been reinforced by 3 inspectors/judges, while the 'foreigners' have been divided into inspectors/judges (2), judges only (9). From Volume XXVIII on they are not listed.

Finally, in each volume there is an 'Extract from the Rules for Registration': progeny of registered parents on both sides automatically eligible; all other ponies to be 'inspected'. Oddly enough, there is no mention that prize winners in Dartmoor classes (1st–4th) are also accepted as 'already inspected'; which, of course, they have been.

So affairs go on until Volume XXIX (1957). There we find the curt statement that 'the stud book is now closed for three years'. The reason for this is that a new scheme is being tried: the Supplementary List. The old, easy way in has been slammed shut, but this little postern has been left open; another kind of inspection, but involving several stages. New blood is thereby not entirely excluded but will be more closely controlled. (For details see Chapter 14, p.84)

These all-too-brief official utterances sketch in the progress of the DPS over the early post-war years. In this connection it is sad to see that the space given by the NPS to interesting details – of ponies and people as well as societies – is shrinking as the number of registrations grows. One by one these wayside flowers have been rooted out. First to go were those frank and uninhibited judges' comments on their classes at the London show. 'They were a poor lot,' said one. Even Dwarka's appearance at one London show drew the comment from Judge Willis that 'although he showed some signs of being "desert-born", his looks did not make up for his defective action.' Good straight stuff.

Too rough for modern sensibilities? So thought the NPS Council apparently, for the following volume's preface says that 'it (has been) deemed inadvisable to publish the judges' reports of the London shows'. Anyway, comment is out; gone too are those pre-First-World-War mini-essays extolling impeccable lineage, wins at home and overseas and a lot more. By Volume XXVII (1953–4) we are down to hard tack: name, number, parentage, owner, breeder; and as a concession, one feels, age and colour.

The message is clear: from now on it's strictly business. 'A studbook,' the editor reminds us in the Preface to Volume XXX (1958–60), 'is primarily a registration of the *blood* in the animals entered and is not at all concerned with their merits … [it is] a guide to *breeders*.' (Her italics.)

A trifle disdainful, perhaps, but perfectly correct all along the line. No longer can we indulge our fancy, call for the bill and pay it. All the same, it is saddening to be deprived of all those adornments; not merely idle chit-chat, but useful background to fill in the wider picture. Well, all that frivolity has been swept away. However, we do enjoy one compensation: we have reached the stage in our story within the scope of what is called, with no more than a trace of irony, living memory. We have, therefore, material and to spare. On the other hand, as we know, memory, consciously or otherwise, does tend to do its best for whoever's doing the remembering. It should therefore be handled with care, best described as with polite scepticism. With this caveat firmly lodged at the back of our minds, visible only to ourselves, let us move on to the next chapter to discover how our subject fared during those years we can at long last look on as truly 'peacetime'.

Widecombe in the Moor

13 THE BREED SHOWS (PART 1)

Of course, the return to peacetime wasn't like switching on a light. Nevertheless, the darkness of wartime was gradually dispelled, so that by the end of the forties austerity was more or less a thing of the past. If we accept the year 1949 as a very approximate milestone, then it is a good year for picking up the threads of the Dartmoor story, the year in which the DPS held its first show at Prince Hall. By then, too, the signs were that the world of the Dartmoor pony was expanding. In contrast to the eleven new registrations in Volume XXIV (1940–44) and the four dozen in Volume XXV (1945–7), Volume XXVI (1948–52) mustered almost 300. There were Dartmoor classes at shows up and down the country. And, if it was still not very easy to get to them, it was becoming easier. With so much activity it is more important than ever that we should keep our bearings.

So, in describing the early post-war years, we have taken as our reference point the breed show. This does not imply the belief that the activities of the DPS began and ended with this annual event. There were other shows, larger and more important in the general pony world, but (dare it be said?) none more important to Dartmoors than this, the show to which the real moorland ponies were taken. For the moor and its ponies it was 'The Show'; unique too, for its offspring the Northern and Southern Darts were thirty years away ahead.

The 1947 Princetown show had been something of an experiment. Its success suggested that in later years they could spread their wings with confidence. By current standards the 1949 programme was ambitious: a class for stallions, three for mares, four for young stock; even some for first-crosses and riding ponies. Back to the style of 1939. Back, too, were the pre-war names: White, Holman, Coaker, Horrell, Croft and, for the first time at a breed show, Sylvia Calmady-Hamlyn herself.

She won, of course. Her winning stallion, Pete, was a four-year-old by Jude out of Peewit by Dinarth Spark. His grandam was Water Wagtail by The Leat; as fine a line-up of classic mountain and moorland ancestry as anyone could ask for.[1]

There were new names too, for time does not stand still, even on the moor. The children that had come with their parents to Lydford in 1939 were now married men and women. One of these won both the brood-mare classes. The schedule said 'up to 11.3' and 'up to 12.2', so there was no reason why Jean Palmer's Yeoland Lady Hamilton should not go in for both. Such latitude may or may not have been the intention of whoever had compiled the schedule. One would imagine not, seeing that the classes for the following year were for 'up to 11.3' and 'over 11.3 and up to 12.2'. Lady Hamilton (11.1) was bred by Ernest White & Son; by Cawsand Dinky out of Daisy XVI.[2]

The breed show was held at Prince Hall over fifteen years. The neighbourhood may have been draughty – where on the moor is not? – but it was conveniently central for those days when transport was scarce. Let us then review the activities during that period.

---

[1] And all wasted, for Pete left no progeny. Given away, he was treated with what can at the best be described as inadequate understanding, so that he became almost unmanageable. He had to be put down.

[2] Cawsand Dinky was unregistered. The Cawsand prefix was used by the Holman family, neighbours of the Whites in pony-loving South Zeal. On the female side we are on firmer ground. Daisy was out of Fairy III, both bred by White & Son and considerable winners before the Second World War. Incidentally, the 'Cawsand' refers to Cawsand Beacon, the hill above Zeals, and has nothing to do with the bay near Plymouth.

First the classes for mares. Over the years the society rang the changes according to interest manifest in the entries for the various categories. At the first three shows the third class was for barren mares. It was won on all three occasions by Syd Horrell's Midget V (actually placed 'equal first' with Anne Bullen's New Moon in 1950). In 1949 and 1950 Midget also won the Championship of the Show. She was foaled in 1937, by Sammy (unregistered at the time, later legitimized as a gelding) in the year her dam, Syd Horrell's Virtuous Lady, won the broodmare class when eighteen years old. Midget did well for her owner-breeder over the years: a win at Bath & West in 1939, three in a row at Roborough (1944–6). Midget's 1942 foal Flash (by 'Dartmoor') also won youngstock classes at Roborough, Princetown, Scoriton and Okehampton.

In 1952 there were only the two open classes (11.3 and 12.2). Then in 1953 a class for novice mares and fillies was introduced. This, though it attracted a wide variety of entries, was not very well filled. It lasted for seven shows, being replaced by one for barren mares with certificates of service, this latter moderately successful.

As might be imagined, there was a wide spread of both age and merit in the novice class, ranging from up-and-coming yearlings acquiring ring experience to game but permanently down-the-line veterans. The first was won by E.W. White & Son's home-bred yearling Juliet VIII (by 'Dartmoor' out of Julia ('Dartmoor')) which earlier in the day had been second to Major Bulteel's

Beltor. In 1954 the winner was Jim Stephens' four-year-old Hele Jenny (breeding given as 'Dartmoor'), followed in 1955 by Tom Holman's five-year-old Cawsand Lass II (probably out of Cawsand Lass, herself by Ranger III out of the legendary Queenie XX, (all Holman-bred).[3] These were followed by two wins by Pat Robinson's yearlings: Jenetta (Jude/Dora) in 1956 and Vean Zelinda (Jude/Zigzag) in 1957; both bred by Sylvia Calmady-Hamlyn. Belinda won again two years later as a three-year-old.

The year 1957 might be termed a 'collector's year', as it saw the first appearance in the ring of ponies actually carrying the Vean prefix: V. Zelinda (as above), V. Wayzgoose (owned by Elspeth Ferguson and, incidentally, the first Vean to appear in

---

[3] *The Queenie line (all so named, being distinguished from each other solely by numbers) came into the Holman family in 1919, round about the time of Thomas Holman's marriage to May Cottle, also of South Zeal. May Cottle's great-uncle John Cottle had a mare called Queenie (the first). She was in foal and when her time was on her she made her way down off the open moor to drop her foal alongside the brook at Ford Cross (near the present course of the A30 road).*

Some say she abandoned it there; others that it actually fell in. At all events, she would have no more to do with it, so that it was Tom Holman's lot to spend a sizeable part of his honeymoon bottle-feeding a foal which its owner presented to him in gratitude. So well did he do this job that Queenie VII (as he dutifully named her) lived right through the next war to die in 1946, having produced her last foal in 1943. The Queenies were undoubtedly survivors.

Midget V (1937)

Vean Blue Jennykin (1956)

the Dartmoor section of the stud book: Volume XXVII (1954)) and V. Wildfire (owned by Joan Montgomery). In this connection, it will have been noted that for many years none of the Vean stallions carried the prefix. Their breeder no doubt felt confident that there was no need for any nominal brand-mark for Jude, Jon, John and the rest; their ancestry was plain enough for all to see. Thus for many years the Vean prefix was only tacked on to ponies sold away from the Vean Stud; a pardonable piece of oneupmanship.

As mentioned above, for the first eleven years of the society's stay at Prince Hall there were two open classes for broodmares with foal at foot (11.3 and 12.2). Of the total of twenty classes after 'Lady Hamilton's Benefit', nine were won by Sherberton mares. The star was Linnet. She won the small mare class three times, was second thrice, third once and only unplaced once when shown. She was by Smokey (unregistered) out of Sherberton Eliza by Brown Berry out of Heatherbelle VI. The Coakers' other big winner was Brownbelle, with no fewer than five firsts in the 12.2 division. Better than Linnet? A matter of opinion, of course, but the pointers are that the competition was fiercer in the 11.3 class.

Brownbelle must have been a good pony. She was half-sister to the Eliza mentioned above and was at least fourteen when she

won in 1957. The youthful John Coaker was undoubtedly in luck when he acquired Heatherbelle in the early thirties, for she was almost certainly by either Dwarka or The Leat. These two were at Tor Royal, where she was bred, at the relevant time – about 1922. Heatherbelle the Sixth: dam, grandam and ancestor of many good ponies.

Among the 'other' winners – the eleven not from Sherberton – was Tom Holman's Betty XXI (foaled in 1945 of unstated parentage). She won the 11.3 class in 1951 and again in 1954 when, for good measure, she edged Sir John Bulteel's John out of the championship. Then there was Sylvia Calmady-Hamlyn's Wild Rose IV, thrice winner of the 12.2 class: in 1952, 1956 and 1959, the last when she was seventeen. Her win in 1956 matched that of her stable-mate Jenny VII in the 11.3s.

The single wins were as follows: in the large class Syd Horrell's Yeoland Beepety Bump (by Y. Lord Nelson out of Bucktor Queen) in 1951; in the 11.3s Joan Montgomery's Halloween II (bred by Newman Caunter and dam of Michelmass – so spelt) in 1957, Elspeth Ferguson's Snipe (breeding not given) in 1958, Mrs Jackson's Chymes (bred by John Coaker by Smokey out of S. Eliza, full sister to Linnet) in 1959. And, of course, there was Sylvia.

'Who was Sylvia?' Who indeed! Long before she won her 11.3

Tom Holman with grandson Peter and (*left*) yearling (?Ranger) and (*centre*) Queenie XXI (1947) at Widecombe Fair

Tom Holman with Queenie XXI (1947) at Widecombe Fair

The Royal Show at Newton Abbot, 1952: Sylvia Calmady-Hamlyn shows Jenny VII and foal Jentyl to the Queen.

class in 1950 she had achieved a kind of vicarious fame, her unorthodox descent being well authenticated, even to the extent of eye-witnesses. Some years back, Caunter Senior (Newman's father) had, in the ordinary way, brought a filly to a local show. And there destiny took a hand. A stallion broke loose and covered her, to the great annoyance of Caunter. A heated exchange ensued with the stallion's owner, who happened to be White of South Zeal. This was showing every sign of escalating, via abuse, to actual blows when the two protagonists were called to order by Sylvia Calmady-Hamlyn, drawn to the scene as a warrior to the sound of the guns. Sizing up the situation, she strode between the two protagonists. Then, observing that the offender was none other than White's champion Boxer, she roundly told Caunter that, far from being irked, he should

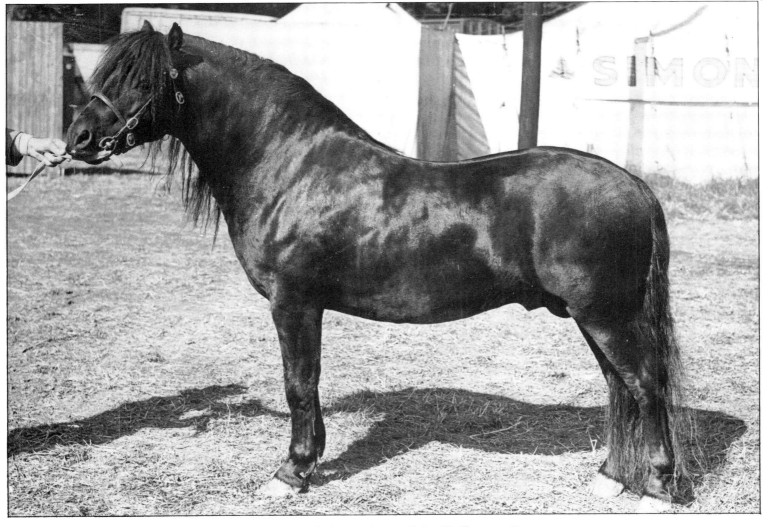

Janus (1945), thrice a winner of the Shalbourne Cup

recognize his luck in obtaining a free service to such a high-class sire and without the bother of transport either, or words to that effect.

However it was, the result was that peace was restored. Indeed, Caunter soon saw the sense of her remarks. To show his appreciation he named the eventual outcome Sylvia in her honour, and Sylvia it was that won the small mares' class in 1950. It was a good class to win too, for she was up against John Coaker's three-times-winner Linnet, as well as Pat Hyett's Cater's Beam, the previous year's three-year-old winner. Sylvia's foals did well too. Of them more later.

In the stallion classes over those first eleven years the Vean stock simply took over: in 1949 Pete as already mentioned, in 1950 Jude (by Dinarth Spark out of Juliet IV), in 1951 Pete

Line-up of stallions at the Royal Show, 1953: (*right to left*) **Pete, John, Janus and Judcock; all Calmady-Hamlyn bred**

John (1944)

again, in 1952 Janus (by Jude out of Dora), in 1953 John (full brother to Janus, shown by Major Bulteel), in 1954 John again, in 1955 Jenyn (by Pipit out of Jenny VII, shown by Pat Robinson), in 1956 Jude again (now fifteen years old), in 1957 Jentyl (full brother to Jenyn), in 1958 and 1959 Jenson (also full brother to Jenyn and Jentyl).

Finally, the show champions. Midget's two wins in 1949 and 1950 have already been mentioned. On the remaining nine occasions the winning stallion claimed the lion's share with Pete, Janus (only three at the time), John, Jentyl and Jenson (twice). It went to the 11.3 mare in 1954 (Betty XXI) and 1956 (Jenny VII), to the two-year-old filly in 1955 (Minerva V).[4]

As it turned out, after the amalgamation of the two open classes for broodmares the society was only able to hold four

more shows at Prince Hall; the level, open and accessible field being no longer available. Those years, however, witnessed the arrival on the showing scene of a remarkable line. We have already met Joan Montgomery's Halloween as the winner of the small mares in 1957. Her nick was Jenyn. By him she produced Michelmass (1958), Spellbound (1960) and Sorceress (1969); no ordinary Dartmoors, being described in an article as 'three of the most outstanding ponies in the breed in recent times'.[5]

Michelmass for a start. He won as a yearling, as a two-year-old and at three when he added the show championship to his class win. He went on in the following years to win the stallion class and, naturally, the championship. After this *tour de force* he left the show-ring to his progeny.

The other two winning stallions during this short, end-of-Prince-Hall period were: in 1960 Jenson completing his hat-trick of first-and-champion and in 1961 Elspeth Ferguson's Dunnabridge Bonny Boy, the latter introducing a rare dash of non-Vean blood. Bonny Boy was bred by Newman Caunter; by Huccaby whose descent has not found its way into the stud book. On the dam's side, however, there is an interesting link with

---

[4] *Minerva was very well bred (by Jude out of Miss Muffet VI). Foaled in 1953 she appears just twice in the youngstock classes, backing her 1955 championship with a win in the three-year-olds in 1956. After this splendid start – nothing. She fades from the show-ring; at least from that of the breed show. Her yearling by Janus is entered in the 1958 catalogue but evidently was not forward. However, she had other foals; notably Whitestone Ragged Robin (by Rose Vean Jack Snipe) after she had travelled to Yorkshire to Hazel Hunter's stud.*

[5] *'The End of an Era', by Pat Robinson* (Dartmoor Diary, *1976*).

Jentyl (1952), a winner of the Shalbourne Cup

Michelmass (1958)

another winner. Bonny Boy was out of Moor Hen III, who was also the dam of Halloween the dam of Michelmass. Nor is that the end of the matter, for Moor Hen was the daughter of Sylvia. Sylvia again! Yes, here is that by-blow of a horse-line romp; not only a winner herself, but the grandam and great-grandam of

winners; indeed, champions. A fortunate escapade indeed!

The 1960 show saw the first truly 'open' class for broodmares, at the single height-limit of 12.2 hh in any case imposed by the rules for registration. In that year, too, a class for barren mares with service certificates for the current year was substituted for the novice mare or filly class that had attracted an average of some seven entries over the previous seven years. This latter started weakly, but built up to around a dozen.

The 1960 winner of the open class was Iris Gould's Fudge III, paying a second dividend on the fiver laid out for her at Ashburton Market. It was a strong class too: Linnet, Betty XXI, Halloween and a dozen more quality mares. The barren winner was Molly Croft's Coronet II, a seven-year-old of distinguished male ancestry: by Storm II by Jef by Jude by Dinarth Spark.

Mrs Jackson's Chymes won the 1961 open class, again over strong opposition from Snipe, Halloween, Hele Judith and her daughter Judith II. Chymes was by Smokey out of Elizabelle. Another Smokey mare won the Barren class: Lady Edith Brooke's seventeen-year-old Cottage Light. Not much support for this latter class, with entries touching rock-bottom at three in 1961 and again in 1962, after which a slow climb. Cottage Light was also Coaker-bred, also by Smokey but out of Prickles (through whom she goes back to Heatherbelle via Brownbelle II). They were a fine pair of veterans, totalling thirty-three years between them, every one of which had been spent, winter and summer, on the high moor above 1000 feet.

Indeed, around the early sixties the older mares were on top. In 1962 the same classes were won by Jim Stephens' ten-year-old Hele Judith (home bred from 'Dartmoors') and Joan Montgomery's eight-year-old Gamma Ray. This was a great breakthrough for Judith which had only once been unplaced in the seven times entered, though it must be admitted that the previous hot competition was no longer there. Still, you can't do better than first … Gamma Ray was bred by J. White & Son by Teignhead out of Julia IV.

The 1963 winners were younger. The open class went to Iris Gould's five-year-old Skaigh Princess, bred by Tom Holman (by Cawsand Boy out of Betty XXI). The barren winner was Violet Dalby's four-year-old Hele Judith V, bred by Jim Stephens (by Sherberton Choirboy out of Hele Judith, dam of a long line of Hele Judiths (II–IX) and herself the previous year's winner of the open class).

So the breed show came to the end of its time at Prince Hall. It was sad to have to leave, but the new tenant had other plans for the field where fifteen shows had been held and the alternative offered was far from suitable, being less easy of access, uneven, unlevel and liberally strewn with gorse-bushes. Luckily the society found a new site in plenty of time for the next year's event, with Mr Mudge at Brimpts above Dartmeet where it had last been held in 1937. In the meanwhile let us retrace our steps across a few years to take a wider view of the society's activities and those of its members.

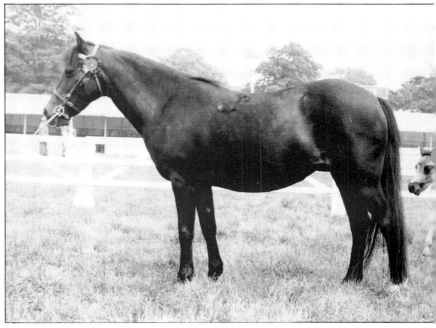

Wild Rose IV (1942) dam of Juniper

Rose Vean Jack Snipe (1958)

Chinkwell Tor U '85

14 POST-WAR ADJUSTMENTS

There was one notable absentee from the 1959 show. For the first time since she herself had launched it in 1931, Sylvia Calmady-Hamlyn was not well enough to face the rigours of a summer day at Princetown. She was now in her late seventies and this was the first public sign that she was nearing the end of her busy road. Within a few months she resigned her secretaryship and from the judges' panel. She died in 1961, but by then there was clear evidence that her purpose had been achieved: the evolution and presentation of the quality Dartmoor to which she had devoted a very large part of her time, skill and fortune over some forty years. She could see it for herself, in her own stud and in the show results; a magnificent bequest to the Dartmoor breed.

So the twin pillars of the Dartmoor Pony Society were no more, for Nora Dawson, the great anchorman, had gone on ahead in the middle year of the war. For close on twenty years the staunch firm of Dawson & Hamlyn had subsidized almost every activity of the society, in particular the annual breed show. Nora Dawson's death had left her partner to carry on as best she could; a tall order, for these were no longer the spacious, free-spending twenties and thirties. Fortunately, help was at hand; in the way most needed too – an injection of solid cash. The unlikely *deus ex machina* was the British Betting Control Board, with an announcement that every year it would grant money to the native breed societies, to be used in mounting shows for their respective breeds; a major windfall and, to say the least, a great relief. Indeed, nothing less than a reprieve, for had it not been forthcoming, with a reasonable certainty of its continuing, the outlook for the DPS would have been bleak. This began in 1950 and has continued ever since – at a steadily rising rate. Breeders of Dartmoors, remember the punters of Britain!

Sylvia Calmady-Hamlyn was gone, but (largely thanks to her) the society was very much alive. Let us take a look at it, from the point of view of our particular interest – the Dartmoor pony itself. We have discussed the breed shows in the forties and fifties: where they were held, which ponies did well and against what opposition, glanced at their breeding and so on. All this mainly enjoyable activity was, of course, brought about by the DPS, now just past its silver jubilee. The organization – and much more concerning breeding, registration and showing the moorland pony – was discussed, argued about, occasionally fought over (one AGM had to be prematurely closed) and finally decided; either at general meetings or at those of the appointed council.

If, then, we are to achieve a picture that is broader and deeper than a show report, we should know more of what went on when the society was in conclave. And for this the best place to search is in the society's minute book, the official and approved record. Did we not learn at our mothers' knees that minutes tell all? Or, if not entirely, then give us an accurate, objective summary, brief but comprehensive, of what went on; the arguments for and against, the protagonists, the motion actually put, the voting numbers, even perhaps who was going to do what in consequence. That is, they *should* do.

We know, too, that it's seldom like that in real life, though we should come to no harm from bearing these precepts in mind. In short, are we here demanding an inhumanly high standard? Is it reasonable to expect that the views of the minute-taker will be held in check, when that minute-taker is also a voting member and, furthermore, the society's chief patron – indeed for many years its sole (or, at the most, joint) backer – as well as its champion against all-comers in the show-ring? Let us, then, take the practical course of reading those minutes (taking care that we ourselves, in turn, are entirely objective). From them we can extract the facts and, as it were, hold the rest up to the light. As, one might add, is usually the case with minutes.

Of course, if they aren't there, they can't be read at all, with or without reservations. Such, indeed, we discover to be the case for all those relating to the first twenty-two years of the society's life. The entry for 9 April 1947 makes this clear: 'The Hon. Sec. reported that the Minute Book and all the Society's papers had been burnt in the Chytane fire.'[1]

Well, there it is; all down in the minutes, so it must be in order, mustn't it? And, if it isn't, what can we do about it today? More to the practical point, though, is the question of how much these shortcomings and lacunae need bother us; that is, in putting together our story of the Dartmoor pony. It would have been nice to have had a full account stretching right back to that first gathering when it was 'decided to form an association', but we can manage without; losing a little, but gripping the main thread. We are after facts; further, facts relating to the pony, rather than to the general affairs of the DPS. For instance, the composition of the society's council may loom large in the minds of members (and, if not, it ought to), but cannot be allowed to distract us from what is our main business. Rather we are interested in such matters as the maximum height for registration, the eligibility of ponies for stud book or register, how well they did and so on. And on these less personal subjects there is every reason to feel confident that the post-1947 minutes, reticent though they sometimes are, will come up with the facts we need.

The height limit for a start. But surely all that was settled as long ago as the mid-twenties, as mentioned in Chapter 11, with 12.2 hh as standard for both stallions and mares? That is true. It is also true that such matters, not being laws of nature, can never be permanently laid to rest. Sure enough, up it popped in 1957, with Jim Stephens of Cornwood moving that 12 hh should be the limit in future. The minutes do not give his reasons, only that John Coaker was against any alteration, arguing that the current 12.2 hh fitted in well with the heights of the riding pony classes (12.2, 13.2 and 14.2 hh then – as they still are). This point may sound strange to modern ears, for today a true 'mountain' or 'moorland' pony – say, a Welsh Mountain or a Dartmoor – wouldn't stand much chance in a class for riding ponies as this term is currently understood. But don't let us forget the lead-rein classes at 12 hh.

Penny II (1960)

The motion was lost by a single vote. However, as it was raised under Any Other Business, the idea may have taken the meeting by surprise. At all events, the close finish encouraged Stephens to try again the following year. This time he went for 11.3 hh (why not stated) and was again defeated (majority not given). It seems that this 1958 A.G.M. was a stormy affair, for under Any Other Business (a nice touch) it is stated that 'the uproar became so hopeless that the Chairman broke up (sic) the meeting'. What the row was about is not stated, but it could not have led to sober debate on heights.

Twelve hands, 11.3 – or 13 hh? There was still talk (no more than that) of raising it, presumably to appease some foreign buyers, but this had not been officially debated. Probably a case could be made for the 12-hand limit[2] – if one were starting with

---

[1] Where Sylvia Calmady-Hamlyn lived before moving to Pearroc Vean.

[2] During the eleven years (1949-59), when there were two classes for broodmares, there were many more entries in the 11.3 class than in the 12.2. The former also provided the show champion on the two occasions when this was awarded to a mare. By no means conclusive, but of interest. Contrariwise, we should not forget the top-grade ponies over the 12-hand mark: Heatherbelle, for instance; The Leat, if it comes to that. Above all, we should bear in mind that a limit is a limit, to allow reasonable latitude; it is not a 'best height'.

Vean Petrina (1960)

a clean sheet. Having had it at 12.2 hh for so long, breeders would undoubtedly face a considerable upheaval. Would this be justified? Moving the goal-posts in the middle of a game is seldom popular with those about to score with them in the original position. Not a decision to be taken lightly.

Then there was colour, another evergreen argument – if such is not a contradiction in terms. As has already been described, it took some years to achieve a precise 'Description' in the stud book. The situation in 1990 is that any colour (other than piebald or skewbald) may be registered. For many years the masthead of

the Dartmoor Section of the *NPS Stud Book* read: 'Colours: bay, brown, black, grey, chestnut; but no colour-bar except piebald and skewbald.' This was continued as long as the Dartmoor Section appeared in the *NPS Stud Book,* the clear inference being that the colours named were 'preferred', but that roans, duns and so on were admissible – just. The latest official utterance to hand comes from the *1990 Spring Sales List.* There under 'The Standard of the Dartmoor Pony' we find 'Colour – bay, brown, black, grey, chestnut, roan. Piebalds and skewbalds are not allowed. White markings on the head and/or legs should be

Vean Mary Rose (1982)

fairly small.' Thus, roan is in at last, only leaving the duns in limbo, presumably acceptable.[3]

One may, perhaps, sum up the rules and guidance on height and colour as follows. Height is a matter of ascertainable fact. A

---

[3] *Duns are certainly rare. There is a 'dun chestnut' in Volume XXI: May V, bred by Frank Webber. She did well too: first as a yearling at the 1933 breed show; first again at Devon County; second as a two-year-old and three-year-old. It is interesting to note that at the breed shows she is always described as 'chestnut'.*

Dartmoor measuring over 12.2 hh will not be eligible for a Dartmoor class, nor for registration. Colour, on the other hand, while also a matter of fact, is also a matter of preference. Most judges prefer the colours listed and, within that list, largely in the order quoted. Likewise, over-large white markings are generally thought to be unsightly. But how much is 'too much', as was asked at the 1963 A.G.M.? 'Excessive white (was) to be discouraged,' said the official description. How much, then was 'excessive'? That, said the chairman, must be left to the judge. A small point, but an important principle: judges are there to judge.

Jenetta (1955)

Turning now to the more general business of registration, we find some change in eligibility. As already mentioned, for some years after the Second World War there were a number of not-too-exacting ways into the stud book, helping to make good the losses suffered during those six years when our interests were otherwise engaged. By 1956 these had been made up, so the society decided to close the register,[4] during which time only the progeny of fully registered sires and dams would be accepted. It was hoped that this emphasis on 'pedigree' would help sales to America, where breeders demanded at least four generations of known descent. Thus the old, single-sentinel gateway was closed and bolted against newcomers. However, the same meeting accepted John Coaker's suggestion of a supplementary register, designed to leave a way still open for the infusion of new or unknown blood; a postern to be carefully guarded under the rules similar to those of the original inspection scheme but more stringent. The scheme was to run as follows, starting in 1961.

---

[4] *To come into force on 30th June 1957 for a 'three-year trial period'.*

It started with a mare; any mare, for at this stage her provenance, if any, was immaterial. She was unregistered, but her owner liked the look of her. He may have *thought* she was a Dartmoor; he may even have known she was, being by and out of registered Dartmoors. What could be done for her? Or, if not for her, then for her descendants? Gone were the days of Good King Edward, when she could have been inspected and in before you could say Calmady-Hamlyn. The new route, via the supplementary register, was lengthy, to be sure, but to stock of merit – and on the female side – it did offer the hope of full registration for their great-granddaughters.

The path to eventual registration underwent some amendment. By 1969, however, the procedure had been reduced to the following. The owner asked the DPS to arrange for his mare's inspection. The three official inspectors had to decide whether she 'looked like a Dartmoor and, in addition, in their opinion was likely to produce a moorland foal if mated with a Dartmoor stallion'. If passed, she became 'SR'. She – or, rather, her line – had climbed the first rung. Once so designated (but not before if the owner wished to continue towards full registration), she could be mated with a registered Dartmoor. If the result was a colt, he could be registered as a gelding, though this was not encouraged.

So they concentrated on the female side. A filly foal was inspected (at two years or over) as her dam had been and, if passed, went into Supplementary Register One (SR1). Once she had achieved this (but not before) she too could be put to a registered Dartmoor. The result of this union was similarly inspected and, if passed, registered as Supplementary Register Two (SR2), though if a male only as a gelding. From then on the SR2 filly was, as it were, up and away. Any of her foals could be fully registered *without further inspection*. As far as her progeny (by a registered Dartmoor, of course) were concerned, an SR2 mare was treated in every way as a fully registered Dartmoor mare.

A long, hard road? Undoubtedly. The whole process from the foaling of the 'likely filly' to the registration of her great-granddaughter would stretch over a dozen years. Unnecessarily long? Evidently the DPS didn't think so. Indeed, they could well have pointed to what had happened in those Edwardian Days aforesaid, when several fully registered Dartmoors hadn't a drop of good moorland – let alone Dartmoor – blood in their veins; the result of trying to progress too quickly.

Well, the society wasn't going to let that happen again. With great skill and restraint the long-sighted breeders had evolved the quality Dartmoor. The pick of these showed that they could hold their own against anything other native breeds could put up

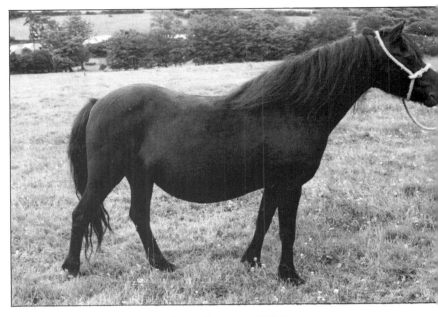

Shilstone Rocks Rainstorm (1964)

Red Hall Aquarius (1950)

against them. Outside or unregistered blood could add an occasional bonus, to be sure, but must be carefully controlled and sparingly used; hence the several stages in the SR process, the increase in the number of inspections as well as in the number of inspectors on each occasion.

This extra care was manifest in the stipulation that the sire at each stage could only be a registered Dartmoor. This ensured that only a small amount of new, even unknown, blood was introduced, rather than the other way round. Simple arithmetic shows that the colt or filly finally accepted into the stud book (the offspring of the SR2 mare) would have *at least* seven-eighths guaranteed Dartmoor blood: from its sire, grandsire and great-grandsire.

The SR scheme offered this chance to the progeny of good but unregistered ponies. It also acted as a safety-net to those that had a perfectly good Dartmoor (in that its sire and dam were registered) but had allowed time to slip by until one morning they woke up to find that the rules put their little champion over the age-limit for registration (currently by the end of the calendar year after the year of foaling). Now they were offered a second chance.

The scheme never attracted many entries, but it was there for those willing to take the trouble. Recently it has received some encouragement from the introduction of the Society's Moor Scheme for bringing in fresh *quality* blood, as described in Chapter 17.

Then there was – and still is – the Part-bred Dartmoor Register (P-BDR). This is quite different from the SR scheme, in that it concerns itself, as one might put it, in breeding *away* from the moor, rather than towards it; a record of out-crosses via *registered* stock. It was started in the late fifties as a private venture by a group of enthusiasts headed by Lady Willingdon with the object of recording out-crosses from the pure Dartmoor pony – on either side. It differs in its function by concerning itself only with the progeny of ponies already registered in one or other of the recognized stud books (GSB, AHSB, NPS or those of the native breeds), the only requirements being at least a quarter fully registered Dartmoor blood (on either side or combined) and not more than a quarter other native blood.

There cannot, of course, be such a thing as a standard part-bred, as a cross with, say, a TB could be quite different from one with a riding pony. An entry in the P-BDR should, therefore, be looked on as denoting that admixture of Dartmoor, the ponies themselves being judged simply as ponies. For those interested there are part-bred Dartmoor classes at a number of the major shows.

It is, of course, the main stud book that concerns us most. This formed part of *The National Pony Stud Book and Register* until Volume 46 (1976), after which the Dartmoor Pony Society issued its own stud book.[5] So let us see what information we can draw from it.

The National Pony Stud Book and Register (to give it its sonorous full title) isn't what it was. But then what is? The details of individual ponies in it have been whittled away until, in the last volume before the DPS launched its own stud book, these had to come down to name, date of foaling, owner, breeder, sire, dam and colour. Older *aficionados* may sigh for the days when the NPS thought nothing of devoting a whole *extra* page to tracing the lineage of The Mikado (Fell, 1889) back to Flying Childers (1715, by the Darley Arabian).[6] But that 1900 biennial listed no more than 127 mountain and moorland ponies all told, in contrast to the 148 *Dartmoors alone* in the latest *annual* issue. So, we must see, there simply isn't room, now that pony breeding has become so popular.

However, there is one snippet of information that can be dug up: where the owners of Dartmoors live. The table below reveals all too clearly the dwindling proportion of owners living in the Dartmoor's home county, expressed as percentages of total registrations.

	Resident in Devon
Polo Pony Stud Book Volume VI (1902)	100 per cent stallions 96 per cent mares
NPS Stud Book Volume XIX (1927)	87 per cent stallions 83 per cent mares
NPS Stud Book Volume XXVI (1952)	85 per cent stallions 70 per cent mares
DPS Stud Book Volume O (1977)	32 per cent stallions 36 per cent mares
DPS Stud Book Volume 8 (1986)	27 per cent stallions 32 per cent mares

---

[5] *The switch from a section in the* NPS Stud Book *to the breed's own stud book went as follows. The DPS series started with 'Volume O'. This says on its cover that it 'contains the Dartmoor Sections of the National Pony Society Stud Book (Vol 47 & 48)'. Actually it comprises the Dartmoor entries that would have appeared in volumes 47 and 48, but at any rate it bridges the gap between NPS vols 44, 45 and 46 (covering the years 1974–6 and the last in which Dartmoors appeared) and DPS Vol 1 (covering the year 1979).*

[6] *Volume VI, pp. 102-3.*

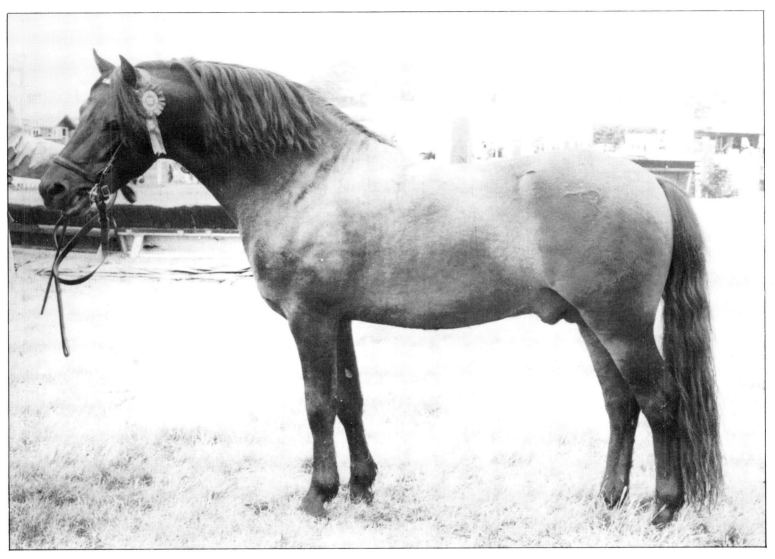

Shilstone Rocks Okement (1966)

Like all seemingly simple statistics, especially those tossing around percentages, these need to be looked at carefully. The point here is not that there are fewer home-grown animals but that there are many more from the far side of the Exe; also that most of these come from newcomers to the Dartmoor world. The causes and results of this shift of emphasis are worth noting. As with most enjoyable activities, pony breeding and showing took a little while to get back into its stride after those six years of austerity. However, when it did, from about 1960 onwards, it made up for lost time. The sixties and seventies were the years of the pony boom, ponies of all kinds. There was transport for them – a bit rough perhaps but serviceable and not at all expensive –

Blythford Scylla (1969)

plus cheap fuel to run it on; there were lots of shows and, with all that transport, many more of them within range. Here was a niche for the Dartmoor; a high-quality animal fit to be seen with in the ring, in hand or under saddle.

All this added up to more participation, more competition and hence the spur to improvement. However, it was not only up-country that saw this greater interest in the Dartmoor. Appendix C lists a score of studs chosen by the society as prominent in post-war breeding. Although the addresses range through Somerset, Surrey, Berkshire and Yorkshire, there are also top-flight establishments in Widecombe, Yelverton and Lustleigh, the important point being that they all have one attribute in common: the desire to breed the best possible pony. No longer would these be seen as just another farm product, but as valuable show-animals. One side-effect was some tightening of the rules governing aspects such as registration, who would be allowed to judge Dartmoor classes – and, contrariwise, whom society members could show under in Dartmoor classes. Also, the geographical spread led to some discussion on where the breed show and the society's meetings should be held, a subject dealt with elsewhere. For all that, it must be seen that this upsurge, which has only fallen off a little during the eighties, cannot be anything but a good thing for the breed.

Dartmoor ponies on the moor, gouache by Peter Upton

Dartmoor ponies on the moor, gouache by Peter Upton

Dartmoor ponies at the Shilstone Rocks Stud, Widecombe

Shilstone Rocks Rainy Day by Peter Upton

Dartmoor mare and sketches of her foal by Jean Palmer

'A young boy on his Dartmoor Pony'
by James Loder (1841)

Dartmoor ponies at the Shilstone Rocks Stud, Widecombe

Judy V   **Wood statuettes**   **Jude**

Jenny VII (2 years)   **Jenny VII**

15 THE BREED SHOWS ———— (PART 2)… ————

Dartmoor cottage · Buckland

NOTE: So far in our story the descriptions of the successive breed shows have included the main details of the various classes at those shows. With an expanding programme and a steadily increasing entry, the time has come – or at any rate we think it has – to divide the record in two: first and in the main text, a general account of the shows or series of shows; second and in Appendices A and B, the outline results and references to individual ponies. We trust that this will make life easier for our readers.

Dartmoor doesn't change. The Brimpts to which the breed show came back in 1964 did not differ greatly from the same high, wind-buffetted ground of twenty-seven years before: an open field with a distinct cant towards Dartmeet 300 feet below. The trouble was that although the moor was the same as ever – and few wished it otherwise – the requirements for even a modest show had altered considerably. For instance, two attributes were now considered essential: accessibility and accommodation, neither notably applicable to Brimpts.

Brimpts was beautiful; it was on the moor, close to the heart of the breed's home over the centuries. But Brimpts was also hard to reach; getting progressively harder as the West Country holiday traffic relentlessly piled up. The lanes between the show-field and the main roads were narrow, winding and steep; it didn't take much to choke them. Thus, it was becoming increasingly clear that a move was essential. But where to?

Newton Abbot Racecourse was available. Not even its most ardent supporters would have called it beautiful – indeed, the more fastidious might have dismissed it as scruffy – but it did at least meet the two desiderata mentioned above. Easy access is, after all, essential for a racecourse, so there was no difficulty there, the ground being not only easy to get in to or out from, but was right alongside big, wide, main roads; a trifling advantage when the alternative might be to have to bump along a few miles of familiar lanes, but a very different matter when tacked onto a long haul. Accessibility was important to the 'foreigners', and, not unreasonably, they said so. Furthermore, Newton had stabling, one half of the 'accommodation' aforesaid; a basic amenity also important to the exhibitors from up-country or from across the Tamar; such exhibitors, in turn, being important to the society if it was to fulfil its declared purpose of extending interest in the breed.

So Newton Abbot it was. For the first time the breed show came down from the moor; from just over 1000 feet up in the clear, open sky to 7 feet above mean sea-level; from the countryside to the outskirts of a town and a stone's throw from the Western Region's main line. Down just about as far as it could go.

But it was still in business. And that was what mattered. Nor did the entries suffer, at any rate to start with. During the seven years at Brimpts the overall total of entries rose from 135 to 185.[1] Entries started well at Newton with 217, possibly encouraged by better access, but fell away to 139 for the sixth year. Oddly enough, there is no evidence of increased support from the 'foreigners' as a result of the move from moor to main line; that is, if we are to go by percentages of entries; no marked trend during the six years (29, 25, 28, 29, 31 and 27 per cent of entries from outside Devon).

The move to Brimpts saw some small adjustments to the various in-hand classes: the yearling colts and fillies were separated and a class for novice mares was added. On the debit side, however, the geldings were not doing so well: no class at all for them as yearlings until 1966 (when they were put in with the

---

[1] *'Entries', here and elsewhere in this account, refer to the number of ponies actually allotted numbers in the catalogue, a rough and ready statistic but one which nevertheless gives a good general idea.*

Oatlands Diggory Delvet (1961)

Oatlands Mr MacGregor (1965)

yearling colts), remaining with the fillies as two- and three-year-olds. Well, it was the old business of supply and demand. Over the half dozen years at Brimpts no more than thirteen geldings were entered all told. Thus, looking at the in-hand programme as a whole, it is fair to say that, by the time the show left Brimpts, the pattern had sorted itself out pretty well, with well-balanced opportunities for stock of all ages.

This happy state had not yet been achieved in the ridden classes. In the years soon after the Second World War the society's attention had been concentrated on basic production rather than ultimate use, a reasonable view of 'first things first'. However, from the early fifties interest was steadily increasing. Its progress can be traced through the ebb and flow of the ridden classes at successive breed shows.

Until the end of the fifties the programme for the breed show was officially entitled 'Catalogue of Dartmoor Pony Show *also* Children's Pony Classes; as though the two events were quite disparate; as for all practical purpose they were. In 1959 there were four ridden classes, all for children: leading rein (11.2 hh children under eight years old), 12.2 hh, 13.2 hh and 14.2 hh; with never a word about 'Dartmoor' or 'registration'.

The year 1960 saw the shift back to moorland. First, the title said 'Catalogue of Dartmoor Pony Show'. Inside there was just one ridden class: for 'fully registered Dartmoor ponies' for children under seventeen. And that was that. True, there were only seven entries, of which five were forward, but it was a start in that it proclaimed the Dartmoor's purpose (or at any rate one of them); it was for *riding.*

While looking at this business of the end-product, it is interesting to trace the official view over the years. It will be recollected that Volume V (1899), which carried the first Dartmoor entries, does not bother with anything more than a description of what this pony *was*, no doubt confident that everyone that mattered (that is, everyone not tainted with the town) would already be aware of what a pony was expected to *do*. So it was not until 1948 (in Volume XXV) that the Dartmoor section of the *National Pony Society Stud Book* deemed it advisable to deal with this aspect. Under 'description of pony' it added: '... essentially a riding pony ... used by moorland farmers ... for carrying them over the rocks, boulders and steep hill-sides, being both sure-footed and active'. Not a word about the little dears. Indeed, it is not until nine years later that this entry is amended to read: 'Essentially a child's riding pony – for which purpose they (*sic*) are bred today.'

This latter-day definition may seem to the modern Dartmoor-owner to be a little too tightly drawn, as surely borne out by the excellent entries in the *open* ridden class over recent years. Also by the increasing enthusiasm for the Dartmoor for driving: on its own, as a pair or even four in hand. Is not one of the breed's greatest assets its versatility?

The ridden classes were a little slow to take root, judging from the numbers entered in the seventies. There does also seem to be some ambivalance in the society's thinking on the whole matter of riding Dartmoors, demonstrated in a discrepancy between what it says about the Dartmoor ('essentially a children's riding pony', as quoted above) and what it offers to competitors in the show-ring, where after 1960 there is no Dartmoor ridden class specifically for children – apart from that for the under-eights in the lead rein. Of course, children do compete in the open ridden class, but this does no more than demonstrate that the Dartmoor is *also* suitable for children. Which indeed it is. All the same, the introduction of ridden Dartmoor classes was a start and in roughly the right direction. It was a tender plant, but it grew, so that in the nineties this side can be described as 'healthy'.

So much for the classes. Let us now look at the site. As already mentioned, the show spent six years on Newton Abbot

Huntspath Heath, ridden by Sarah Goodman

Racecourse; accessible, accommodating but somehow not quite what was wanted; a waning in enthusiasm reflected in the falling number of entries. So it was up sticks again and move on? And, again, where to? Now into the early seventies, the requirements for a showground had grown far beyond the original open and fairly level field, thus narrowing the choice. This was additionally circumscribed by the strongly expressed insistence on keeping it in Devon (everyone – well, pretty well everyone – was agreed on this) and, apparently, by the depth – or, rather the shallowness – of the society's pocket; plus, of course, accessibility and accommodation.

From the point of view of pocket, it was at first maintained that the society should eschew anything involving heavy overheads. When the hon. show secretary reported in 1976 that the fee for Bicton was £100 per day, the council agreed 'not to pursue the idea'. The discussion, if any, is not recorded. It was then decided to stay on at Newton, at least for a further year.

However, things did not quite work out as planned. To start with, there had been some coolness between the society and the racecourse. This arose from a letter written by an individual member to *Horse and Hound*, which had some hard things to say about the amenities and conditions at Newton, including a particular complaint about the dust raised by contractors' lorries. Thus, the council did not find it irksome to have to comply with the opinion voiced at the Annual General Meeting that the council should 'reconsider the proposed site and date for 1977'.

And so the breed show came to Okehampton, at the invitation of the town's rugby football club. Of course, the simple amenities were hardly geared to a pony show, Okehampton was a long way from almost anywhere except Cornwall, but it was somewhere. At least it was handy to the A30 road, whose modernization was almost complete. Stabling was 'by arrangement'.

So the business staggered along for another three years. Then, at the A.G.M. and after due warning, the motion was tabled to the effect that the 1980 show (and, by inference, those that followed) should be 'easily accessible from a motorway' and 'with loose-boxes available on the ground; even if this meant taking the show out of Devon'. This last was, of course, the crux of the matter, as no doubt was intended. Out of Devon? Never! But what about nearby Somerset? Taunton Racecourse had everything needed and was very close to the M5. Or perhaps the society would like to make the Southern Show at Ascot its premier event? And it was at this precise moment that the society's patron made her nicely timed interjection. 'How,' asked Lady Devon, 'about Bicton?' How, indeed? Had they, perhaps, been too hasty in casting aside this possibility? True, it would cost £150 (like everything else it had gone up), but wasn't it worth it? She felt certain that members would be willing to help towards this outlay. She herself would be happy to contribute £25. Perhaps others would follow suit.

And so they did – or promised to. Thus, Bicton it was, on an immediate while-the-iron-was-hot show of hands. Well, near enough. What actually happened was that the members 'asked the council to consider Bicton for 1980'. Which, with commendable speed, it did that very afternoon, declaring for Bicton by an 11-1 majority. Where the show still is in 1990.

Have the wanderings of the Dartmoor Pony Society's Breed Show ended after half a century? At least the signs point to a long-term resting-place, as this most attractive and peaceful

Shilstone Rocks Easter Day (1978)

Shilstone Rocks Darkness (1966)

Shilstone Rocks Fury (1971)

At Bicton there is much to gladden the heart and ease the burden of the exhibitor, who is, after all, the most important human participant at such events. He arrives to find all the parking room in the world; good, firm ground too with a convenient slope down towards the hard road. He chooses a shady tree, runs his box beneath its branches and that is that. Moreover, from where he is, the rings are all in plain view, so he can carry on grooming, walking a restive colt around or just sitting in his cab, while keeping an eye on how the classes are running. There are rows of loose-boxes, lavatories galore, snack bars and a restaurant, a public-address system to keep him awake and possibly *au courant*, benches at the side of the main ring; indeed, every reasonable aid to modern equine civilization.

The actual classes at Bicton have differed little from those of the preceding years, though with some adjustment in the cases of mares and geldings. On the mares' side for the first three years (1980–82) there were three classes: open, novice and barren. From 1983 the barren class was divided into 'with certificate of service' and 'without'.

Then there were the geldings. For some years there had been some unease among the more experienced and responsible breeders over the large number of indifferent and even thoroughly unsuitable colts that were being left as entires and used for breeding; an irresponsible policy – or, rather, lack of it – to be discouraged. One way to further this was to remind owners that geldings were, from one point of view, the end-product – a pony to be ridden. Thus various permutations were tried to encourage gelding-owners to bring them to the show-ring. If we look back to the early years at Brimpts, we find them in with the fillies as two- and three-year-olds but nowhere else, the yearling class being simply headed 'colts'. Gradually the hoof was eased in to the doorway. In 1965 we find a yearling gelding, even though the title remains 'yearling colts'. He was bottom of the line, but never mind; the breach had been made, for in 1966 the class was officially catalogued as for 'colts and geldings' and Katkin of Torr was *not* bottom. Since then the yearling class has always been for all males.

For the years 1980–84 the older geldings remained with the fillies. In 1981 the geldings of four or more joined the barren mares. Then in 1985 there was a big change-round (apart from the yearlings): a separate class for geldings of two and three and another for four and over. The younger class only lasted for a couple of years, then the previous in-with-the-fillies-system came back.

An unconscionable amount of chopping and changing? Not really, for it can be held that the only practical way of discovering

haven in Devon's countryside surely combines as many desirable qualities as can reasonably be expected in an imperfect world. Of course it isn't perfect, but it stands up well to comparison which is what matters. For instance, although it is only about 9 miles from Junction 30 on the M5 (good), there is no denying that the lanes do become a bit narrow in the immediate vicinity of the showground (not so good, especially as viewed by impatient townsmen). However, that is the price for being in the *real* country, with never a railway, motorway or housing estate in sight or earshot. True, it collects a black mark from the traditionalists for not actually being on the moor. But it *is* in Devon, its home county. And where on the moor would one find the combination of Bicton's excellent amenities and its rural peace?

demand is to try out the various permutations. One can best describe the response as 'mixed'. That for the yearlings (in with the colts) was poor: a total of nine entered in the years 1980–88, of which fewer than half were forward; not exactly a crowd. In the classes for two- and three-year-olds the situation on this side remained fairly static, except that in 1988 alone there were nine geldings in these two classes. However, the idea of giving the older geldings a class to themselves seems to have caught on; 7 in 1985 when it was introduced, 13 in 1986 and again in 1987, 11 in 1988, 9 in 1989. The DPS might reasonably claim that the breed show gives a fair crack of the whip to all concerned. Now it is up to the exhibitors to fill those classes.

There is plenty of scope for all kinds of mares too, with four classes in the most recent schedules: for those without foals or certificates of service, for those without foals but with current certificates, for novices with foal at foot and the open class (with foal at foot). Apart from a falling-off among the novices (single figures since 1982) there has been a steady average of over forty each year. However, probably the most encouraging sign is the burgeoning of the ridden classes. Ten years ago there were 13 entries all told in the 2 ridden classes (leading rein and open); at the 1989 show there were 40 entries (for leading rein, open and novice). This is, of course, good news as demonstrating the ultimate purpose of the Dartmoor – for riding or driving. Taking the riding side, is it not pertinent to ask: 'ridden by whom?'

The question is relevant because it does seem that the statement in the stud book that the Dartmoor is 'essentially a child's riding pony'[2] finds no echo in the breed show schedule (apart from the leading-rein class). Surely the two should be brought into line? Not a burning issue, but a detail to be tidied up; and, in so doing, possibly helping the society to decide on where the emphasis should lie. Even if the open class is retained – after all, the 'Darty' was the traditional mount on the moor – it does seem reasonable to have a class for children *only*.

[2] *In the preamble to the Dartmoor section in Volumes 44–6 of the* NPS *Stud Book, the last volume before the DPS started its own stud book. This latter does not publish any 'description', so presumably the purpose quoted above still stands.*

Raybarrow Pool (1953), FS No. 20 – later gelded

16 . . . AND THE OTHER SHOWS

Most owners of Dartmoors look on the breed show as their premier event. A win there imparts prestige to the pony concerned and, who knows, might enhance its market value. There are, of course, plenty of other events open to them up and down the country. These range from major shows (though not many of them north of Yorkshire) right down the line to those jogging along happily to the theme of 'Now, dear, let Muriel have a go!' Somewhere there is a niche for everyone, a chance to find glory at any level between a national championship and tossing apples from pony-back into buckets.

It would be agreeably comprehensive if we could follow the fortunes of the Dartmoors at them in the same way as we have at the breed show, but this is not practicable between the covers of a single volume. To trim our report to the main theme we must prune and prune again. Fortunately, the first step has been taken for us. Since the sixties the DPS has classified certain events as 'star shows' from the point of view of the breed. These are nominated annually from among those scheduling at least four in-hand classes exclusively for Dartmoors and covering all ages and sexes, the list being published in *Dartmoor Diary*.[1]

Stars they are indeed, so far as the breed is concerned: judges strictly from the society's 'A' panel and with an embargo on any single judge officiating at more than one star show in any one season. Nor are the benefits to the winners confined to such abstractions as prestige; there is hard cash as well. As has been mentioned in Chapter 14, every year the DPS, along with the other native-pony societies, receives a grant from the 'Betting Levy Board. This hard cash – the society's share is currently a hefty £2000 plus – is in turn doled out to the needy in, among other forms, sire premiums, foal premiums, sire super-premiums and mare premiums; all based on the results at the star shows. The scheme works as follows: a Dartmoor stallion winning his class or one of whose progeny (other than a foal) wins its class at any of these events becomes a premium stallion. His owner receives a tenner and the owners of foals sired by him after becoming a premium stallion each get a fiver (not more than two foal premiums per member/stud).

Very pleasant for the recipients, but there is more in the offing. If a stallion's progeny (other than foals) win two classes at one or more star shows he can become a super-premium stallion: £25 to his owner, foal premiums as before, but also mare premiums of £25 (maxima as for foals) to be claimed by owners of mares covered during the following season. There is only one small string: premium and super-premium stallions must be declared to be available at public stud in the next season following the award. Incidentally, a premium stallion is one for the duration of the scheme, but a super-premium has to re-qualify annually – if his owner wishes to continue to enjoy the benefits.

Dartmoor Diaries over the eighties report an average of about nine super-premium awards each year. Those delving a little deeper may discover discrepancies between star-show winners

---

[1] *Dartmoor Diary, the society's magazine, established in 1971 and published annually in the New Year ever since; a most useful compilation of such facts as results at the three shows, together with articles on the Dartmoor pony both past and present.*

Senruf Grebe (1973), winner of the Ridden Championship at Olympia, 1979, Nicola Furness up

Hisley Polonaise (1982), a winner of the Lord Arthur Cecil Trophy

and actual awards, accountable to those eligible but not standing at public stud. In 1988 there were sixteen star shows, including of course the breed show and the Northern and Southern Dartmoors (more of which anon). Again, lack of space decrees that we can only look at one of these, which must serve as our example of 'Dartmoors at the Big Shows': how they did among themselves and, possibly of even greater moment, how the breed showed up against the others. For this we look at the National Pony Show.

Like so many of the national events, the NPS moved about the country until well after the Second World War, finally (we hope) settling on the Three Counties Ground at Malvern, where it has now (1990) been since 1971. To be sure, there is always argument on the choice of a site (especially when it looks like being long term or even permanent), but there is much to be said for Malvern, both abstract and concrete.

First, about the ground itself. It is level, well laid out and with all the amenities. Well, so have a lot of other large showgrounds. Yes, but it also enjoys the added 'amenity' of being almost uniquely easy to get into and away from. Then, on atmosphere, let it only be suggested that, if Bicton is cosy – at the DPS Show there is a marked family atmosphere – Malvern is magnificently spacious; even the NPS comes nowhere near to filling it; there is room and to spare. And, of course, the ground is well placed on the map of England and Wales, being, as near as makes no difference, at its geographical centre. Finally, those able momentarily to lift their eyes above their charges' ears are rewarded by the splendid backdrop of the Malvern Hills filling the western skyline. Is it too much to hope that he (or, more likely, she) would echo Wordsworth – at least phonetically correctly?

> 'Dull would he be of soul who could pass by
> A site so touching in its majesty.'

At all events, and down to earth again, we find that the NPS offers all the competition the most ardent exhibitor could wish for: not as many classes for Dartmoors as at Bicton but, taking the whole affair further and higher, inter-breed championships and, at the top of the range, a qualifying round for the national in-hand championship for 'light horses and ponies', currently (1990) sponsored by Judy Creber. It is, of course, in these supra-breed contests that the NPS – and most of the other major shows – score over Bicton. In them the representative of the Dartmoors (and the record shows they are in the top flight) can offer himself – or herself – for judging against the best of the other breeds: or, indeed, anything in hand.

Kilbees Mr Jingle (1970), a winner of the Shalbourne Cup

It is fair to claim that Dartmoors have done well since the Second World War: the Lord Arthur Cecil Cup for mares 6 times and the Shalbourne Cup for stallions no fewer than 11 times out of 41 shows. The female winners were: Snipe in 1958, Rosevean Quail in 1963, Miss Muffet of Robins in 1966, Whitmore Honeymoon in 1976, Hisley Caviar in 1985 and Hisley Polonaise in 1987; on the male side Jude in 1951 and 1953, Janus in 1952, 1956 and 1958, Jentyl in 1962, Hisley Woodcock in 1969, 1971 and 1974, Kilbees Mr Jingle in 1973 and Allendale Vampire in 1986.

These are followed in importance by the Best of Breed (see Table 1). These reveal, one imagines, nothing we did not know already: the early dominance of the ponies actually bred by Sylvia Calmady-Hamlyn, followed by a gradual broadening out, though still tracing back to the 'J class' stallions in almost all cases. Possibly a more rewarding investigation lies in the classes and entries themselves: which categories were catered for and how well they were filled.

Table 1

NATIONAL PONY SOCIETY SHOW 1948–89 – BEST DARTMOOR

Year	Name	Sire	Dam	Breeder
1948	John	Jude	Dora IV	Sylvia Calmady-Hamlyn
1949	Jenny VII	Jude	Dora IV	"
1950) 1951) 1953)	Jude	Dinarth Spark	Juliet IV	"
1952) 1954) 1956) 1957) 1958)	Janus	Jude	Dora IV	"
1955	Jon	Jude	Dora IV	"
1959	Jenson	Pipit	Jenny VII	"
1960) 1962)	Jentyl	Pipit	Jenny VII	"
1961	Blue John	John	Belstone	Sir John Bulteel
1963	Rosevean Quail	Vean Partridge	Snipe	Elspeth Ferguson
1964	Boveycombe Gemini	Jenyn	Fudge III	Iris Gould
1965	Michelmass	Jenyn	Halloween II	Joan Montgomery
1966	Miss Muffet of Robins	Janus	Widecombe Fair	Diana Davies
1967	Vean Zaffer	Petroc	Vean Zelinda	Patricia Robinson
1968) 1969) 1971) 1974)	Hisley Woodcock	Jenson	Dunnabridge Wigeon	(Ann Jones (Patricia Roberts
1970	Hisley Quince	Peter Tavy II	Queenie XXIII	(Ann Jones (Patricia Roberts
1972	Whitmore Honeymoon	Janus	Honeybags	Imogen Slade
1973	Kilbees Mr Jingle	Jentyl	Red Hall Auriga	Lady Willingdon
1975	Boveycombe Leo	Jude	Fudge III	Iris Gould
1976	Kilbees Mr Pickwick	Jon	Vean Blue Jennykin	Lady Willingdon
1977	Allendale Flauros	Huntspath Holly	Whitmore Titania	Paul & Jo Carter
1978	Hisley Pedlar	Lammermuir Rambler	Hisley Quince	(Ann Jones (Patricia Roberts

Year	Name	Sire	Dam	Breeder
1979	Vean Zennor	Vean Zaffer	White Willows Radiation	Patricia Robinson
1980) 1981) 1985)	Brandsby Tornado	Petroc	Shilstone Rocks Bay Wind	June Little
1982	White Willows Darwin	Shilstone Rocks Baccarat	White Willows Radium	Joan Montgomery
1983	Shilstone Rocks Hosanna	Shilstone Rocks Fury	Huntspath Hannah	Elizabeth Newbolt-Young
1984	Hisley Caviar	Hisley Pedlar	Blachford Brandween	(Ann Jones (Patricia Roberts
1986) 1987)	Allendale Vampire	White Willows Darwin	Allendale Black Magic	Paul Carter
1988	Shilstone Rocks Another Bunch	Shilstone Rocks Fury	Whitmore Honeybunch	Elizabeth Newbolt-Young
1989	Hisley Salvo	Hisley Woodcock	Hisley Serenade	(Ann Jones (Patricia Roberts

**Hisley Caviar (1974), a winner of the
Lord Arthur Cecil Trophy**

**Hisley Woodcock (1962), three times winner
of the Shalbourne Cup**

Whitmore Honeymoon (1960), a winner of the Lord Arthur Cecil Trophy

Allendale Vampire (1980)

For almost a decade after the Second World War had ended, classes were few and poorly supported – at least by later standards. Until 1961 there were only three Dartmoor in-hand classes with about a score of entries between them, reaching an all-time low of nineteen in 1961. What could be done to pump some life into the business? Which was to come first, the chicken or the egg? Or, in more specific terms, did it rest with the NPS to lay on more classes or was it up to the exhibitors to show by their numbers that they deserved more? Or a bit of both?

In the event both parties appear to have rolled up their sleeves. There were more classes (up to 4 in 1962, 5 in 1975, 6 in 1984); the entries crossed the half-century line in 1969 and, though they see-sawed between the mid-thirties and the mid-seventies (as such things tend to do) they never again sunk down to those dreadful 'teens.

So today in the nineties the Dartmoors enjoy half a dozen in-hand classes: stallions and colts of two years or over, yearlings, two- and three-year-old fillies and geldings, mares without foals

Vean Zaffer (1960)

and geldings of four years or over, mares with foals at foot, a separate class for those foals (provided they are by registered Dartmoors). This is exactly on par with the Connemaras, Fells, Highlands, New Forests. The Dales and Exmoors have only two classes each, but then their enthusiasm is not marked. On the other hand, the Welsh Sections 'A' and 'B' have seven classes each (an extra class for yearling and two-year-old colts). And we must admit that this is fair, with 150 entries in the 'A' and 'B' Section classes last year; the corresponding fifty-four fielded by the Dartmoors, while creditable, is hardly in the same league.

And then there were the ridden classes. As has already been mentioned, the ridden mountain and moorlands did not excite any great interest until shortly before the Second World War. Even after that distraction, there was a tendency to lump similar (and not so similar) breeds into a single catch-all class. First the 'small breeds' (Dartmoors, Exmoors, Shetlands, Welsh 'A' and 'B') went into a single class, superseded in 1958 by the narrower and slightly ill-assorted trio of 'Dartmoor-Exmoor-Shetland'.

Predictably, the class for 'small breeds' in the early years after the war was dominated by the Welsh Section A. In 1955 there were four Welsh at the top of the line, the winner being Criban Biddy Bronze, which went on to win the open 12.2 hh class; twenty ponies entered, only two of which can be identified as

Dartmoors. After that the classes were reallocated, the Welsh (A and B) getting a class to themselves, as did the Dartmoors, Exmoors and Shetlands. The odd result was that the *total* entry fell: from 20 in 1955 to 4 (all Dartmoors) and 7 (Welsh, Sections A and B). The setback was only temporary; from the mid-sixties the Dartmoor-Exmoor-Shetland entry averaged 14.

During these two decades the Dartmoors kept their end up, but did not always have it their own way at the start. In 1963 they filled the first four places, headed by Oatlands Timmy Tiptoes, backed by Toffee, Spellbound and Oatlands Jeremy

Rose Vean Quail (1959), a winner of the Lord Arthur Cecil Trophy

Langfield Canth (1983), Supreme Championship, National Pony Show, Country Life Cup, 1988, Chris Farnaby up

**Shilstone Rocks Quercina (1971), ridden by Lizzie Loriston-Clarke, Supreme Champion, Ridden Mountain and Moorland Pony –
National Pony Society Show, when owned by Mrs R. M. Taylor.**

Fisher; all of which have already been brought to the reader's notice. Timmy Tiptoes won again in 1966, but the following year the Exmoors levelled the score with their own 1-2-3-4 order. Then came three wins by Dartmoors Riddle-me-ree (by Cawsand Boy II out of Oakheath Spillikins, bred by Joan Cave-Penny). After that an almost unbroken sequence of Dartmoors: Whitestone Ragged Robin (1971) with Riddle-me-ree down in third place; Senruf Abelia (1972); five Shilstone Rocks victories in a row (Okement in 1974 and 1977, Quercina in 1975, 1976 and 1978);[2] White Willows Wizard in 1979, followed by a hat-trick by Allendale Exorcist in 1980, 1981 and 1982, again with a Shetland in second place (Bard of Transy).

The year 1984 saw further preferment for the ridden native ponies, with classes for each of the breeds and sections of those breeds, twelve classes in all. The response from the Dartmoors might be seen as a little slow, but perhaps they were taken by surprise. There were only five entries that year, the class going to Senruf Grebe (by Hisley Woodcock out of Blachford Greta, bred by Colin and Margaret Furness), but an encouraging twelve in 1985, when Boveycombe Redwing (by Shilstone Rocks Fury out of Boveycombe Heron, bred by Iris Gould) pointed the way to more future support. She beat Pat Campbell's Cruachan Dunnock (by Oatlands Diggory Delvet out of Cruachan Grouse).

[2] *Let us here join in a cheer for a gallant loser: Hannibal of Hinton, Shetland, on each of these five occasions second to Okement or Quercina.*

The Dartmoor Pony Show at Ascot, 1952: line-up of brood mares, (*from right*) Jenny VII, Cherrybrook, Linnet, the foal in the foreground is Jentyl.

Senruf Graduate (1981), Mrs Jo Green, whip (owner)

Two of the last three years of the period under review, 1987 and 1988, brought wins for Paul and Madge Taylor's home-bred Langfield Canth (by Shilstone Rocks Fastnet Fury out of L. Noilly Prat). In 1988 Canth was also Ridden Mountain and Moorland Champion, beating the Connemara Chiltern Sika. This latter achievement was a most welcome feather in the Dartmoor hat, for until recent years the record in the championship had been poor. Indeed, it was not until 1975 in the post-war shows that a Dartmoor notched up the supreme win with Shilstone Rocks Quercina. Quercina was reserve the following year and champion again in 1978, a fine record. The only other Dartmoor Ridden Champion was Allendale Exorcist (1980). Still, with Canth's win in 1988, the breed can point to four names on the Country Life Cup over the last fourteen years. Indeed, 1988 was an excellent year for Dartmoors at Malvern: in addition to Canth's win, there was the double triumph of Shilstone Rocks Another Bunch in the Overall Mountain and Moorland Championship and in the Lloyds Bank Qualifier.

The uninitiated might well ask how Another Bunch could win the supreme after having been reserve in the female championship only a few minutes earlier – and under the same judge. The answer lies in the fact that at this show there are, *inter alia*, two knock-out competitions running side by side: The Female Mountain and Moorland Championship open to the *best mare* in each breed and the Supreme Mountain and Moorland Championship open to the *champions* of each breed. On this occasion the champion mare was not the champion in her breed, (Welsh Section D), being reserve to the stallion. Thus, she could compete for the mares championship, but not for the mountain and moorland supreme. Bad luck on Tydfil Magic Princess; good luck for Another Bunch. But all perfectly fair and in order. Wanted: some generous patron to present a cup for the Supreme Mountain and Moorland Pony. At present all that comes to the winner is a rosette. A cup, as well as being nice for the champion's owner, should make sure that this award is mentioned in the 'mountain and moorland championships', thus lightening the burden of the researcher.

At this point we must leave the star shows. Including the NPS these currently number sixteen: West Midland Stallions, Ponies (UK) Spring, Ponies (UK) Summer, Devon County, Bath & West, East Anglian Native Ponies, South of England, Three Counties, Royal, Great Yorkshire, Northern Dartmoors, Southern Dartmoors, DPS, NPS North of England, Nottinghamshire.

Of these, however, two do call for interpretation into our story: the Northern and Southern Dartmoor Shows, started in 1977 and 1978 respectively so as to bring a Dartmoor-oriented show within reasonable travelling distance of those far from the home ground in Devon. The Southern show follows in the footsteps of the 1952 show organized at Ascot by Sylvia Calmady-Hamlyn; the Northern breaks new ground. These shows are quite independent of the society's breed show, currently at Bicton, being run by their own committees. There are, of course, close links and for some years the show champions at the Northern and Southern Shows competed at Bicton for an inter-show championship.

---

[3] *Authority:* Dartmoor Diary *1990*

17 THE WAY AHEAD

Hullaby Bridge

o'86

So, in the nineties, our story catches up with the present day. We are at now; that magical, ever-moving watershed hovering for an instant between was and will be. Not that this achievement means that the history of the Dartmoor pony is complete, all ends neatly tucked away and nothing more to be said. History, even on such a modest scale as that of our subject, marches relentlessly on, taking the world with it. All the same, we can at this point legitimately look about us, take stock and even hazard a few guesses about which way our little Dartmoor is going; which way we should like it to go, so far as we humans have any real, long-term say in the matter.

Before we do so, however, there is one quite important loose-end to be tied. Today most of us think of the Dartmoor as a riding pony; for riders of all ages, but mostly for children. Yet when our Saxon forefathers put their ponies to work – and for many centuries after – it was most exclusively in the role of hauler or carrier, the side that has only recently, since the Second World War, returned to any kind of prominence in and around the show-ring.

Of course, the load-*carrier*, as distinct from the hauler, plays a very small part in modern transport, but the Dartmoor between the shafts has always been with us. For a start, there was Blackdown, the great matriarch and dam of the immortal Leat, earning her keep pulling the Princetown fish-cart. And many more. All the same, strictly utilitarian. It was not until the late seventies that there appeared evidence of a change in this attitude in the form of including driving at any of the Dartmoor shows. The Southern Darts took the lead in 1978, followed by the breed show itself four years later. The Northern show put on a class for a single year in 1985. At Ascot driving lasted until 1983, but that at Bicton, though a later started (1982), is still going, its average entry being nine.

Maybe nine doesn't sound very many, especially when one bears in mind that latterly this class has been split into three sections (pure-bred singles, part-bred singles and pairs/teams), the only requirement for the latter two being a quarter or more of registered Dartmoor blood (as for the part-bred register). On the other hand, we should remember that the exhibitors set themselves a very high standard of turn-out, which can only be achieved by great enthusiasm, backed by lavish outlay of time, energy, organization and, let's face it, a tincture of hard cash.

The class is for 'private driving', with the accent on 'private'. 'Show wagons and commercial vehicles' are barred – what is the shade of Blackdown saying about that? – though commercial sponsorship of individuals is allowed. Reconciling the irreconcilable? But then what event can keep going today without such infusions? And is not a driving class a very pleasing sight at a show, as well as underlining the versatility of the Dartmoor; in short an excellent shop-window?

And then there are the private drivers; the really private ones that run their ponies between the shafts and enjoy an outing through the lanes. How many of these? Impossible to say, but let us hope that, even in this high-tech age, there are plenty of people wishing to enjoy this simple and inoffensive recreation. Recreation? Isn't that just what it is? A leisurely drive behind a willing pony in the open air (best of all on the open moor), diametrically opposed to being cooped up in a stuffy saloon, cannot but revive mind, body and spirit. The driver and his companions return with no records smashed but with a gentle sense of achievement, that driver and pony have worked happily together to a common purpose. A pat of gratitude, even a lump of sugar, for the prime mover? Certainly! But who ever thought of stroking the bonnet of a motor car?

So let us hope that 'private driving' is here to stay. There is reason to believe that it is in good heart. More and more major shows have classes for it; the NPS, for instance, had eleven entries for its small (13.2 hh) mountain and moorland 'private driving and road drive' in 1988; the Bath & West included a non-Hackney private-driving class (14 hh) as well as two scurries (one for 12 hh pairs which attracted twenty entries). Mind you, there's a world of difference between a scurry and a sedate drive down the lane to the village, but it's all 'driving'. On the subject of this highly skilled sport, it was not possible to discover a Dartmoor in the Bath & West event, but it does seem that it's tailor-made for him …

Turning back to generalizations, we must ask ourselves what the future holds for this valiant little animal. From which we must further ask what are we, collectively and individually, doing to help. Perhaps we should start by reminding ourselves of the purpose – stated and implied – of the association directly concerned, the Dartmoor Pony Society, now well into its second half-century. In broad terms, this is to serve the interests of the Dartmoor; the pony that should be able not only to survive on the uplands from which it takes its name but also to thrive in these or similar surroundings; a pony for use too, as every pony should be; on the one hand to be ridden or driven for pleasure, the rider or driver bearing in mind that such pleasure should be shared; on the other to provide the means of transmitting through its progeny the characteristics engendered by its tough environment. All said before, but worth repeating; especially when trying to peer into the future.

In speaking of 'characteristics' we are not so much concerned with those easily observable or quantifiable, such as height and colour. In any case these have already been discussed in Chapter 14. Rather we are interested in those intangibles that make a pony what it is, especially those that fit it for a rugged environment, as mentioned just above.

So next we should address ourselves to the question: what *is* a Dartmoor? A combination of abstractions. If it is registered – or if both parents are registered – then that is sufficient. But what if, like so many good ponies owned by moorland farmers, it is 'known' to be of pure descent, it looks right and exhibits all the characteristics of the Dartmoor pony as upheld over the last sixty-odd years? Moreover, living on the high moor, it is imbued with the hardiness so much admired in the breed. And isn't this what we need?

This aspect was taken care of in the early days by admitting ponies after official inspection, later through the supplementary register, as outlined in Chapter 14. Finally, the SR was discarded and the *DPS Stud Book* became a closed register, just like the GSB. Well, such is no longer the case, for the supplementary register has been re-opened in concert with the society's latest venture, the DPS Moor Scheme which we now consider.

For many years – indeed, almost continuously since the society's foundation – many Dartmoor breeders and potential breeders, both on and away from the moor, have held to the idea of the Dartmoor running on its own native heath with the object of ensuring that its original qualities should not be lost or obscured by other more showy attributes. It was, they said, all a matter of environment. They were right, of course – up to a point. Very well, then if environment was all they wanted, wasn't there plenty of that around? There was; thousands of unfenced acres on which the commoners enjoyed grazing rights and to spare. Unhappily, this inviting space was already occupied – though many would say 'infested' by a most undesirable equine riffraff; every kind of cross-bred, in-bred, diseased pony having but one characteristic in common, unsuitability to mate

Elizabeth Newbolt-Young, aided by daughter Alona with Shilstone Rocks Downpour and Brandsby Cyclone at Wylye Driving Trials 1989

with any animal with the least claim to quality. To have turned out a Dartmoor – a proper Dart as outlined above – with these ragamuffins would in one generation have set at nought all the careful breeding of the previous half-century. The way out of this apparent impasse was to keep the two kinds of 'ponies on Dartmoor' apart; in other words, the establishment of one or more enclosures having all the attributes of the high moor but safe from the attentions of the *canaille* just mentioned.

Easy to say, hard to put into effect, being beyond the unaided resources of the society. Thus the DPS was greatly cheered when the Duchy of Cornwall, the National Parks Authority and the Ministry of Agriculture, headed by the Duchy as landlord of Dartmoor Forest, in 1988 announced their willingness to back what came to be known as the Dartmoor Pony Society Moor Scheme. The Duchy would provide the land and the three sponsors would help to prepare the site with fencing and so on, the DPS would run it and the ministry would help to monitor its working.

The moorland known as Brownberry Newtake[1] was offered by its tenant: some 83 acres bordering the north side of the Two Bridges-Dartmeet road (B3357). It has, indeed, all the basic qualities to make even the toughest Dartmoor pony feel at home: 1100 feet (335 metres) above mean sea-level at Newlyn, trees (of which surprisingly there are a few in the relatively sheltered parts) bowed to the prevailing south-westerly gales; genuine moorland and no place for the pampered to loiter, even on a sunny day; in short, just the spot to tone up the systems of real Dartmoors.

Considerable effort is going into making it suitable for its purpose from a number of angles. For instance, the whole will be bounded by a dry-stone wall; not only accepted as the best method of keeping ponies (or other stock) within bounds, but also the traditional and most attractive fencing (in its broad sense) thus presenting the ponies to the public against their proper traditional background.

This last is far from insignificant. The society – and some others – have for many years chafed under the realization that a false picture of 'the Dartmoor pony' is being painted. The generality,

travelling across the moor in their motor cars have, until now, only encountered the scrub animals referred to above. It is understandable that they should think of them as 'Dartmoors'. When the media make play of neglected livestock in winter snowstorms, again it is this sorry tribe that is brought into their lounges by television. Anything, therefore, that can be done to

Mares at Brownberry Newtake in 1988, looking across the West Dart to Sherberton

Huccaby Newtake in 1989, near Dartmeet

---

[1] *A 'newtake', as defined by Eric Hemery in* High Dartmoor *(Hale, 1983), originally meant 'eight acres . . . of waste or forest ground' which a son had the right to enclose on succeeding his father as holder of an ancient tenement. And, if the reader wishes to know about ancient tenements, he cannot do better than read further in Hemery's comprehensive work. Hemery notes that recently – that is, since about 1700 – a 'newtake' has been applied loosely to any moorland enclosed by a tenant, which is what Brownberry is.*

dispel this misapprehension is to be applauded such as the sight of the well fed, well cared-for ponies on Brownberry.

The scheme is aimed at the moorland farmer. If he has a 'good type of Dartmoor' but unfortunately cannot produce acceptable evidence of its being a 'pure Dartmoor' he can submit it for inspection, very much in the same way as for the original supplementary register. Indeed, as already mentioned, this register has been re-opened to include these animals, except that now any mare or filly accepted will spend the summer months (May to September) on Brownberry with a selected registered Dartmoor stallion, any female offspring being inspected and, if passed, entered in the supplementary register.

Mrs P. Thomas driving her Dartmoor four-in-hand, to win her class at the Windsor International Driving Trials 1989, left leader Vean Patrick, right leader Stanwyke Corn Bunting, left wheeler White Willows Wallaby, right wheeler Harts Bugle.

So far the number involved is small, minute when compared to the total of 'Dartmoor type' on and around the moor; the first batch comprising fifteen mares and a stallion. However, it is a pilot scheme and, if successful and more suitable animals are forthcoming, it can easily be augmented. In terms of actual real estate, eyes are already being turned on Huccaby Newtake (site of the one-time Huccaby Races) right alongside Brownberry. Thus current plans (1990) extend the scheme to comprise two groups, one at each enclosure, each of about twenty mares and its own, carefully chosen, registered stallion. Numbers would undoubtedly cut down overheads per mare; desirable, provided this is not at the expense of quality. For 'quality' is what the moor scheme is all about.

The society sees the matter as follows. In its council's opinion, modern registered Dartmoors 'exist on a disturbingly narrow genetic base', backing this opinion with the fact that analysis of the entries at recent Breed, Northern and Southern shows reveals that 'virtually every pony there can trace descent to Sylvia Calmady-Hamlyn's Jude.' There is, in consequence, room – indeed, need – for the establishment of what it calls 'a fresh genetic pool from which all breeders may draw, thus allowing studs away from the moor to introduce new bloodlines to their stock.' In short, a return to the *fons et origo* by means of *good*, moorland-bred stock; calling a halt to the drift away from 'true moorland characteristics', possibly lured by the belief that wins in the show-ring come more easily to larger, rangier animals.

Thus the Dartmoor Pony Society's Council is determined that the execution of the scheme shall be worthy of its inspiration and directed to this long-term purpose of improving the breed. In practical terms this means very careful inspection of candidate mares by inspectors not easy to please, still less to deceive, followed up by monthly inspections by a DPS Council Member accompanied by a Ministry of Agriculture vet.

As well as looking over the stock, the vet will also observe the state of what is fashionably called 'infrastructure'. This, it turns out, is not a NATO airfield planned for Postbridge, but no more than the various permanent fixtures and amenities; in this case which herbage is sought by the ponies and which shunned, another and useful step in the never-completed enquiry into what is needed to make a Dartmoor what it is – and keep it so. The society can fairly claim that this venture is far from being a slapdash, corral-'em, chuck-'em-out-and-leave-'em response to a passing whim, but a carefully organized and monitored operation to maintain (or regain?) contact with the Dartmoor pony's home ground; the upland that gave it its name – and much else in danger of being lost or cast aside.

There is a spin-off too in the gossamer world of public relations. As mentioned above, the generality can see for themselves what real Dartmoors are like; that wherever the writ of the DPS runs the ponies are well cared for. To this end, the Dartmoor National Park Authority plans to include Brownberry (and any other similar intakes) in its organized walks. Well, it all helps.

In contrast to this 'back to the moor' movement there is the whole question of what might be termed the epicentre of the Dartmoor Pony Society, its geographical focus given practical expression in the selection of meeting-places and the venue for the breed show itself. Current membership of the society is spread pretty evenly up and down the country, even stretching as far as Scotland. A case for more central locations? Not so, say the West Countrymen. It is true that the breed show is no longer held on the actual moor, but the move (still within the county of Devon) was dictated by the practical need for accessibility and accommodation, as already discussed. The Dartmoor pony is part and parcel of the West Country and would lose all its individuality if it moved away.

Well, there it is, like the height question, a matter for discussion. Happily it is no business of this chronicle to come down on one side or the other, it being essentially concerned with the *pony* rather than its sometimes intransigent owners.

So what does the future hold for the Dartmoor pony? That it is thriving at the present time is surely beyond dispute. It is increasingly in demand and, as the record shows, is holding its own in competition with other native breeds and, for that matter, with ponies of any kind, no matter how assiduously plaited and polished. But is that the real answer, albeit pleasing to owners, breeders and admirers? Is not the real question whether, despite all pulls in other directions, it can maintain its unique character? And in this surely the Dartmoor Pony Society is right in putting the moor scheme right at the top of its list of priorities.

It was said at the start of this chapter that our arrival at 'now' did not spell the end of the Dartmoor pony's story. All the same, there is an attractive completeness in this business of re-forging the link with its own home ground; a link essential to the well-being of the breed. Long may it remain strong and bright!

BRIMPTS AND NEWTON ABBOT
(1964–1976)

In these Appendices are the outline results of the classes at the later breed shows from 1964 onwards: who won, how he (or she) was bred, which ponies she (or he) beat; details of interest indeed, an essential part of our story, but tending to clog the main flow of narrative if included in the text. So here they are in appendices, part and parcel but by no means the whole answer in the search for excellence. They guide and illuminate, but they must not be allowed to dictate. Never should it be claimed that the breed show is the final forum in which the breed is judged. Many excellent Dartmoors have never been near it, yet have proved their merit elsewhere and in competition with other breeds, which, of course, they cannot do at the breed show.

Nor do these appendices lay any claim to completeness, only to painting a fair general picture of the kind of Dartmoor favoured by competent judges, together with the winners' parentage to whet the appetite of those interested in bloodlines. For greater detail the student should consult such contemporary publications as the Dartmoor Diary, the society's annual since 1971; back numbers of Horse and Hound or – possibly most rewarding of all – the marked catalogues of the form-watchers. These last will have the facts, and more.

Brimpts (1964–1970), in hand

1964

At the first post-war breed show at Brimpts (1964), Lady Willingdon's Red Hall Auriga (by Janus out of Cottage Garden) was Best Broodmare and Champion of the Show. Indeed, it was a good day all round for the Kilbees Stud, which also collected the prizes for yearling fillies with Kilbees Skylark (by Jentyl out of Dunnabridge Tansy) and for three-year-old fillies with Janessa (by Janus out of Off Ration); a good day too for the Red Hall (Reiss) breeding, with Mandy Ferguson's Red Hall Aries (by Jon also out of Cottage Garden) Best Two-year-old Filly and Reserve Champion; perhaps most notable of all for the Vean sires, with all but one of the winners descended from one or other of them.

The Certificated Barren Mare winner was Miss Benson's Whitsun (by Jenyn out of Hele Juliet II), which beat the Coakers' Sherberton Titwillow (by Hele Romeo out of thrice-winner Linnet). Both were four-year-olds, which suggests that the 'barren' label (while technically correct) might have been slightly misleading, at least to the generality.

In the youngstock classes there were only five entries of yearling colts, the winner being Jean McMillan's Lakehead Little Joker (by Jester IV out of Yeoland Beepety Bump and bred by George Shillibeer of Bellever) over the Jordans' home-bred Moortown Lad (by Brown Berry III out of Granite II). However, the Jordans were more fortunate in the class for older colts, winning with the Lad's full brother Moortown Berry. This was a very strong class (judged with hindsight), for he beat the Reeps' Easter, Iris Gould's Boveycombe Leo and George Shillibeer's Hisley Woodcock.

The winning stallion was Veronica Ker's Witchcraft (by Vean Wildfire out of Halloween; Wildfire, incidentally, the first Calmady-Hamlyn stallion to carry the Vean prefix). This was another strong class, for Witchcraft had to beat Cawsand Cavalier, Brown Berry and Petroc.

1965

In 1965 the broodmare class was won by Margaret Furness's Syrup (by John out of Treacle), which beat her full brother Toffee II in the championship. So it was worth their while to come all the way from Berwickshire – a mark, too, of the widening interest in showing Dartmoors. Neither John's nor Treacle's breeding is registered, John's not at all, Treacle's merely as 'Dartmoor', in 1944 and 1942 respectively. However, John is known to be by Jude out of Dora IV.[1]

The 1965 youngstock classes were well filled, except for the older colts where there were only two. Still, that was enough for Moortown Lad to reverse the previous placings, with Lakehead Little Joker below him. Mrs Oakey's Pieman (by Jenson out of Heather Queen, the latter bred by Tom Holman out of the twentieth of the famous Queenie line) was Best Yearling Colt, ahead of the Hayes' Phantom (by Jenyn out of Halloween). The yearling filly class (twenty-one entries) went to Joan Montgomery's Telstar (by Michelmass out of Gamma Ray, the latter's breeding being in contrast to the sire's: by Teignhead bred by John Rowe from 'Dartmoors' out of E. W. White & Son's Julia IV). Second was the Reeps' Shilstone Rocks Windswept (by Jude out of Zippee bred by Tom Wicks).

---

[1] *For full details of Dora's distinguished descendants, see the article 'The End of an Era' in the* Dartmoor Diary *for 1976. A foundation mare if ever there was one.*

RedHall Auriga (1959)

In the class for two-year-old fillies and geldings, Lady Willingdon's Kilbees Skylark repeated her previous year's win, second being Mrs Oakey's Teddy Bear (full brother to her yearling winner). Molly Croft's Jurston Springtime (by J. Spindrift out of May Queen VII) won the three-year-olds, with the Jones-Roberts Hisley Caprice (by Jenson out of Oatlands Appley Dapply) second. The 1964 two-year-old winner, Red Hall Aries, had been entered but was not forward.

For the mature animals there were four classes all told: the broodmares already mentioned, the barren mares and stallions as before and, in addition, one for novice mares (with foal at foot). The entries for the barren class were slowly recovering after touching rock-bottom with three in 1961 and 1962. The winner (of nine) was the Jones-Roberts Rose Vean Teal, beating Mrs Oakey's Heather Queen. Teal was by Jenson out of Snipe. Snipe too had had her hour. In 1958 as a four-year-old of unknown breeding – not even the name of her breeder is revealed – she had won the 11.3 hh mares' class; moreover, against a galaxy of talent: Betty XXI, Hele Judith and Halloween for starters; Linnet too, though she was fourteen by then.

The novice class attracted thirteen entries, Ann Jones and Tish Roberts won with Whitmore Honeymoon (by Janus out of Honeybags), a five-year-old with a future in the hands of Jean McMillan. Second was Syd Horrell's Higher Tor Dawn Skies, five years old by his own Marksman out of Daybreak.

Toffee took the stallion prize, as noted above, with the Jones-Roberts Cawsand Cavalier second and the Jordans' Brown Berry III third. Boveycombe Leo had been entered but was not forward; his time was yet to come.

1966

There were thirty-eight entries in the three 1966 classes for mares, with the main class going to John Holman's Cawsand Sundew, a four-year-old newcomer to the breed show, by Dunnabridge out of the 1963 winner Skaigh Princess (also Holman-bred though then shown by Iris Gould). Whitmore Honeymoon was second. Another Dunnabridge mare won the novice class, the Jones-Roberts Hisley Quill (four years old, by Dunnabridge out of Queenie XXIII), followed by Mrs Oakey's eight-year-old Heather Queen (by Raybarrow Pool by a Dartmoor out of Chymes, ex Queenie XX). Lady Willingdon's Red Hall Auriga (Champion in 1964) won the barren class, beating Mrs Northen's Gorringes Tabaqui (by Oatlands Jeremy Fisher out of Oatlands Jemima Puddleduck and bred by D. C. Bradford). Auriga was Reserve Champion of the Show.

In the Youngstock classes, the Reeps' Hele Hussar (by Jasper out of Hele Judith IV and bred by Jim Stephens) was Best Yearling Colt and Syd Horrell's Higher Tor Midget the Best Yearling Filly. Remember Midget who swept the board in 1949–51? This is her great-great-granddaughter via Midget VI, Marksman and Dawn Skies; all home bred. Alas, this was the best she ever achieved, being no better than fourth as a two-year-old and third as a novice mare in 1970.

The class for older colts was won by the Jones-Roberts Lammermuir Rambler (by Julus out of Plymouth Rock), not forward as a yearling and now ahead of Pieman, the 1965 winner. In the two-year-old fillies, Joan Montgomery's Telster (by Michelmass out of Gamma Ray) beat the Reeps' Shilstone Rocks Windswept (by Jude out of Zippee) and in the three-year-olds Lady Willingdon's Kilbees Skylark (by Jentyl out of Dunnabridge Tansy) beat the Hayes's Whitestone Tudor Rose (by Rosevean Jack Snipe out of Vean White Rose); Telstar's second win, Skylark's third.

The 1966 show saw the first victory for the Jones-Roberts stallion Hisley Woodcock. Home bred by Jenson out of Dunnabridge Wigeon, he was first and Show Champion in 1966, 1968 and 1969. In 1966 Cawsand Cavalier was once again runner-up, with Boveycombe Leo third.

1967

Once again, too, numbers were up in the three 1967 classes for mares (42, with a satisfactory 32 forward). In the absence of the previous year's winner of her class, Whitmore Honeymoon moved up to first, but to show this was no case of Buggins' Turn, took the Show Championship as well – and with the magnificent Michelmass in reserve. Second broodmare was Mary Bienkowska's Mayflower X (ten years old, by Pixie III out of Mayfly V both bred by Mrs Simmons).

The class for barrens went to Jim Stephens' Hele Judith (now aged fifteen), with the Shillibeers' Lakehead Raindrop second (by Jester IV out of Yeoland Beepety Bump); that for the 'novices'[2] to the Jones-Roberts Dartmoors Huccaby Baby (by Huccaby out of Juliet VIII, eight years old), above Margaret Furness's four-year-old Senruf Juliet (by Jude out of Boveycombe Gemini).

Michelmass had not been forward to contest the stallion class in 1966 when Woodcock had won, but made his first appearance at Brimpts in 1967 to take the class, with Woodcock second and Cavalier third, although he had to be content with being Reserve Show Champion to Whitmore Honeymoon. Five stallions were forward, all winners: with Margaret Furness's Toffee II fourth, Iris Gould's Boveycombe Leo fifth.

Honeymoon's yearling by Jenson, Crimchard Bright Spark, was first in the colt class, followed by the Reeps' Shilstone Rocks Darkness (by Easter out of Midgehope Melissa), this order being unaltered the following year. Joan Montgomery's White Willows Violet Ray (by Michelmass out of Gamma Ray) was best of the thirteen yearling fillies, Mrs Calmady-Hamlyn's Boveycombe Jouster (bred by Iris Gould, by Jude out of Skaigh Princess) won the older colts' class, Violet

---

2 *Over the years there have been many young ponies rightly described as novices, also some pretty ancient ones, the record going to a nineteen-year-old in 1968, where it collected the ninth rosette. Do we applaud these game veterans as they totter round the ring (hoping perhaps that one or two standing above them will drop in their tracks) or do we enquire into the actual purpose of a novice class?*

Dalby's Crookety Teasel (by Cawsand Prince out of Fair Diana, whose full sister Candytuft was Second yearling filly) was Best Two-year-old Filly, above another Whitmore Honeymoon product (by Cawsand Cavalier), Hisley Hazelnut (not shown as a yearling, now owned by Jean McMillan).

In the class for three-year-old fillies Margaret Furness's Midgehope Jonquil (by Whitemore Arbutus out of Sherberton Judy) was placed above Telstar, last year's class-winner.

1968

This year saw Hisley Woodcock back at the top: Best Stallion and Show Champion. Next in his class were Boveycombe Leo (Reserve Show Champion) and Cawsand Cavalier. A slight increase in the entries for the mares classes, but not much more than half forward (27 out of 46).

In the novice class the Reeps' Shilstone Rocks Windswept beat Major & Mrs Hayes's Kilbees Firenzi. Telstar, to which she had been second as a yearling and two-year old (not forward at three), was down the line this time. Heartened, no doubt, by this new order, Windswept went on to take second place in the next class (Open Broodmares with foal at foot) to the Jones-Roberts Hisley Quill, the novice winner of two years back.

There were only three barrens forward out of the five entered, the prize going to Joan Cave-Penny's Dartmoors Little Madam, a six-year-old by Cawsand Boy out of Miss Muffet X (Holman bred). Better news from the youngstock, however, with numbers back to over fifty after the previous year's dip below that magic number. Lady Willingdon's Kilbees Bullfinch (by Dunnabridge Bonny Boy out of Venetia) was Best Yearling Colt, with Mrs Morris's Whitmore Glen Mist (by Red Hall Perseus out of Whitmore Honeymead) second. The Hayes's Gin Fizz (by Oatlands Diggory Delvet out of Martine II) was Best Yearling Filly, ahead of Kilbees Bay Leaf (by Jon – not to be confused with John – out of Dunnabrdge Tansy) in a class of fifteen.

As a two-year-old Jean McMillan's Bright Spark held onto his previous year's win over the Reep's Darkness, but there were several changes in the 1968 line-up of two-year-old fillies, as the 1967 yearling winner was not entered and the 1968 winner, Lady Willingdon's Kilbees Jenny Too (also by Jon, but out of Vean Blue Jennykin), had not competed in 1967. Mrs Oakey's Sweetie Pie, at second (third in 1967), provided the only continuity among the winners. So much for 1968.

1969

The status quo was maintained in the 1969 stallion class, with Woodcock again also Show Champion and Leo in second place. In the Open Broodmares, however, a number of changes: Windswept to win (and to stand Reserve of the Show), Lady Willingdon's Janessa (not placed since her win as a three-year-old in 1964) in second place, Quill (last year's winner) down the line.

Crimchard Highlight (Honeymoon's yearling by Woodcock) won the colts' class, Lady Willingdon's Kilbees Jolyon (full brother to the winner of the three-year-olds) in second place. Among the fillies, the Bittleford

Kilbees Jenny Too (1966)

Boveycombe Leo (1961)

Coakers' Bittleford Queen Bee (by Jonaca bred by Mrs Oakey and unshown, out of Cater's Beam) was first in a strong class of fifteen (ten forward), with the Jordans' Moortown Lady (by Blachford Elvan out of Moortown Queen) at second.

Jean McMillan's Bright Spark made it three-in-a-row when he won the class for older colts; again beating a Shilstone Rocks entry, though this time it was S.R. Okement (third the two previous years). Okement was by Petroc out of Caroline II, the latter a Teignhead mare out of Chymes. Both these ponies did well later.

There were fifteen entries in the two-year-old filly class, of which thirteen were forward. Joan Montgomery's White Willows Radium (by Michelmass out of Gamma Ray) won after having been fifth the previous year but with that year's opposition not entered. Second was the Reeps' Shilstone Rocks Cavalina (by Cawsand Cavalier out of Fall Out).

The Hisley Stud scored a left-and-right in the three-year-old class, winning with Quadrille (fourth in 1968) and second with Sweetie Pie (by Jonaca out of Heather Queen) a consistent performer over the years.

The entries for the mares' classes totalled forty-nine. In the novice class the Jones-Roberts Hisley Quince (by Peter Tavy II out of the gallant Queenie XXIII, the Whites' prize-winner by Boxer) was put above White Willows Pepita (by Michelmass out of Hele Juliet III and shown by Mrs Crookes). Firenzi, second novice in 1968, was not forward; she did well later.

There were eleven barren mares entered, though again there were only three forward, with Whitmore Honeymoon ahead of Telstar. In the open class, however, there were sixteen present out of the twenty-three entered. And here the Reeps's Windswept came into her own, having won the novices mare and been second in the open class in 1968. She was Reserve Show Champion to Hisley Woodcock. Running ahead of our story for a moment, we find her winning the open class in 1970 and again in 1972; a fine record.

Hisley Woodcock won the stallion class again in 1969 and, with it, the Show Championship for the third time in four years. And once again Boveycombe Leo was second to him.

1970

The year 1970 proved to be the last year at Brimpts. The in-hand classes were well filled (a record 113 all told, 35 yearlings alone), though it was a little disappointing to have only four stallions to admire in the ring. The Yearling Colts class went to Lady Willingdon's Kilbees Mr Pickwick (by Jon out of Vean Blue Jennikin, hence full brother to Jolyon and Jenny Too already mentioned). Second was Mrs Corry's Huntspath Holly (by Red Hall Aquarius out of Huntspath Josephine, bred by Mrs Titler), a pony which was to do well for the Carters in years to come. The Best Yearling Filly prize went to Joan Montgomery's White Willows Sorceress (product of the famous Jenyn-Halloween nick). This time she beat Mrs Sutcliffe's Boveycombe Cygnet (by Shilstone Rocks Darkness out of S.R. Sanduck).

John and Louise Fleming's Parkland Paragon (by Blue John out of Red Hall Aries) won the class for two- and three-year-old colts, with the Jones-Roberts Hele Lancer in second place and the 1969 yearling winner (Crimchard Highlight) in third. Nor were the first and second yearling fillies of 1969 present to compete with Joan Montgomery's White Willows Cinderella (by Michelmass out of Cawsand Princess and fourth the previous year), who took the prize for two-year-old fillies above Hisley Reverie (by H. Woodcock out of Plymouth Rock and third in 1969) in a class of sixteen (only half forward). Jean McMillan's Gin Fizz (by Oatlands Diggory Delvet out of Martini II) won the class for three-year-old fillies. She had been sixth as a two-year-old and now leap-frogged Jenson's Daughter (third in 1969) and Crookety Gipsy Moth (fourth in 1969 and now sadly at the bottom of the line). Second was Molly Croft's Spindleberry (by Jon out of Spindle). By and large a good entry for the youngsters, though a disappointing proportion not forward.

The Best Novice Mare was the Jones-Roberts Blachford Brandween (by Huccaby out of Hele Judith II, bred by Wing Commander Passy). She was eight at the time – which is elderly for a novice – and did not appear again at the breed show, although entered once (in 1974). Second was Mrs Barraclough's Vean Zena (by Jentyl out of Vean Zelinda, a six-year-old bred by Pat Robinson). The Jones-Roberts team also won the class for barren mares with Penny II (by Grey Wethers out of Queenie XXIII, whose daughter Hisley Quadrille was third), ahead of Joan Montgomery's Telstar (which had won as a yearling and again as a two-year-old).

There were nine mares forward in the open class, which was won again by Shilstone Rocks Windswept, ahead of John Holman's Cawsand Sundew (by Dunnabridge out of Skaigh Princess) and Jean McMillan's Whitmore Honeymoon.

Finally there were the stallions; only four of them (all forward), with first place going to Iris Gould's Boveycombe Leo, who had been knocking at the door for some years against the strong opposition of Michelmass and Woodcock (neither entered in 1970). Second was Jean McMillan's Crimchard Bright Spark (who had won his yearling and two/three-year-old classes from 1967 to 1969).

Ridden Classes 1960–70
(see Chapter 15)

Classes for ridden Dartmoors started in 1960. The winner that year was Joan Montgomery's Vean Wildfire (by Pipit out of Wild Rose IV and four years old at the time), with Jean McMillan's ten-year-old gelding Pip (by Jude out of Peewit III) second in a class of seven. In 1961 the ridden class, now open to riders of any age as it is today, attracted ten entries (five forward) and was won by Elspeth Ferguson's Dunnabridge Bonny Boy (that year's stallion winner). Two two-year-olds had also been entered, but were not forward. In 1968 the lower age-limit was set at three years old.

The winner in 1962 was another entire (and future winner of the stallion class), Margaret Furness's Toffee II (by John out of Treacle). Mr Morrish's Jan Stewer (also by John out of Widdecombe Heather Belle) was in second place, pushing Pip down to third. There were only six entries, but ten in 1963 (all but one forward) when the prize went to Joan Montgomery's Spellbound, now three years old and with a record of first-second-second in the youngstock classes. Toffee was second.

The first lead-rein class (1964) went to Veronica Ker's thirteen-year-old Lady Jane Grey (yet another John foal, out of Smoke), with Mr Harvey's Brown Heath (by Raybarrow Pool out of the venerable Brownie XVIII, the latter foaled in 1942). Brown Heath went on to win the open ridden (Dartmoor) class, ahead of Mrs Martin's Oatlands Tommy Brock (by Julus out of O. Mrs Tittle-Mouse). Spellbound was third in each class, an unusual position for her. However, she was back on top the following year, winning both the 1965 ridden classes above Brown Heath. The entries sagged a bit in 1965, but were up again the following year (from fifteen to twenty-three), when Spellbound again won both classes and again beating Brown Heath. In 1967 she was only entered for the lead rein. This she won, with Margaret Furness's Senruf Stormcock (by Vean Vencock out of Syrup, the latter Show Champion in 1965 and full sister to Toffee) in second place. Mrs Oakey's four-year-old Teddy Bear (by Jenson out of Heather Queen) won the open ridden class, with Iris Gould's Boveycombe Leo (Champion in 1970 and 1974) second.

Only three of the open ridden class came into the ring in 1968 (five entered), when Brown Heath won at last, being placed above Jill Cameron's Dartmoors Riddle-Me-Ree (by Cawsand Boy II out of Oakheath Spillikins) which in 1969 was placed above Joan Montgomery's Telstar in a well-supported class of thirteen, all but two forward.

The 1968 lead-rein class was won by Mr Stear's Cloudy, a three-year-old gelding by Beverley Valerian out of Jurston Mary Tavy. Cloudy also won in 1969 (for *Mrs* Stear) and in 1970 (for the Coakers), beating Teddy Bear (now owned by Mrs Griffey) in 1968 and 1970 and Joan Montgomery's White Willows Thomas (by Cawsand Black Velvet out of Cawsand Cavella) in 1969.

Riddle-Me-Ree had a good record too in the open: second in 1968, first in 1969, first in 1970 when he beat Anne Belam's thirteen-year-old Sherberton Honour (by S. Extra Dry out of S. Paulina).

A class for 'Handy Ponies' was introduced in 1969 and was well supported for thirteen years. Initially it was only for registered Dartmoors, but was extended to include those in the supplementary register. It died in 1981, being revived in 1983 as 'Child's First Pony' (*not* to be led) and open to first-crosses. We therefore note it as an offshoot but space does not allow more than that.

Newton Abbot (1971–76): In Hand

As already told, the numbers for the first year on the racecourse were well up almost all round. There were fourteen yearling colts (nine forward) in a class won by the Jones-Roberts Hisley Pedlar (by

Lammermuir Rambler out of Hisley Quince the 1969 novice winner), with Peter Honey's Walreddon Musketeer (by Cawsand Cavalier out of Dusk IV) second. Of the twenty yearling fillies entered, thirteen were forward, first being Margaret Furness's Senruf Eliza (by Shilstone Rocks Vendetta out of Midgehope Jonquil), above Joan Montgomery's Meldon Sparkle (by Boveycombe Jouster out of Twinkle, this latter a minuscule nineteen-year-old at the time of foaling who had measured just over 9 hh as a yearling; Twinkle herself being 'about 11.3' at that age).[3]

In the class for two-year-old fillies Sorceress followed up her win as a yearling, holding off a challenge of newcomers led by Mrs Mills's May Marguerite (by Cawsand Cavalier out of Hele Janet). There were twelve entered in the class for older colts, which was won by Mary Bienkowska's May Musketeer (another Cavalier foal out of May Belle). Violet Dalby's Shilstone Rocks Horizon took the three-year-olds' prize (and the Youngstock Championship) over Margaret Furness's Senruf Abelia.

Among the mares, Kilbees Firenzi (last seen as second novice in 1968 and now owned by the Robertses of Detling) won the barren class, ahead of the Flemings' Park Jane Again (by Jentyl out of Black Jane), while Alison Taylor's five-year-old Winkie Pop III (by Oatlands Diggory Delvet out of Off Ration) won the novice class with Violet Dalby's Crookety Candy Tuft (by Cawsand Prince out of Fair Diana) in second place.

In the main class for broodmares with foal at foot (of whose twenty entries only nine were forward) Jean Cooke's Whitmore Honeymoon repeated her triumph of 1967; that is, with the Show Championship as well. She beat Spellbound in the class and Shilstone Rocks Okement in the championship. The latter (owned by the Reeps, by Petroc out of Caroline II) beat Michelmass and Bright Spark. This was clearly Okement's day, so far as the stallion placings were concerned, for he had been below Bright Spark at the four previous shows.

There were three dozen fewer entries in 1972; at 181 all told a trifle above the Brimpts average. Shilstone Rocks Fury won the yearling colts' class (by S.R. Darkness out of Fall Out), with the Flemings' Boveycombe Buckthorn (by B. Leo out of Pillar) in second place. Fourteen fillies faced the judge in their yearling class, which was won by Joy Dammers' Catesby Honey Pot (by Mr McGregor out of Honey Bee III), ahead of Jean Cooke's Crimchard Happy Talk (her Honeymoon foal by Hele Lancer). In the class for two- and three-year-old colts the Carters' Huntspath Holly moved up from his previous year's seventh place to win from Violet Dalby's Crookety Cavalcade. Holly was by Red Hall Aquarius out of Huntspath Josephine; Cavalcade by Cavalier out of Crookety Candytuft. In the classes for older fillies, the Holmans' Cosdon May (by B. Leo out of Skaigh Princess) beat Mrs Dammers' Catesby

---

[3] *From then on a contrast between the two winning yearlings: nothing further on Eliza at the breed show, but a great deal on Pedlar. He won the stallion class three times: twice with the Show Championship; the last in 1982, after he had gone north to join the Langfield Stud.*

Orchis (by Whitestone Ragged Robin out of Honey Bee III). The 1971 winner had not been entered and the second that year was not placed. The class for three-year-old fillies went to a scion of Sid Horrell's Midget line: Higher Tor Midget's daughter H.T. Bridget (by Cawsand Cavalier), followed by Sorceress (the previous year's winner when Bridget was seventh). These classes for two- and three-year-old fillies were, of course, also open to geldings. They have not been mentioned, as very few were ever entered: 8 out of a total of 63 in 1971 and 1972 combined; one was fourth, the rest nowhere.

There was a good turn-out for the novice mares; class (16 out of 21 entered, of which over half were aged 4 or 5). The winner was, appropriately, a newcomer: Mrs Leasor's Hambledon Juno (by Jenson out of Sooty of the Barn), beating Violet Dalby's Shilstone Rocks Horizon and a number of other good ponies too. (She tried again the following year, but was down the line.)

Only six entries for the barren class (all present); won by Mary Bienkowska's May-Belle (by Jenson out of Mayfly V) ahead of the Reeps' Fall Out. There were eighteen entries in the main broodmare class, but sadly only six forward. the Reeps' Windswept scored her third win as a broodmare (plus one before then as a novice), with Mrs Corry's Huntspath Josephine (by Witchcraft out of Jacaranda) second, the latter having only been fourth in the novice class.

Bright Spark won his class again (Leo being the only other stallion entered) and went on to be Show Champion, with Juno Reserve. It was very disappointing to have so few in this class, but that seems to be the form for stallions: over the decade 1963–72 an average of six. There are a number of reasons for this scarcity compared with the mares, the most obvious being that there are fewer of them. Add to this the generally accepted opinion that there is more all-round sweat to getting a stallion ready for a show, taking him there, taking (or being taken by) him in, round and out of the ring and finally home again; that for a reigning champion there is no way to go but down the line, and we can see why many stallion-owners delegate the blazoning of his fame to his progeny.

Honeymoon may have been short of a foal but, having won the 1973 barren class, she was good enough to take the Show Championship as well. Sorceress was second to her in the class (fourteen entered and eleven forward). Mrs Leasor again won the novice class, this time with Gaulden Gin Fizz (by Diggory Delvet out of Martini II). Shilstone Rocks Whirlwind was second. There were twenty-five entered in the main class (sixteen forward), won by Sorceress's thirteen-year-old full sister Spellbound. Gin Fizz was second.

Hisley Woodcock returned after a three-year gap to take the stallion class and stand reserve to Honeymoon. Shilstone Rocks Okement was second. A strong class (nine entries, nine forward) in every sense.

In the youngstock classes, Jean Cooke's Crimchard Fanfare (by Bright Spark out of Fair Joanna) was Best Yearling Colt, above the Jones-Roberts Hisley Royalty (by H. Woodcock out of Plymouth Rock), the Holmans' Cosdon May Queen (by Brown Berry III out of Skaigh Princess) being Best Yearling Filly, with Violet Dalby's Crookety Dawn Chorus (by Leo out of S.R. Horizon) second. Hisley Pedlar (who had not been entered in 1972) won the class for older colts, with Syd Horrell's

Higher Tor Flash (by White Willows Macbeth out of H.T. Midget) second.

Eleven out of the seventeen entered in the two-year-old fillies' class faced the judge: the Reeps' Shilstone Rocks Dark Phantome (by Darkness out of Betwitched) ahead of Jean Cooke's Crimchard Happy Talk (a Honeymoon foal by Hele Lancer). The three-year-old winner was the Holmans' Cosdon May, repeating her 1972 win. She had been entered as a yearling in 1971 but had not been forward, so missed the youngstock 'grand slam'. But then she would have had to beat Senruf Eliza (entered as a three-year-old but not forward). Too many 'ifs', but offering some amusement to students of the might-have-been.

The 1974 show included the last appearance in the ring of Boveycome Leo, now aged thirteen. He took the stallion prize and went on to be a Show Champion, a repeat of his 1970 performance. This time he beat five-year-old Shilstone Rocks Achilles (by Red Hall Aquarius out of Fall Out, now owned by Jean Cooke), Hisley Pedlar and Huntspath Holly; a creditable performance, so if it was Leo that stuck another year on his age in the catalogue we can surely forgive this minor vanity. He had been entered for every breed show since 1962 and had been forward every time but one. High marks, at least for tenacity.

Reserve was the winning broodmare, Cosdon May, continuing her successful career. She beat another four-year-old Catesby Orchis (by Whitestone Ragged Robin out of Honey Bee III). Third was a contemporary of Leo's – Honeymoon. May had, of course, won the novice class. The barren class went to Mr McKinlay's Penny II, yet another fourteen-year-old, by Grey Wethers II out of the redoubtable Queenie XXIII, with Molly Croft's Jurston Maytime (by Jenson out of May Queen VII) second.

The Youngstock Champion was Shilstone Rocks Dark Mountain (by Darkness out of Huntspath Hannah). She was a three-year-old, but this was her first appearance at the breed show.

The 1975 show saw the first appearance in the ring – at least at the breed show – of ten-year-old Oatlands Mr McGregor (by Jentyl out of O. Mrs Tittlemouse) to win the stallion class against Woodcock (now thirteen) and Achilles (second the previous year); a late starter, you might say; bred by Jane Dod, he went to Mrs Hollingworth in 1972.

Hisley Siskin (by H. Woodcock out of Sweetie Pie and shown by the Jones-Roberts twins) was Best Novice Mare. A five-year-old, she had only been shown once before (as a yearling). In a class of fourteen (nine forward) she beat Park Jane Again and Crimchard Trilling Lark. Kilbees Firenzi, now eleven, repeated her 1971 win in the certificated barren class, beating Winkie Pop III (Novice winner in 1971). Finally, in the open class Whitmore Honeymoon once again won, though this time she had to allow her stable-mate, a two-year-old colt and Youngstock Champion Crimchard Firefly, to stand reserve to Mr McGregor.

And so on to 1976, the last year at Newton, when Hisley Pedlar won the stallion class. He had done well as a youngster, winning as a yearling and as a three-year-old, his two appearances, the latter bringing him also the Youngstock Championship. He stood third to Leo and Achilles in 1974, was not entered in 1975, then on to winning in 1976. In this

Senruf Abelia (1968)

class of four (three forward) he beat Mrs Bruce's White Willows Satellite (by Red Hall Aquarius out of Telstar). He went north at the end of the year to join the Langfield Stud, returning just twice to take the stallion class and Show Championship.

Among the mares, Iris Gould's Boveycombe Heron (by B. Leo out of Shilstone Rocks Sanduck) won the novice class, with Elizabeth Newbolt Young's S.R. Rainstorm second (by Easter out of Jurston May Storm of Shilstone Rocks, possibly the longest tally in the stud book). Joy Dammers' Catesby Honey Set (by Oatlands Mr McGregor out of Honey Bee III, a four-year-old) won the class for barren mares with certificates, ahead of the Jones-Roberts ten-year-old Sweetie Pie (placed as a filly and also as a mare in 1975 and 1976). The open class went to Elizabeth Newbolt-Young's Shilstone Rocks Whirligig (by S.R. Darkness out of S.R. Whirlwind) a four-year-old making her first appearance as a broodmare. In the youngstock, Allendale Flauros (by Huntspath Holly out of Whitmore Titania) clinched his 1975 yearling win by taking first place in the class for two- and three-year-olds and the Youngstock Championship, with his full brother A. Exorcist (yearling) standing reserve.

Whirligig was Reserve Champion, but who was Champion? The unexpected (but perfectly legitimate) answer turns out to be Alison Taylor's *ridden* five-year-old Shilstone Rocks Quercina (by S.R. Okement out of S.R. Cavallina). Like Whirligig, she was making her first appearance at the breed show. At this opportune moment, let us turn to the ridden classes at Newton.

Ridden Classes (1971–76)

The first year at Newton saw the strength of the Open Ridden Class maintained at thirteen entries and that of the Lead-rein class slightly increased to eleven; figures maintained for the following three years, after which there was some falling off. In that year Joan Montgomery's White Willows Cinderella (by Michelmass out of Cawsand Princess) won the Lead-rein class, with Margaret Furness's Senruf Stormcock (by Vean Vencock out of Syrup) second. The Senruf stable scored a left-and-right in the open class with Senruf Abelia (by Whitemore Arbutus out of Boveycombe Gemini) and Senruf Butterscotch (by Toffee II out of Liberty Light).

The 1972 show saw two newcomers at the heads of their lines: Mrs Wright's Annwood Venture (by Jester IV out of Jurston Veronica) followed by White Willows Cinderella in the lead rein; Mrs Ireland's Phantom (by Jenyn out of Halloween) above Dr and Mrs King's Oatlands Tom Titmouse in the open.

In the following year, Annwood Venture won again, this time above Dr and Mrs King's Oatlands Joshy Campbell (by Whitestone Ragged Robin out of O. Pig Wig) in second place. The open class went to Shilstone Rocks Okement, shown by Mary Houlden and with a fine record from his in-hand classes, incuding Best Stallion in 1971 and second to Woodcock in 1973. Second was White Willows Wizard (full brother to Phantom, the previous year's winner). Wizard came back in 1974 to win for Mrs Starry in the lead rein, above the Kings' Oatlands Constable Crabtree (by Crimchard Playboy out of O. Mrs Tittlemouse). Phantom repeated his 1972 win in the open class, with the Kings' Oatlands Tom Titmouse (by Zaffer out of O. Mrs Tittlemouse) in second place.

The Dod breeding was still evident in the 1975 winners. Joy Dammers' Catesby Honeypot (by Oatlands Mr McGregor out of Honeybee III) won the open class above Elizabeth Reep's Shilstone Rocks Barbados (by Easter out of Molasses); Mrs Hurndall-Waldron's Quillet Avena (by Cawsand Cavalier out of Quickbeam) was above Mrs Renny's Dream III (by Oatlands Diggory Delvet out of Off Ration) in the lead rein (this sadly now down to seven entries with four forward).

The trend was still downwards in 1976, when Mrs Brigg's Chark John Jo (bred in County Wexford by Janus out of White Willows Spook by Mr and Mrs Spring) won a lead-rein class of seven, ahead of J.R. Young's Strode Mermaid (by Cawsand Cavalier out of SR2 Strode Rose, bred by Angela Mills). There were ten entries in the open class, which was won by Alison Taylor's Shilstone Rocks Quercina, who then went on to be Show Champion (as already mentioned), the first ridden pony to do so. She was by S.R. Okement out of S.R. Cavallina and beat Oatlands Tom Titmouse, who seems stuck in second place.

OKEHAMPTON AND BICTON
(1977–1988)

Okehampton (1977–79), in hand

As mentioned earlier, classes for Dartmoor males are seldom large, even for yearlings. At the first show on the ground of the Okehampton Rugby Football Club in 1977 there were four yearling colts forward out of an entry of seven. The winner was the Jones-Roberts Hisley Prospect (by former champion H. Woodcock out of H. Penny), with the Syddalls' Oakfield Wigeon (likewise home bred by Oatlands Mr McGregor out of Boveycombe Capricorn) second. The Best Yearling Filly in a slightly larger class (eight forward out of eleven) was Jean Palmer's Yeoland May (by Whitestone Bayard out of Yeoland June), ahead of Joan Montgomery's Shilstone Rocks Enchanté (by S.R. Fury out of S.R. Enchanted).

Prospect's stable-mate Allendale Flauros (by Huntspath Holly out of Whitmore Titania) won the class for older colts and went on to take the Show Championship. John Holman's Cawsand Dancer (by C. Hail out of C. Sundew) was second in this class (three forward out of four).

The entries for the two classes for older fillies were more encouraging: twenty-two all told, though only fourteen forward. Cilla Harrison's Crimchard Honeylove (by Shilstone Rocks Achilles out of former champion Whitmore Honeymoon) won the two-year-old class, ahead of Violet Dalby's Crookety Jasmine (by Walreddon Musketeer out of C. Candytuft); the three-year-old winner being S.R. Bagatelle (by S.R. Darkness out of Whitmore Jokari), ahead of Pat Robinson's Vean Floradora (by Whitestone Ragged Robin out of White Willows Radiation). Flauros won the Youngstock Championship.

A disappointment in the entry for barren mares with certificate of service: only two forward, the winner being Molly Croft's Shilstone Rocks Nerezza (by S.R. Darkness out of S.R. Cavalina). The novices made up for this: ten forward out of eleven; won by Jean McMillan's Crimchard Trilling Lark (by 1972 Champion C. Bright Spark out of Senruf Trillion). The Lark beat Elizabeth Newbolt-Young's Shilstone Rocks Rainy Day.

The open class for mares was the largest and best filled: eleven forward out of thirteen. It went to the Jones-Roberts eleven-year-old Sweetie Pie (by Jonacs out of Heather Queen). She had been edging forward for some time: third in the open in 1975, second as a barren in 1976. This time she beat Spellbound and Sorceress too.

Jean Cooke's Crimchard Firefly (by C. Bright Spark out of Fair Joanna) followed up his wins as a yearling in 1974 and Reserve Champion in 1975 by winning the stallion class over another four-year-old, Pat Robinson's Whitestone Bayard (bred by Hazel Hunter; by Petroc out of Shilstone Rocks Bay Wind). He just failed to collect the Championship, being reserve to three-year-old Flauros.

At the 1978 show there were four stallions forward out of the eight entered, the class going to Hisley Pedlar, now standing at the Langfield Stud in Lancashire. He beat Flauros whose day as a stallion was yet to come, to become Champion of the Show with Sweetie Pie reserve.

The entries in the mare classes were up a quarter on the previous year. The barren class went to Joy Dammers' Catesby Honey Pot (by Oatlands Mr McGregor out of Honey Bee III), second being Iris Gould's Boveycombe Heron (by B. Leo out of S.R. Sanduck). Jean Cooke's Crimchard Fantasia (by S.R. Darkness out of C. Fantasy), four years old, won the novice class, with Elizabeth Newbolt-Young's S.R. Rainy Day (by S.R. Okement out of S.R. Rainstorm) in second place; eight forward out of ten.

There were fifteen entries in the open class, though only eight forward. Still, it was a strong class, being won for the second year in succession by Sweetie Pie. Cosdon May, who had won in 1974, was second, Margaret Furness's Senruf Abelia third, Catesby Honey Set (the barren winner's full sister) fourth and Spellbound, now fourteen, fifth. The Youngstock Championship went to Joy Dammers' two-year-old colt Catesby Crusader II (by Mr McGregor out of Busy Bee V), with the yearling colt Hisley Cognac as reserve (by H. Pedlar out of Blachford Brandween).

The 1979 show saw two seconds move up. Flauros won the stallion class in the absence of Pedlar the previous year's winner, but Cosdon May was not only preferred to the 1978 winner but to Sorceress as well. Flauros was Show Champion, with May in reserve. Boveycombe Buckthorn (by B. Leo out of Pillar) was the second-placed stallion.

Bicton (1980–89), in hand

Flauros won again at the first Bicton show, being above Brandsby Tornado (by Petroc out of Shilstone Rocks Bay Wind), the latter making his first appearance at the breed show. Unfortunately, there were only three stallions forward out of an entry of seven.

The Langfield Stud's Stokeleigh Wild Rose (by Petroc out of Whitestone Rock Rose) was Best Barren Mare, with Mrs Ogle's Skerraton Camilla (by Crimchard Bright Spark out of Skerraton Wheal Caroline) second; a well-filled class with ten forward out of twelve. Vanessa Goodland's Shilstone Rocks Dark Phantome (so spelt) (by S.R. Darkness out of S.R. Bewitched) won the novice mares' class, above the Abrahalls' Boveycombe Cygnet (another Darkness mare, out of S.R. Sanduck); another well-filled class, thirteen forward out of seventeen. The open class went to Bob and Jean Cooke (*née* McMillan) with Crimchard Fantasia (yet again by S.R. Darkness, out of C. Fantasy).

Entries for the youngstock classes were also up. Jean Palmer's White Willows Prospero was Best Yearling Colt in a class of ten. He was bred by Joan Montgomery by Shilstone Rocks Fury out of the 1973 winning mare Spellbound, the latter incidentally now twenty years old. Second was Elizabeth Newbolt-Young's Shilstone Rocks Fastnet Fury.[1] Shilstone Rocks Stud won the class for yearling fillies with Witching Hour (by S.R. Fury out of S.R. Planchette), also the Yearling Cup.

There were three entries for the older colts' class, which went to Michael and Jean Syddall's Oakfield Robin (by Oatlands Mr McGregor out of Whitmore Calluna), which beat Elizabeth Newbolt-Young's Shilstone Rocks Cloudburst II (by S.R. Fury out of S.R. Rainstorm). The entries for the 2-year-old fillies were a little up; a class of six won by the Jones-Roberts Hisley Champagne (by Allendale Flauros out of Blachford Brandween); those for the three-year-olds better still, thirteen entered with a dozen forward and won by Vanessa Goodland's Mistress Mary of Plovers (by Shilstone Rocks Achilles out of Plovers Bo-Peep) with Shilstone Rocks Cottage Bunch (by S.R. Baccarat out of Whitmore Honeybunch) second. Mistress Mary collected the Youngstock Cup too, with Oakfield Robin as reserve. Flauros was Show Champion, with Fantasia reserve.

There was a splendid turn-out for the barren mares' class in 1981. If we are to believe the marked catalogue, no fewer than twenty-eight of the thirty entrants were forward; even though this included four geldings, an encouraging sign of steadily growing interest. It went to Shilstone Rocks Rainy Day, a nine-year-old, winner as a two-year-old and second novice in 1977 and 1978. Anyway, she won all right this time and was Reserve Champion. Second was the Langfield Stud's Stokeleigh Wild Rose, winner the previous year. Mary Houlden's White Willows Magic was Best Novice Mare in a class of fourteen (ten forward). Magic was by Shilstone Rocks Darkness out of W.W. Sorceress. Second was Elizabeth Newbolt-Young's S.R. Legatee (by S.R.

Baccarat out of Jurston Maystorm of S.R.). The open winner was the Jones-Roberts' Hisley Caviar, which had been second in 1980 and novice winner in 1979, with White Willows Sorceress (Youngstock Champion as a yearling in 1970, winning two-year-old filly, but after that never quite fulfilling that early promise) in second place, though she produced some winners (e.g. White Willows Magic).

The Jones-Roberts three-year-old filly Hisley Serenade (by Allendale Flauros out of Sweetie Pie) was Youngstock Champion, with S.R. Fastnet Fury in reserve. The yearling classes were well filled, being won by Elizabeth Newbolt-Young's S.R. Deluge (colts) and Peter Honey's Walreddon Starlight (by Boveycombe Leo out of W. Dawn). S.R. Witching Hour, now two years old, again won her class.

There were only two forward in the stallion class. There Mary Houlden's six-year-old Allendale Exorcist was first and Show Champion, thus making it three in a row for the Allendale breeding (Flauros in 1979 and 1980). Exorcist is by Huntspath Holly out of Whitmore Titania.

The 1982 class for mares without foals and geldings was again well filled: nineteen mares and six geldings entered, of which all but one mare were forward. It went to Iris Gould's Boveycombe Heron (by B. Leo out of Shilstone Rocks Sanduck), with the Syddells' Oakfield Linnet (by Oatlands Mr McGregor out of Ellimore Tavy) second.

Sad to relate, only Belinda Salem's Langfield Lucy Locket (by Beverley Peacock out of Stokeleigh Tuffet) entered the ring in the novice class. However, a much better turn-out for the open class: sixteen entered and all forward. The winner, Shilstone Rocks Another Bunch (by S.R. Fury out of Whitmore Honeybunch), was well rewarded, for she was Reserve Show Champion and then, in one of those capricious reversals of fortune, was awarded the 1982 Inter-Show Championship, swapping places with Hisley Pedlar, the stallion class winner. The Langfield Stud's Stokeleigh Wild Rose (by Petroc out of Whitestone Rock Rose) was second mare and John Jordan's Catesby Crusader II (by Oatlands Mr McGregor out of Busy Bee V) second stallion.

An additional class for mares was introduced in 1983. This was done by dividing the mares without foals between those with service certificates and those without (plus older geldings). Mrs Briant's Cotswold Finale (by Shilstone Rocks Wild Wind out of Whitmore Moorhen), an eight-year-old newcomer, won the uncertficated class of seventeen (all of whom appear to have been forward). Mrs Mills's seven-year-old gelding Shilstone Rocks Arbutus (by Whitmore Arbutus out of White Willows Pepita) was second. The certificated winner was the Jones-Roberts Hisley Cherry Brandy (by H. Woodcock out of Blachford Brandween), with Stokeleigh Wild Rose (second barren in 1981) in second place.

There were ten mares entered in the novice class (at least six forward), the winner being Elizabeth Newbolt-Young's Hosannah (spelt thus in the catalogue but, one is glad to see, correctly in the stud book). She had not appeared until she was three when she won. The Jones-Roberts Hisley Serenade was second; five years old, by Allendale Flauros

---

[1] *Named after the weather encountered by husband Rod in the Fastnet Race at the time of foaling.*

Hisley Serenade (1978)

Brandsby Tornado (1975)

out of Sweetie Pie. She too had won as a three-year-old.

Another Bunch repeated her 1982 win in the open class and went on to be Show Champion, with the stallion Springs Nougat in reserve. Boveycombe Heron was second mare (by B. Leo out of S.R. Sanduck); she had won the novice class in 1976. The second stallion was Brandsby Tornado (by Petroc out of S.R. Bay Wind), Inter-Breed Champion in 1981.

Next year Tornado won, ahead of White Willows Darwin in a class of five, all forward. Darwin, shown by the Jones-Roberts team, is by Shilstone Rocks Baccarat out of W.W. Radium. Tornado also won the Championship, with Another Bunch (who won the certificated mares' class) in reserve.

Pat Price's Senruf Jingle was second to Another Bunch. She is by Cawsand Cavalier out of Joybelle of Torr. In the mare and gelding class Eileen White's Crimchard Fairy Tale (by Shilstone Rocks Achilles out of C. Fantasia) won, above the Syddalls' Oakfield Linnet (second in 1982). Hosanna endorsed her 1983 novice win by winning the open, beating Hisley Caviar the winner three years before. There were only seven entries (all forward) in the novice class, which went to Iris Gould's

Boveycombe Bunting (by Shilstone Rocks Darkness out of B. Heron) above Martin Ball's Pantmanr's Junket (by S.R. Jehovah out of Park Barn Dance).

In the youngstock classes, Hisley Salvo (by H. Woodcock out of H. Serenade) won the yearling colts, with Langfield Canth second. The Best Yearling Filly was Cilla Harrison's Plovers Pat-a-cake (by White Willows Darwin out of Millcroft Pinkle Purr) with Mrs Ross's Heatherden Charm second. Mrs Hattan's Shilstone Rocks Tamarisk (by S.R. Cloudburst II out of White Willows Radium) won the class for older colts with Anne Rigby's Dykes Timkin second. Hisley Polonaise won the class for two-year-old fillies (second as a yearling in 1983), with Jimmy Vickers' Jurston Starlight second. June Little's Brandsby Honeybunch (by B. Cyclone out of Catesby Honeyset) was Best Three-year-old. Polonaise was Youngstock Champion, with Hisley Salvo reserve.

Tornado won the stallion class again in 1985, but had to stand Reserve Champion to Hisley Caviar, who had also won the open class in 1981. Mary Houlden's Allendale Vampire (by White Willows Darwin out of Allendale Black Magic) was second stallion. Caviar's runner-up was Another Bunch, the winner in 1982 and 1983.

Mary Bienkowska's May Tinkerbelle (by Allendale Flauros out of Maybelle) won the uncertificated mares' class, the Faradays' Torfield Quicksilver second (by Flauros out of Hisley Quadrille). Pat Price's Park Barn Dance (by Kilbees Mr Jingle out of Hambledon Juno) won the certificated class, White Willows Halloween III being second. The novice winner was Hisley Cherry Brandy (by H. Woodcock out of B. Brandween).

Only two colts and a gelding forward in their class and the gelding won: Pat Ogle's Skerraton Comfrey (by Crookety Cavalcade out of S. Camilla), with White Willows Macbeth II second. Five yearling fillies forward out of fourteen; Cilla Harrison's Plovers One-a-Penny (by Torfields Pennyworth out of Crimchard Honeylove) ahead of Shilstone Rocks Gentle Fury and taking the Yearling Cup. The new classes for geldings only attracted thirteen entries between them.

Hisley Salvo, now a two-year-old, repeated his 1984 win in the class for older colts, with Jean Cooke's Crimchard Free 'n' Easy (by Shylock out of C. Fantasia) second. Only three forward out of seven.

However, the filly classes were much better filled: ten forward in the Two-Year-Olds, won by Mrs Marshall's Wendel Seaspray (by S.R. Fastnet Fury out of Langfield Green Ginger), with Pat Robinson's Vean Floribunda (by S.R. Easter Day out of V. Flora Dora) second; nine forward out of eleven in the three-year-olds, won by the Jones-Roberts Hisley Polonaise (two-year-old winner in 1984), with Mrs P. Morris's Senruf Atalanta (by C. Firefly out of Senruf Abelia — a newcomer) second. Salvo was Youngstock Champion; a good day for the Hisley Stud.

The year 1986 saw the continuation of two classes exclusively for geldings: for two- and three-year-olds, won by the Misses Booths' White Willows Cymbeline in a class of six; for four-year-olds and older, won by Mrs McKeough's Cruachan Dunnock in a class of seven. However, the yearling classes were slightly up; Bob and Margorie Rigby's Boveycombe Buoy (by Hisley Woodcock out of Boveycombe Bunting) winning the colts' class, with Pat Robinson's Vean Black Jack (by Shilstone Rocks Easter Day out of Vean Dorelia) second; Jean Palmer's Yeoland Juliet (by White Willows Prospero out of Vean Honeysuckle) winning the fillies class, with Joan Montgomery's White Willows Bewitching (by W.W. Darwin out of W.W. Sorceress) second.

The class for older colts was won by Paul and Madge Taylor's three-year-old Langfield Canth, which had been second as a yearling. Second was Mrs Moon's Pantmanrs Joyride (by Brandsby Tornado out of P. Junket). Nicola Tyler's Vean Dorabella II (full sister to Vean Black Jack) won the class for two-year-old fillies, with Mrs Challoner Tucker's Stonehealed Demetria (also by Easter Day, out of Whitmore Venus) second. Cilla Harrison's Plovers Pat-a-Cake won the three-year olds; she had been first as a yearling. Pat Robinson's Vean Floribunda, second as a two-year-old, was again second.

There were fifty entries for the four classes for mares in 1986, of which thirty-six were forward. Mary Bienkowska's May Tinkerbelle again won the uncertificated class, second being Pat Ogle's Skeraton Camilla (by Crimchard Bright Spark out of S. Wheal Caroline). The winner of the certificated class was the Faradays' Torfield Quicksilver

(by Allendale Flauros out of Hisley Quadrille), with Penny Harrison's and Mrs Silvester's Wynhill Cherry (by Boveycombe Buckthorn out of Whitmore Tia Maria) second. Pat Price's Stonehealed Tarantella (by S.R. Easter Day out of Park Barn Dance) won the class for novice mares, with Mrs Challoner Tucker's Shilstone Rocks Witching Hour (by S.R. Fury out of S.R. Planchette) second. The open winner was Meg Gould's Boveycombe Bunting (by S.R. Darkness out of B. Heron), with Langfield Green Ginger (jointly owned by the Taylors and Miss Raphael, by Hisley Pedlar out of Stokeleigh Wild Rose) in second place.

There were four stallions forward, with Allandale Vampire scoring his first win (and the championship) at the breed show. He had been second the previous year and third as a four-year-old the year before that. Second was Mrs Green's Senruf Graduate (by Whitmore Arbutus out of Blachford Greta). Tornado was not present to defend his title. Tarantella was Reserve Champion.

Nineteen-eighty-seven was very much the stallions' year, with Tornado winning the Show Championship and the second stallion, Mrs Jones's Nappa Country Boy (a five-year-old by Brandsby Cyclone out of S.R. Country Bunch, a newcomer bred by June Coates of Hereford) standing reserve.

Mrs Tucker's Witching Hour, second novice in 1986, won the barren class, the Harrison-Silvester Dunros Missy Mouse (by Huntspath Holly out of Dunros Peppermint) being second in a class of seventeen. The certificated class went to the Jones-Roberts Hisley Caviar, now twelve years old, with Mrs Green's Dunmere Tamarisk (by Jurston Blue Tit out of J. Vernal) second. Pat Robinson's Vean Mary Rose was Best Novice Mare, her first appearance at the show after winning as a yearling. The Andersons' Haven Halina (by S.R. Darkness out of Huntspath Hannah) was second. Finally, the open class for mares went to the Jones-Roberts Hisley Serenade which had been Youngstock Champion in 1981, second being the Vanstones' Senruf Jingle (by Cawsand Cavalier out of Joybelle of Torr, fifteen years old).

In the yearling colt class Alison Taylor's and Martin Ball's Langfield Roth (by S.R. Fury out of Langfield Noilly Prat) beat Mrs Tucker's Harleston Pilot (by Brandsby Cyclone out of S.R. Witching Hour); Meg Gould's and Mrs Jackson's Boveycombe Seal (by Brandsby Cyclone out of Boveycombe Bunting) won the yearling fillies' class, June Little's Brandsby Serenade (by B. Tornado out of Blythford Scilla) being second. The older colts' class went to Miss Mizzi's Whinberry Quality Way (by Allendale Flauros out of Springs Quality Street), with Mrs Jones's (of Carlisle) White Willows Witchdoctor second. The two-year-old class for fillies was won by Jean Palmer's Yeoland Juliet (by W.W. Prospero out of Vean Honeysuckle), the Taylor-Ball's Pantmanrs Jaunt (by Brandsby Tornado out of P. Junket) being second. The Taylors' Langfield Miz Sophie (by Hisley Pedlar out of Ryland Castanet) took the three-year-old-filly prize, Mrs Tucker's Stonehealed Demetria again being second. There were no classes especially for young geldings, but the one for four-year-olds and over again attracted thirteen entries. It was won by Mrs Vigus's Abthorpe Allblack (by S.R. Darkness out of Catesby Catrena), with Mrs Compton's Allendale Vulcan (by W.W. Darwin out of Huntspath Josephine) second.

Cosdon May (1970)

Crimchard Bright Spark (1966)

Pantmanrs Jaunt (1985)

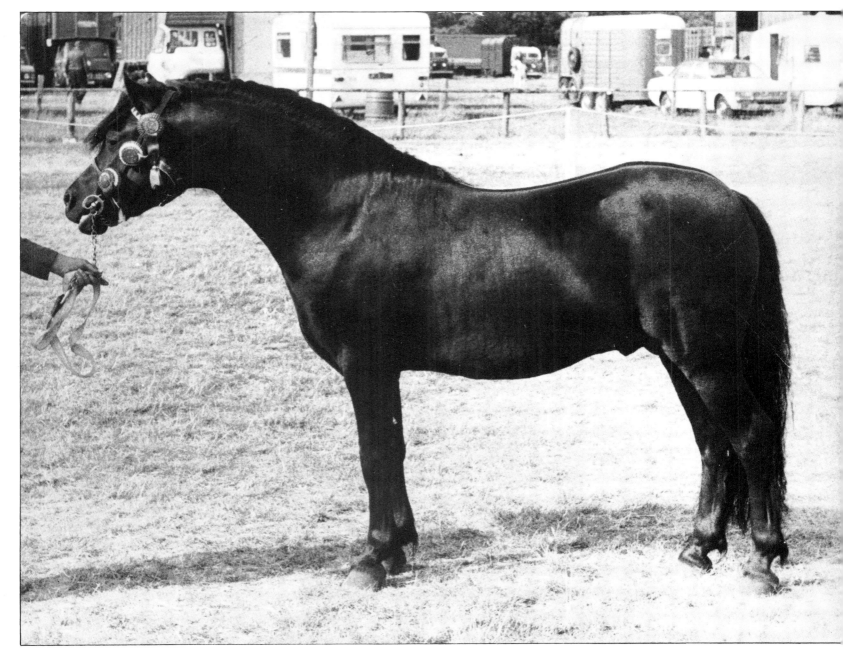

Allendale Flauros (1974)

The total entry for the 1988 breed show ran pretty level with that for the previous year. Elizabeth Newbolt-Young's Shilstone Rocks Nicodemus (by Brandsby Cyclone out of S.R. Dark Mountain) beat Mrs Challenor-Tucker's Harleston Bard (by White Willows Darwin out of Torfield Tomasina) in the yearling colts, while Joan Montgomery's White Willows Spellbound (by W.W. Darwin out of W.W. Halloween III) beat Anne Bubear's Langfield Greenacres (by L. Canth out of L. Green Ginger) in the yearling fillies. Alison Taylor's and Martin Ball's Langfield Roth (by Shilstone Rocks Fury out of Langfield Noilly Prat) beat Patricia Robinson's Vean Black Jack (by S.R. Easter Day out of V. Dorelia) in the class for two- and three-year-old colts. Probably the class with the highest quality was that the two-year-old fillies and geldings, being won by Ann Jones' and Patricia Roberts' Hisley Charisma (by H. Salvo out of H. Caviar) above Elizabeth Newbolt-Young's Shilstone Rocks Musada (by Brandsby Cyclone out of S.R. Dark Mountain), these two eventually standing champion and reserve in the youngstock. The class for three-year-old fillies and geldings went to the Taylor-Ball's Pantmanrs Jaunt (by Brandsby Tornado out of P. Junket) above the Bubear gelding Pumphill Beau Sabreur (by Oatlands Mr McGregor out of Allendale Black Magic). The class for four-year-old-plus geldings went to Pat Ogle's Skerraton Comfrey (by Crookety Cavalcade out of S. Camilla) above M. Dallyn's Crimchard Martell (by Shilstone Rocks Darkness out of C. Moonlark).

There were only three novice mares, first place going to the Newbolt-Young's S.R. Snowfall (by S.R. Darkness out of S.R. Rockfall) ahead of Vanessa Parkinson's Plovers April Showers (by S.R. Cloudburst out of Tomatin Early Dawn). The open class, as though to make up for this, produced the Show Champion, Elizabeth Newbolt-Young's Shilstone Rocks Another Bunch to back up her NPS win, with Patricia Robinson's Vean Mary Rose as Reserve Show Champion (by S.R. Fury ex Whitmore Honeybunch and by S.R. Easter Day ex Vean Dorelia respectively). Best of the stallions was Mrs Green's Senruf Graduate (by Whitmore Arbutus out of Blachford Greta), second being the Furnesses' Senruf Taurus II (by Senruf Solomon out of Senruf Tiffany).

The schedule for 1989 followed the lines of the previous year, with entries well up. The class for yearling colts and geldings went to Miss Dunn's and Miss Lanfear's Hisley Sorcerer (by H. Woodcock out of Hisley Serenade) above Carole Rigby's Dykes Acanthus (by Langfield Canth out of Stokeleigh Muffet); Mrs Challoner Tucker's Hisley Charmer (by H. Salvo out of H. Caviar) winning the filly class ahead of Jim Holman's Cosdon Princess (by Catesby Crusader II out of C. May); well filled classes (25 entries all told).

The Furnesses' Senruf Gladiator (by Hisley Pedlar out of Blachford Greta) took the prize for two- and three-year-old colts, above Alison Taylor's and Martin Ball's Langfield Roth (by Shilstone Rocks Fury out of L. Noilly Prat) and went on to win the youngstock championship. In the class for two-year-old fillies and geldings the Goodman-Houseman White Willows Spellbound repeated her 1988 win, above the Taylors' Wendel Sea Dragon (by Langfield Canth out of Wendel Sea Spray); the class for three-year-olds went to Elizabeth Newbolt-Young's Shilstone Rocks Masada (by Brandsby Cyclone out of S.R. Dark Mountain), above

the Jones-Roberts Hisley Charisma (by H. Salvo out of H. Caviar), Masada being Reserve Youngstock Champion. Over forty female young stock entered, which is encouraging.

The ages in the class for mature geldings ran from four to twelve. There were nine entered, the prize going to Mrs Bubear's Pumphill Beau Sabreur (by Oatlands Mr McGregor out of Allendale Black Magic) with the Silvester-Harrison Wendel St George (by Springs Nougat out of Langfield Green Ginger) second; both four-year-olds.

There were four classes for mares. Vanessa Parkinson's Horselode Hermione (by Catesby Pip out of Felstead Fianna) won the class for barrens, with Mrs McKinlay Clark's Piers Aspen (by Huntspath Holly out of Vean Zena) second. The best mare with certificate of service was the Jones-Roberts Hisley Stardust (by H. Woodcock out of H. Serenade). Elizabeth Newbolt-Young's Shilstone Rocks Rain Again (by Whitmore Arbutus out of S.R. Rainstorm) was second. In the class for novice broodmares Mrs Morris's Radway Rosie (by S.R. Jehovah out of Senruf Amanda) beat Penny Harrison's Plovers One-a-Penny (by Torfields Pennyworth out of Crimchard Honeylove). Finally, in the open mares' class the previous year's winners maintained their positions: Another Bunch first (and Reserve Supreme Champion), Mary Rose second.

There were ten entries in the stallion class, which went to Paul and Madge Taylor's Langfield Canth (by S.R. Fastnet Fury out of Langfield Noilly Prat). He displaced Senruf Graduate, the 1988 winner, and went on to take the Supreme Championship.

Okehampton (1977–79), Ridden

The first of the three breed shows at Okehampton saw wins for White Willows ponies in both ridden classes. The open went to the Milkwood Stud's White Willows Wizard (which had also won in 1974), second being Paul Carter's Catesby Bullfinch (by Oatlands Mr McGregor out of C. Ptarmigan). White Willows Ophelia (by Cawsand Cavalier out of Spellbound) won the leading-rein class for Mrs Cardwell, above Mrs Bienkowska's May Jonquil (also by Cavalier, out of Hele Janet). Entries were down: four for the open (three forward) and five for the leading-rein class (all present)

The next year was not much better: thirteen all told (nine forward). In 1978, too, the lower age-limit for the open was raised to four years. This class was won by Elizabeth Newbolt-Young's Shilstone Rocks Whirligig (by S.R. Darkness out of S.R. Whirlwind) above Jackie Baggott's Millcroft Missy Munchkin (by Crimchard Bright Spark out of Rosevean Curlew). In the leading-rein class (three forward out of four) the winner was Jill Cameron's Broadfield Popples (by Oatlands Jeremy Fisher out of Dartmoors Little Miss), with J.R. Young's Strode Mermaid (by Cawsand Cavalier out of Strode Rose) second.

Nineteen-seventy-nine, the last year at Okehampton, saw a slight revival: nine entries in the open with seven forward, won by Joan Montgomery's Catesby Miss Perkins (by Mr McGregor out of Busy Bee V) with Mrs Roeves's White Willows Wizard, the 1974 and 1977 winner, in second place. The leading-rein class mustered five out of six and went to Mrs Lane's Hayborough Sara (by Whitestone Ragged Robin out of Red Hall Sagitta), with Cilla Harrison's Tomatin Early Dawn (by Higher Tor Skylark out of Winkie Pop III) second.

Bicton (1980–89), Ridden

The 1980 lead-rein winner was Mrs Calder's Blachford Impact (by Cawsand Prince out of Blachford Brandween), with Mrs Cardwell's Ophelia, winner in 1977, second. The open went to Iris Gould's Boveycombe Redwing (by Shilstone Rocks Fury out of B. Heron), with Mrs Roeves's Catesby Miss Perkins (the 1979 winner) second.

A second win for Mrs Calder's Impact in 1981, with Mrs Peters' White Willows Adelaide (by S.R. Fury out of W.W. Radium) in second place. In the open class Mary Houlden's Allendale Exorcist demonstrated his versatility, winning there as well as in the stallion class and, for good measure, coming second to Hisley Saga in the Working-hunter Ponies. Second to him was Iris Gould's Boveycombe Bunting (by S.R. Darkness out of B. Heron). Entries were well up: twenty-one in the open and eight in the lead-rein class.[2]

Exorcist's double in 1982 was for the open ridden and the W.H.P. Although the latter is outside the strict terms of our report, it is interesting, surely, in underlining the point that the pure-bred Dart is not just for show. Second to him in the open was full brother Allendale Flauros. Mrs Mills' Shilstone Rocks Arbutus (by Whitmore Arbutus out of White Willows Pepita) won the lead-rein class, Elizabeth Newbolt-Young's Shilstone Rocks Brighter Day (by S.R. Baccarat out of S.R. Rainy Day) being second.

A class for novice ridden ponies (three years and over) was introduced in 1983, the age-limit for the open class being also brought down to three years, though the latter reverted to four-year-olds and over in 1989.

The result in the lead-rein classes was an exact repetition of the previous year: Arbutus followed by Brighter Day. There were seventeen entries in the new novice class, which went to Miss Hillyard's Oakheath Peep Bo, a ten-year-old mare by Jurston Storm Petrel out of Sherberton Tit Willow, second being Mrs Briant's Cotswold Finale, class winner for uncertificated mares. Eight of the novices also competed in the open, Peep Bo coming second to Hisley Pedlar, the Langfield Stud's formidable thirteen-year-old stallion and former Show Champion (1978). The total number of entries in the ridden classes this year was thirty-eight, a considerable improvement on the nine of 1977.

___

[2] *From 1981 the breed show winners were eligible to complete in the NPS Ridden Mountain and Moorland Championship at Olympia. This extra carrot may have had something to do with the larger entries. However, the reason need not detain us. The fact is that they went up and have stayed up, which is all to the good. (The NPS also holds a Ridden Mountain and Moorland Championship at Malvern, for which DPS Breed Show winners do not qualify as such.)*

The entries for the 1984 ridden classes matched those of 1983. Six lead-rein entrants faced the judge, who put Eileen White's Crimchard Fairytale (that year's uncertificated mare winner) at the top of the line, with Mrs Booth's White Willows Banquo (by Boveycombe Leo out of Spellbound) second. Mrs McKeough's Cruachan Dunnock (by Oatlands Diggory Delvet out of C. Grouse) won the novice class with lead-rein winner Fairytale second. The open class went to Tansy Ballhatchet's Hornton Nimbus (by Shilstone Rocks Wild Wind out of Hornton Thrift), with Mrs Rylah's Senruf Grebe (an eleven-year-old stallion by Hisley Woodcock out of Blachford Greta) second.

Linda Sobey's and Mrs Healey's Stonehealed Trista Bella (by Whitestone Bayard out of Cosdon Trissie) won the 1985 lead-rein class, with White Willows Banquo (now owned by the Misses Booth) again second. Mrs McKeough won again in the novice class, this time with Cruachan Dunnock (by Oatlands Diggory Delvet out of Crimchard Windsong), with Trista Bella second. In the open Penny Harrison's Boveycombe Redwing (by Shilstone Rocks Fury out of B. Heron) was first and the Rosses' Kirtley Ladybird (by Whitestone Tarragon out of Dunros Squirrel) second.

Tansy Ballhatchet's and Miss Child's Allendale Mystique (by White Willows Darwin out of Hisley Champagne) won the lead-rein class in 1986, second being John and Diana Coaker's Arscott Lucky Lady (by Crimchard Windrush out of Shilstone Rocks Milady). The novice class went to Mrs Bruce's Blairhill Bellona (by White Willows Satellite out of Lakehead Belinda), her Blairhill Blue Moon (full sister) being second. Finally, Mrs Rylah's Senruf Grebe bettered her 1984 position in the open class, second being Elizabeth Newbolt-Young's Shilstone Rocks Cloudburst II (by S.R. Fury out of S.R. Rainstorm). Novice Bellona was third.

In 1987 there were no fewer than sixty-one entries in the ridden classes (for registered Dartmoors). Nicola Tyler's Senruf Astra (by Crimchard Firefly out of S. Abelia) won the leading-rein class, Mrs Faraday's Shilstone Rocks Mountain Sweet (by Whitmore Arbutus out of Huntspath Hannah) being second. The Taylors' winner of the Three-Year-Olds, Langfield Miz Sophie, won the novice ridden class, Eileen White's Crimchard Fairytale being second. The open went to Penny Harrison's Boveycombe Redwing (by S.R. Fury out of B. Heron), with Mrs. Compton's Allendale Vulcan, second in the older geldings, also second in this class.

The entries for 1988, at fifty-three, were only a little down on the previous year's. The leading-rein class was won by Mrs Smith's Crimchard Fair Maid (by Shilstone Rocks Fury out of Crimchard Fantasy); second Linda Sobey and Jill Healey's Stonehealed Trista Bella (by Whitestone Bayard out of Cosdon Trissie). The novice class went to Miss Matthews' Skerraton Camilla (by Crimchard Bright Spark out of Skerraton Wheal Caroline), above Mrs Faraday's Torfield Quicksilver (by Allendale Flauros out of Hisley Quadrille). First in the open class (and Ridden Champion) was Penny Harrison's and Mrs Silvester's Wynhill Cherry (by Boveycombe Buckthorn out of Whitmore Tia Maria), second was the Furnesses' Senruf Taurus II (by Senruf Solomon out of Senruf Tiffany) in a class of twenty-one.

The classes for 1989 followed the same pattern as in the previous year. The lead-rein class went to Mrs Rowell's Stonehealed Hector, with Mrs Silvester and Miss Harrison's Wynhill Cherry second. Mrs Jones's Nappa Country Boy won the class for novices, with the Brown's Wrydecroft Pippa second. In the open class Wynhill Cherry came first (Hector was not entered) and Mrs Silvester's and Miss Harrison's Wendel St George second.

Before leaving the breed shows, we should record the presence of a notable veteran at the penultimate show of our review: Cosdon May, aged eighteen and brought in a cattle lorry by James Holman himself; novice and open winner in 1974, Reserve Champion to her sire Boveycombe Leo (she was out of Skaigh Princess). She was third in her class this time – to the Supreme Champion Another Bunch and Reserve Champion Mary Rose. The writer happened to be passing as she came out of the box on arrival; as spry as ever, moorland born and bred for generations.

A SCORE OF DARTMOOR STUDS

The Oxford Dictionary tells us that a 'stud' is a 'number of horses kept for breeding'. Well, we probably knew that already. What is interesting about this entry, however, is that it relegates to second meaning 'place where these are kept'. And surely the O.E.D. has, as usual, got it right? Pride of place for the live creatures that are at the heart of the matter – indeed, they *are* the matter. Then, and only then, should we comprehend all the associated bricks and mortar, grazing, fencing, even the grooms and – dare we add? – the stud owners themselves. In so doing we shall get our priorities right and also exhibit a seemly humility, an attribute that can well do with any airing in these publicity-seeking days. A stud stands for horses – or, as now, ponies.

Before we move on to take a brief look at each of this score of prominent studs[1], it would be wise to remind ourselves that the phrase 'foundation stock' has two meanings, depending on whether it refers to an individual line or to a stud as a whole. In connection with a line, we mean here the forebears, male or female, beyond which it is not possible to trace antecedents, moving backwards up the tree. For example, the famous Dora lacked any documented pedigree (no insurmountable obstacle in those days of registration-by-inspection) and was therefore the 'foundation mare' of her line. On the other hand, when applied to a stud as a whole, the phrase's meaning is slightly different, in that 'foundation' refers to the stud and not to any line. For instance, Huntspath Holly and Whitmore Titania are the foundation stock of the Allendale Stud (see below). On the other hand, Allendale Black Magic and the rest are not 'foundation', in that they were bred *by* the stud.

One last general word. The details given below are brief, no more than sketches. Should the reader feel that he is not getting his money's worth, we would plead that this work is – or sets out to be – the story of the Dartmoor pony. To list more than these few distinguished ponies would make it unduly long. To those that want to discover more about 'which was bred where and how' two sources are open: the stud book and the stud owners. Telephone numbers in the *Dartmoor Diary*.

---

[1] *Studs nominated by the society, details supplied by stud owners.*

The Allendale Stud

Great Shefford, Newbury, Berkshire
Founded in 1970 by Paul Carter

Foundation Stock

Huntspath Holly: stallion, 1969; by Red Hall Aquarius out of Huntspath Josephine, bred by Mrs Titler
Whitmore Titania: mare, 1969; by Whitmore Arbutus out of Imp of Torr bred by Imogen Slade

Notable Allendale Stock

Allendale Black Magic: mare, 1973
Allendale Flauros: stallion, 1974 } by H. Holly out of W. Titania
Allendale Exorcist: stallion 1975
Allendale Vampire: stallion, 1980; by White Willows Darwin out of A. Black Magic
Allendale Vulcan: gelding, 1980; by W.W. Darwin out of Huntspath Josephine

The Boveycombe Stud

Nutcombe, Lustleigh, Newton Abbot, Devon
Founded in 1955 by Iris and Meg Gould

Foundation Stock

Jude: stallion, 1941; bequeathed by Sylvia Calmady-Hamlyn
Fudge III: mare, 1955; believed by Silver Dollar, bred by Mann of Widecombe
Skaigh Princess: mare, 1958; by Cawsand Boy II out of Betty XXI, bred by Thomas Holman
Pillar: mare, 1964; by Michelmass out of Hele Juliet III, bred by Joan Montgomery
Shilstone Rocks Sanduck: mare, 1965; by Red Hall Aquarius out of Dunnabridge Wild Goose, bred by Elizabeth Newbolt-Young

Notable Boveycombe Stock

Boveycombe Gemini: mare, 1959; by Jenyn out of Fudge III
Boveycombe Leo: stallion, 1961; by Jude out of Fudge III
Boveycombe Heron: mare, 1971; by Leo out of S.R. Sanduck
Boveycombe Bunting: mare, 1975; by S.R. Darkness out of B. Heron
Boveycombe Redwing: mare, 1976; by S.R. Fury out of B. Heron

The Brandsby Stud

The Lane, Guilsfield, Welshpool, Powys
Founded 1970 by June Little

Foundation Stock

Shilstone Rocks Bay Wind: mare, 1966; by Boveycombe Leo out of Jurston Windrift, bred by Tim and Elizabeth Reep
Blythford Scilla: mare, 1968; by Blue John out of Azalia, bred by Mrs Fulford
Whitestone Mentha: mare, 1969; by Jentyl out of W. Mint, bred by Hazel Hunter
Park Jemima Jane: mare, 1970; by Parklands Paragon out of Black Jane, bred by John and Louise Fleming
Catesby Honey Set: mare, 1972; by Oatlands Mr McGregor out of Honey Bee bred by Joy Dammers

Notable Brandsby Stock

Brandsby Tornado: stallion, 1975; by Petroc out of Shilstone Rocks Bay Wind
Brandsby Cyclone: stallion, 1978 ⎱ by B. Tornado out of
Brandsby Storm Cloud: stallion, 1982 ⎰ Blythford Scilla

The Cawsand Stud

Hazelwood, Gidleigh, Chagford, Newton Abbot, Devon
Founded 1877 by the Holman Family
Present owner: John Holman

Foundation Stock

The Queenie line of Cawsand ponies is known to go back to 1877, being then introduced by John Cottle, Mrs Holman's uncle. More recently, the following were acquired:
Queenie VII: mare, 1919; by Cannon Ball out of Queenie; bred by James Cottle
Chymes: mare, 1945; by Smokey known to be out of Sherberton Eliza, bred by John Coaker

Notable Cawsand Stock

Queenie XX: mare, 1943; known to be by Punch out of Queenie VII
Cawsand Boy II: stallion, 1955; by C. Boy out of Queenie XX
Cawsand Cavalier: stallion, 1960; by Huccaby out of Betty XXI
Cawsand Sundew: mare, 1962; by Dunnabridge out of Skaigh Princess
Cawsand Dancer: stallion, 1974; by C. Hail out of C. Sundew

Comment (see also 'The Cawsand-Cosdon connection' under the Cosdon Stud) John Holman writes that the South Zeal ponies were 'mainly sired by the society stallions, which ran over Cawsand on South Tawton'; this 'society' being a local association of breeders started about 1906 and lasting until shortly before the First World War, its purpose being to provide high-quality sires of true moorland type. It was not connected with the present DPS, which did not exist until the mid-twenties.

He further reports (May 1988) that 'the line of (Queenie) ponies is still going strong'. It is indeed; with Cawsand Silver Queen (out of C. Black Queen, out of C. Queenie, out of Queenie XX) in the 1981 Volume of the *DPS Stud Book*; incidentally, next to the entry for Cosdon May's foal, Cosdon Mayling.

The Cosdon Stud

High View, South Zeal, Okehampton, Devon
Established 1969 by Betty Holman and James Holman

Foundation Stock

Skaigh Princess (1958): bred by Thomas Holman; by Cawsand Boy II out of Betty XXI (sold to Iris Gould 1961-2, bought back in 1970)

Notable Cosdon Stock

Cosdon May: 1970, by Boveycombe Leo out of Skaigh Princess
Cosdon May Queen: mare, 1972; by Brown Berry III out of Skaigh Princess
Cosdon Miss Vicki: mare, 1977 ⎱
Cosdon Mayling: mare, 1980 ⎰ by Crookety Cavalcade out of C. May

The Cawsand-Cosdon Connection

John, James and Betty Holman are the children of Thomas Holman of King's Arms, South Zeal, and later of Whitecombe, South Zeal. Thomas Holman died in 1959, when his elder son, John (christened Thomas John), inherited the Cawsand Stud. James and Betty founded the Cosdon Stud in 1969, taking as their prefix the old name for Cawsand, the hill rising on the southern side of the A30 road near South Zeal.

James's son Peter and John's daughter Diana Alford (who has the Shelly Stud) will carry on the Cawsand line into the fourth generation of the family ownership. As a tail-piece to the Cawsand-Cosdon story, it is interesting to find that Skaigh Princess, James Holman's foundation mare, brings together the bloodlines of the Queenies and Betties originated by Tom Holman.

The Crimchard Stud

Pretty Oak, Chard, Somerset
Established 1960 by Jean Cooke (née McMillan)

Foundation Stock

Peewit III: mare, 1939; by Dinarth Spark out of Water Wagtail by The Leat; bred by Sylvia Calmady-Hamlyn and Nora Dawson

Fair Joanna: mare, 1956; by John out of Widecombe Fair; bred by Glenda Spooner

Whitmore Honeymoon: mare, 1960; by Janus out of Honeybags; bred by Mrs Peter Slade

Notable Crimchard Stock

Crimchard Bright Spark: stallion, 1966; by Jenson out of Whitmore Honeymoon

Crimchard Trilling Lark: mare, 1971; by C. Bright Spark out of Senruf Trillion

Crimchard Fanfare: stallion, 1972 } by C. Bright Spark out of
Crimchard Firefly: stallion, 1973 } Fair Joanna

Crimchard Fantasia: mare, 1974; by Shilstone Rocks Darkness out of C. Fantasy

Crimchard Fairy Tale: mare, 1978; by S.R. Achilles out of C. Fantasia

Crimchard Free 'n' Easy: stallion, 1983; by White Willows Shylock out of C. Fantasia

The Hisley Stud

Lower Hisley Farm, Lustleigh, Newton Abbot, Devon
Founded 1959 by Ann Jones and Patricia Roberts

Foundation Stock

Queenie XXIII: mare, 1948; by Boxer out of Countess VIII; bred by E.W. White & Son

Jenson: stallion, 1954; by Pipit out of Jenny VII; bred by Sylvia Calmady-Hamlyn

Hele Judith II: mare, 1956; by Hele Romeo out of Hele Judith; bred by Jim Stephens

Dunnabridge Wigeon: mare, 1956; by Huccaby out of Dunnabridge Goose Girl; bred by Newman Caunter

Heather Queen: mare, 1958; by Raybarrow Pool out of Queenie XX, bred by Thomas Holman

Notable Hisley Stock

Hisley Woodcock: stallion, 1962; by Jenson out of Dunnabridge Wigeon

Hisley Quince: mare, 1964; by Peter Tavy out of Queenie XXIII

Hisley Pedlar: stallion, 1970; by Lammermuir Rambler out of H. Quince

Hisley Caviar: mare, 1975; by H. Pedlar out of Blachford Brandween

Hisley Serenade: mare, 1978; by Allendale Flauros out of Sweetie Pie

Hisley Cherry Brandy: mare, 1979; by H. Woodcock out of B. Brandween

Hisley Polonaise: mare, 1982; by H. Woodcock out of Torfield Pretty Penny

Hisley Stardust: mare, 1984; by H. Woodcock out of H. Serenade

The Jurston Stud

Middle Venton, Drewsteignton, Exeter, Devon
Established 1938 by Molly Croft

Foundation Stock

Dawn V: mare, 1938; by and out of Dartmoor ponies; bred by W. Mortimore

Mary Tavy II: mare, 1939; by Dartmoor pony; bred by C. Doidge

Hornbeam: mare, 1945; by and out of Dartmoor ponies, bred by Whitley

May Queen VII: mare, 1954; by Cawsand Boy out of Queenie XX; bred by Thomas Holman

Notable Jurston Stock

Storm II: stallion, 1949; by Jef out of Dawn V

Coronet II: mare, 1953; by Storm II out of Hornbeam

Jurston Tiara: mare, 1968; by Jenson out of Coronet II

Jurston Blue Tit: stallion, 1972; by Crimchard Bright Spark out of J. Tiara

The Kilbees Stud

Kilbees Farm, Winkfield, Windsor Forest, Berkshire
Founded in 'the late fifties' by Lady Willingdon

Foundation Stock

Jon: stallion, 1950; by Jude out of Dora IV; bred by Sylvia Calmady-Hamlyn

Dunnabridge Bonny Boy: stallion, 1955; by Huccaby out of Moor Hen III; bred by Newman Caunter

Red Hall Auriga: mare, 1959; by Janus out of Cottage Garden; bred by Mrs Reiss and Mrs Strettle

Rose Vean Quail: mare, 1959; by Vean Partridge out of Snipe; bred by Elspeth Ferguson

Notable Kilbees Stock

Kilbees Jenny Too: mare, 1966 } by Jon out of Vean Blue Jennykin
Kilbees Mr Pickwick: stallion, 1970 }

The Langfield Stud

Broad Carr Farm, Langfield, Todmorden, Lancashire
Founded 1973 by Paul and Madge Taylor

Foundation Stock

Blachford Brandween: mare, 1962; by Huccaby out of Hele Juliet II bred by Wing Commander Passy

Ryland Castanet: mare, 1967; by Oatlands Diggory Delvet out of Peppa; bred by Mrs M. W. Evans

Hisley Pedlar: stallion, 1970; by Lammermuir Rambler out of Hisley Quince; bred by Ann Jones and Patricia Roberts

Stokeleigh Muff's Pet: mare, 1975; by Petroc out of Miss Muffet of Robins; bred by Miss S. M. Raphael

Stokeleigh Wild Rose: mare, 1975; by Petroc out of Whitestone Rock Rose; bred by Miss S. M. Raphael

Shilstone Rocks Fastnet Fury: stallion, 1979; by S. R. Darkness out of S. R. Rockfall; bred by Elizabeth Newbolt-Young

Notable Langfield Stock

Langfield Noilly Prat: mare, 1979; by Hisley Pedlar out of S. Muff's Pet
Langfield Green Ginger: mare, 1979; by Hisley Pedlar out of S. Wild Rose
Langfield Chanel: mare, 1982; by S.R. Fastnet Fury out of B. Brandween
Langfield Canth: stallion, 1983; by S.R. Fastnet Fury out of L. Noilly Prat
Langfield Miz Sophie: mare, 1984; by H. Pedlar out of R. Castanet
Langfield Roth: stallion, 1986; by S.R. Fury out of L. Noilly Prat

The Oatlands Stud

Oatlands Chase, Weybridge, Surrey
(later: Stonehouse Farm, Halstead, Sevenoaks, Kent)
Founded in 1950 by Jane Dod (née Durrant)

Foundation Stock

Folly III: mare, 1934; ? bred by Mrs Wright of Chagford
Cicely Parsley (late Sprite II): mare, 1934; ? bred by Mrs Wright
Jemima II: mare, 1936; by Wee Devil out of Little Charm bred by Mrs Wright
Mrs Tiggywinkle: mare, 1936; by Wee Devil out of May V, bred by Mrs Wright
Miss Muffet: mare, 1936; by Dartmoor out of Starlight XV out of Sparklet II by The Leat, bred by Mrs Wright
Cherry Brook: mare, 1948; bred by Anne Coaker (breeding not given)

Notable Oatlands Stock

Oatlands Tabatha Twitchit: mare, 1951; by John out of Miss Muffet
Oatlands Mrs Tittlemouse: mare, 1953; by Jon out of Cherry Brook
Oatlands Jeremy Fisher: Stallion, 1954; by John out of Cherry Brook
Oatlands Diggory Delvet: stallion, 1961 ⎫ by Jentyl out of
Oatlands Mr McGregor: stallion, 1965 ⎭ O. Mrs Tittlemouse

Note: Several of the foregoing were initially registered without the prefix. Cherry Brook is variously spelt in the stud book as one or two words (two in the original registration). Note also that John and Jon are two different animals (both bred by Sylvia Calmady-Hamlyn).

The Senruf Stud

Cockerdale Farm, Oldstead, York
Founded 1961 by Colin & Margaret Furness

Foundation Stock

Toffee II: stallion, 1956; by John out of Treacle; bred by Lord Wilton
Syrup: mare, 1957; full sister to Toffee II
Boveycombe Gemini: mare, 1959; by Jenyn out of Fudge III, bred by Iris Gould
Whitmore Arbutus: stallion, 1959; by Janus out of Honeybags, bred by Imogen Slade (now McKinlay-Clark)
Blachford Greta: mare, 1967; by Cawsand Prince out of B. Brandween bred by Wing Commander Passy

Notable Senruf Stock

Senruf Abelia: mare, 1968; by Whitmore Arbutus out of Boveycombe Gemini
Senruf Grebe: stallion, 1973; by Hisley Woodcock out of B. Greta
Senruf Gorse: mare, 1978; by W. Arbutus out of B. Greta
Senruf Astra: mare, 1980; by Crimchard Firefly out of S. Abelia
Senruf Graduate: stallion, 1981; by W. Arbutus out of B. Greta

The Sherberton Stud

Great Sherberton, Princetown, Yelverton, Devon
First registration of Dartmoors by Frank Coaker in Volume XXI (1931–3) of the *NPS Stud Book*, but the Coaker family had been breeding Dartmoors for generations before then. Stud inherited by Frank's children John and Anne (now Anne Belam of the Haida Stud); present owner Diana Coaker, John's widow

Foundation Stock

Heatherbelle VI: mare, 1922 (about); bred at Tor Royal possibly by Dwarka
Brown Berry: stallion, 1929; breeding not stated
Smokey: stallion, age not recorded; ⎫ bred by George Smith
Icicle: stallion, 1946 ⎭ of Hexworthy

Notable Sherberton Stock

Dolly Grey VI: mare, 1925; by Dartmoor, out of Dolly Grey II
Peewit: stallion, 1929; by Dartmoor, out of Granite
Trump: stallion, 1929; by Dartmoor, out of Dolly Grey VI
Gem III: mare, 1930; breeding not stated
Brownbelle II: mare, 1935; by Brown Berry out of Heatherbelle VI
Linnet: mare, 1944; thought to be by Smokey out of Sherberton Eliza
Cherry Brook: mare, 1948; breeding not in stud book but known to be out of mare bought by Mrs Coaker Snr (*see also Oatlands Stud*).

The Shilstone Rocks Stud

Chittleford Farm, Widecombe in the Moor, Devon
Founded in 1960 by Elizabeth Newbolt-Young

Foundation Stock

Zippee: mare, 1951; by and out of Dartmoor ponies; bred by T. Wicks
Whitmore Honeybunch: mare, 1958; by Janus out of Honeybags; bred by Imogen Slade (now McKinlay-Clark)
Jurston May Storm of Shilstone Rocks: mare, 1960; by Storm II out of May Queen VII, bred by Molly Croft
Fall Out: mare, 1963; by Michelmass out of Gamma Ray, bred by Joan Montgomery

Notable Shilstone Rocks Stock

S.R. Windswept: mare, 1964; by Jude out of Zippee
S.R. Okement: stallion, 1966; by Petroc out of Caroline II
S.R. Darkness: stallion, 1966; by Easter out of Midgehope Melissa

S.R. Cloudburst II: stallion, 1970; by Petroc out of S.R. Rainstorm
S.R. Fury: stallion, 1971; by S.R. Darkness out of Fall Out
S.R. Rainy Day: mare, 1972; by S.R. Okement out of Jurston May Storm of S.R.
S.R. Another Bunch: mare, 1976; by S.R. Fury out of Whitmore Honeybunch
S.R. Easter Day: stallion, 1978; by S.R. Darkness out of S.R. Rainy Day
S.R. Hosanna: mare, 1979; by S.R. Fury out of Huntspath Hannah
S.R. D Day: stallion, 1980; by Catesby Cockspur out of S.R. Rainy Day

The Vean Stud

Until 1959: Pearroc Vean, Buckfast, Devon
1959–82: Bettman's Wood, Biddenden, Kent
From 1982: Hackpen Barton, Ashill, Cullompton, Devon
Established as a Dartmoor Stud by Sylvia Calmady-Hamlyn with the registration of Kezia in Volumes XVI-XVII (1919–1921); bequeathed to Patricia Robinson

Foundation Stock
Scintilla: mare, 1914; breeding not recorded
Judy V: mare, 1915; by Dartmoor out of Dartmoor, bred by Edmund Northey
The Leat: stallion, 1918; by Dwarka out of Blackdown, bred by Edward, Prince of Wales
Dora IV: mare, 1938; breeding not recorded
Wild Rose IV: mare, 1942; breeding not recorded

Notable Vean Stock
Juliet IV: mare, 1923; by The Leat out of Judy V
Sparklet II: mare, 1923; by The Leat out of Scintilla
Peewit III: mare, 1939; by Dinarth Spark out of Water Wag Tail
Jude: stallion, 1941; by Dinarth Spark out of Juliet IV
John: stallion, 1944; breeding not recorded (by Jude out of Dora IV)
Jenny VII: mare, 1945; by Jude out of Dora IV
Pipit: stallion, 1947; by Jude out of Peewit III
Janus: stallion, 1949; by Jude out of Dora IV
Jon: stallion, 1950; by Jude out of Dora IV
Jenyn: stallion, 1951; by Pipit out of Jenny VII
Jentyl: stallion, 1952; by Pipit out of Jenny VII
Jenson: stallion, 1954; by Pipit out of Jenny VII
Petroc: stallion, 1955; by Jude out of Peewit III
Jenetta: mare, 1955; by Jude out of Dora IV
Vean Blue Jennykin: mare, 1956; by Pipit out of Jenny VII
Vean Zelinda: mare, 1956; by Jude out of Zigzag

Vean Petrina: mare, 1960; by Petroc out of Jenetta
Vean Zaffer: stallion, 1960; by Petroc out of Vean Zelinda
Vean Mary Rose: mare, 1982; by Shilstone Rocks Easter Day out of Vean Dorelia
Vean Floribunda: mare, 1983; by Shilstone Rocks Easter Day out of Vean Flora Dora

The White Willows Stud

Yelverton, Devon
Founded 1957 by Joan Montgomery

Foundation Stock
Halloween II: mare, 1952; by Gay Boy out of Moorhen III; bred by Newman Caunter[1]
Gamma Ray: mare, 1954; by Teignhead out of Julia IV, bred by J. White
Jenyn: stallion, 1951; by Pipit out of Jenny VII, bred by Sylvia Calmady-Hamlyn (on loan from Patricia Robinson)

Notable White Willows Stock
Michelmass: stallion, 1958
Witchcraft: stallion, 1959 ⎫
Spellbound: mare, 1960 ⎬ by Jenyn out of Halloween II
White Willows Radium: mare, 1967; by Michelmass out of Gamma Ray
White Willows Sorceress: mare, 1969; full sister to Michelmass, Witchraft, Spellbound
White Willows Darwin: stallion, 1976; by Shilstone Rocks Baccarat out of White Willows Radium

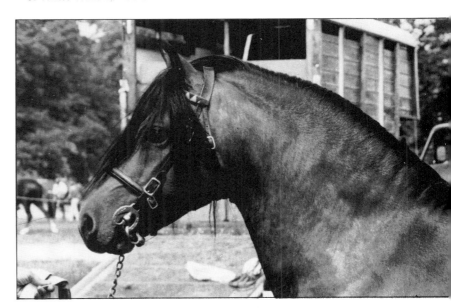

White Willows Darwin (1976)

[1] *From DPS certificate issued to Halloween's grandson, W.W. Prospero. The entry for Halloween in the stud book (Vol XXIX, page 25) gives no breeding at all. Moorhen, incidentally, was foaled in 1946 to Sylvia (see Chapter 13, page 74).*

White Willows Prospero (1979)

The Whitestone Stud

Cross Hills, Sutton under Whitestone Cliffs, Thirsk, North Yorkshire
Founded in 1959 by Hazel Hunter

Foundation Stock

Minerva V: mare, 1953; by Jude out of Miss Muffet VI, bred by Elspeth
  Ferguson
Genevieve II: mare, 1956; by Jenyn out of Sweet Brier; bred by Joan
  Montgomery
Fair Joanna: mare, 1956; by John out of Widecombe Fair, bred by
  Glenda Spooner
Vean White Rose: mare, 1957; by Pipit out of Wild Rose IV, bred by
  Sylvia Calmady-Hamlyn
Rose Vean Jack Snipe: stallion, 1958; by Janus out of Snipe, bred by
  Elspeth Ferguson

Notable Whitestone Stock

Whitestone Mint: mare, 1959; by Janus out of Minerva V
Whitestone Ragged Robin: stallion, 1961; by Rose Vean Jack Snipe out
  of Minerva V
Whitestone Bryony: mare, 1962 ⎫ by Rose Vean Jack Snipe
Whitestone Tudor Rose: mare, 1963 ⎬ out of Vean White Rose
Whitestone Rock Rose: mare, 1964 ⎭

Whitmore Arbutus (1959) at 22 years old

Whitestone Bayard; Stallion, 1973; by Petroc out of Shilstone Rocks Bay Wind

The Whitmore Stud

West Ford Farm, Cheriton Bishop, Exeter
Founded in 1957 by Xonia Slade and Imogen Slade now owned by Imogen McKinlay Clark

Foundation Stock

Honeybags: mare, 1945; by Dartmoor out of Treacle, bred by Major Bulteel
Sooty of the Barn: mare, 1947; by and out of Dartmoors, bred by I. S. Edwards
Josie: mare, 1957; by Julus out of Mahjong, bred by Mr & Mrs A.R.B. Owen

Notable Whitmore Stock

Whitmore Honeybunch: mare, 1958
Whitmore Arbutus: stallion, 1959
Whitmore Honeymoon: mare, 1960 } by Janus out of Honeybags
Whitmore Honey Dew: mare, 1962
Whitmore Titania: mare, 1969; by Whitmore Arbutus out of Imp of Torr
Whitmore Royal Prince: stallion, 1983; by White Willows Othello out of Whitmore Jubilee

The Yeoland Stud

Yelverton, Devon
Later: Holdscroft Farm, Marshwood, Dorset
Founded in 1944 by Jean Hyett and Patricia Hyett (now Jean Palmer and Patricia Robinson) since 1959 Jean Palmer on her own

Foundation Stock

Bucktor Queen: mare, 1924, by Dartmoor pony out of Virtuous Lady; bred by Syd Horrell
Yeoland Lady Hamilton: mare, 1935; by Cawsand Dinky out of Daisy XVI bred by E.W. White & Son
Yeoland Lord Nelson: stallion, 1939; by Grey Wethers out of Princess; bred by F. Webber
Yeoland Pussy Willow: mare, 1942; by Dartmoor pony out of Y. Lady Hamilton; bred by E.W. White & Son
Cater's Beam: mare, 1946; by Young Joe out of Little Princess; bred by F. Webber

Notable Yeoland Stock

Yeoland Beepety Bump: mare, 1946; by Y. Lord Nelson out of Bucktor Queen
Catkin: mare, 1947; by Dartmoor pony out of Y. Pussy Willow
Yeoland Horatia: mare, 1947; by Y. Lord Nelson out of Y. Lady Hamilton
Yeoland Belinda: mare,1967; by Vean Zaffer out of Vean Gentian
Yeoland May: mare, 1976; by Whitestone Bayard out of Yeoland June
Yeoland Juliet: mare, 1985; by White Willows Prospero out of Vean Honeysuckle

FOUR ESTABLISHMENTS HORS CONCOURS

Little Lyndridge

Okehampton, Devon
Founded 1922-4 by Joan Vinson-Thomas

As mentioned in the text (Chapter 11, p. 59), the life of Little Lyndridge was short but glorious, a mere matter of some eight years when its ponies won virtually everything they went in for. Then, in 1930 a blanket of silence, not yet dispelled.

His Nibs of Lyndridge (1921, by and out of Dartmoors, bred by Albert Hodge of Higher Halstock, Okehampton) was the most notable of its foundation stock – his many successes are recounted in Chapter 11.

So far it has not been possible to trace any modern descendants of this stock. For all that, it is felt that no history of the Dartmoor pony is complete without a mention of the Lyndridge Stud.

Foundation Stock

His Nibs of Lyndridge: stallion, 1921 (see above)
Lyndridge Sally: mare, 1920, bred by H. Ewens of Pothanger, Okehampton
Lyndridge Tinkle: stallion, 1925; by The Leat out of D. Tinsel, bred by C. Jordan of Bratton, Clovelly

The Lyndridge prefix was used for almost all the ponies registered by the Little Lyndridge Stud, irrespective of whether these were home grown or from elsewhere. The record shows that most of the important prizes were won by one or other of the trio named above.

The Leighon Stud

Manaton, Newton Abbot, Devon
Founded in 1944 by Sir John Bulteel

Foundation Stock

Burnt Sugar: mare, aged; by Dartmoor out of Dartmoor
Chinkwell: mare, aged; by Dartmoor out of Dartmoor
Granite: mare, aged; by Dartmoor out of Dartmoor
Treacle: mare, 1942; by Dartmoor out of Dartmoor
John: stallion, 1944; out of Dora, bred by Sylvia Calmady-Hamlyn
Jamaica Inn: mare, 1945; by Dartmoor out of Burnt Sugar
Tiny: stallion, 1948; by Joe out of Betty XXI, bred by Tom Holman

Notable Leighon Stock

Bellever: stallion, 1945; by Dartmoor pony out of Chinkwell
Honeybags: mare, 1945; by Dartmoor out of Treacle
Mountain Sweet: mare, 1948; by Bellever out of Treacle
Plymouth Rock: mare, 1949; by Bellever out of Treacle
Off Ration: mare, 1951; by John out of Burnt Sugar
Honey-Locust: mare, 1951; by John out of Honeybags
Mahjong: mare, 1951; by John out of Chinkwell
Mewstone: mare, 1953; by John out of Plymouth Rock

Sir John bred Dartmoors for only a decade, but in that time produced some first-class ponies, starting in many cases from unnamed, even unknown, sires and dams (with the exception of John, acquired about 1950). He was also fortunate in the number of filly-foals in those early years which enabled him to build up his stud. (Volume XXVI of the stud book (1948–52) lists five colts and no fewer than twenty-four fillies; not conclusive, but a strong pointer.) The descendants of Plymouth Rock, Mountain Sweet (full sisters), Honeybags and Mahjong are winning today.

The Higher Tor Stud

Rixhill, Tavistock
Founded in 1920 by Sydney Horrell

Foundation Stock
Polly V: mare, 1905; bred by J. Hopper of Tavistock
Virtuous Lady: mare, 1919; by Little Star (1899) by Star, out of Polly V

Notable Higher Tor Stock
Bucktor Queen: mare, 1924; by Dartmoor out of Dartmoor
Moorman: stallion, 1924;
Silver Leaf II: mare, 1926; out of Virtuous Lady
Bucktor: stallion, 1928; out of Virtuous Lady
Sammy II: stallion, 1933
Midget V: mare, 1937; by Sammy II out of Virtuous Lady
Daybreak: mare, 1944; by Sammy II out of Midget V
Higher Tor Marksman: stallion, 1957; by Jenyn out of Midget VI
Higher Tor Dawn Skies: mare, 1960; by Higher Tor Marksman out of Daybreak
Higher Tor Midget: mare, 1965; by Peter Tavy out of Higher Tor Dawn Skies

Syd Horrell epitomized the moorman breeder of Dartmoors. He bred many good ponies from sires and dams he chose without reference to any stud book. He didn't bother to register his Higher Tor prefix until 1960. A Member of the DPS council since the twenties, a panel judge for over thirty years, he was made an Honorary Life Member in 1973 after over half a century's association with the breed. Probably his best known Dartmoor was Midget V, DPS Show Champion in 1949 and 1950. Her memory is kept green by her portrait on the cover of each year's *Dartmoor Diary*.

Tor Royal

Princetown, Yelverton, Devon
Founded in 1916 by H.R.H. The Prince of Wales (later King Edward VIII) as Duke of Cornwall

Tor Royal was not a Dartmoor stud in the accepted sense, in that its purpose was other than to breed Dartmoors as such. True, it bought a number of Dartmoors and even bred a few, but only to serve as out-crosses to produce polo ponies, pack horses and the like.

It is not surprising, therefore, that few Tor Royal Dartmoors made any mark on the pony world. The Sherberton Stud bought Heatherbelle VI at the dispersal sale in 1931 – she was a big winner in the early thirties – and that was about all. Yet not quite.

Whatever the original intention, there was one happy outcome, for at Tor Royal there was bred the pony that many Dartmoor experts would maintain was the greatest Dartmoor of them all and from which almost every high-quality Dartmoor alive today is descended.

The circumstances of The Leat's birth have been recounted in the main text; we repeat them in outline to emphasise the uncertainty inherent in all such matters. He was one-half pure Arab (from Dwarka), one-quarter roadster (from Confident George), one-quarter Dartmoor (from an unnamed 'Dartmoor pony' grandam). Result: the incomparable Dartmoor.

FOUNDATION STOCK AND THEIR PROGENY

By Peter Upton

Note:

Foundation ponies of the Dartmoor breed are the original ponies registered in the *Dartmoor Pony Stud Book* from which all present-day ponies can be traced. Ponies are listed in order of registration. These tables do not include all the offspring of any one mare or stallion, but a selection of the more important lines.

Upper case indicates a stallion
Lower case indicates a mare

* indicates a FOUNDATION pony
FS indicates a FOUNDATION stallion
FM indicates a FOUNDATION mare

Each indentation from the left indicates one generation

DARTMOOR FOUNDATION STALLIONS

FS No.   1 LITTLE STAR
2 THE LEAT
3 GREY WETHERS
4 JOLLY JANKIN
5 PUNCH
6 BROWNBERRY
7 SAMMY II
8 JUDE
9 JULIAN II
10 CHRYS
11 FOXTROT
12 YEOLAND BOB-A-NOB
13 GAY BOY IV
14 BELLEVER
15 ICICLE
16 SILVER DOLLAR
17 TEIGNHEAD
18 HELE ROMEO
19 RANGER III
20 RAYBARROW POOL
21 SHERBERTON NEWMAN
22 TINY

FS1 LITTLE STAR 315. Vol. 8. br. Foaled 1897. 12.1½hh.
White spot on heel

Sire: BOLD VENTURE. br.13hh. D.P.
ex. bl. D.P.12.1hh
Dam: Star. bl. 12.1½hh. D.P.

Breeder:
Delia Doidge,
Lamerton Villa,
Nr. Tavistock

Sire of: Virtuous Lady. b. 1919 (Polly V *FM1)

————

FS2 THE LEAT 1068. Vol.18. b. Foaled 1918. 12.2hh.
White hind heel

Sire: DWARKA b. 1892. 14.1½hh
(A desert-bred Arab)
Dam: Blackdown *FM3

Breeder:
H.R.H. The Prince of Wales,
Duchy Stud, Tor Royal,
Princetown
Owner:
Miss S. Calmady-Hamlyn

Sire of: Juliet IV br. 1923 (Judy V *FM2)
Sparklet II gr. 1923 (Scintilla *FM5)
Water Wagtail bl. 1924 (Scintilla *FM5)

————

FS3 GREY WETHERS 1307. Vol. 19. gr. Foaled 1924. Brand C-H

Sire: South Tawton Assoc.
br. Stallion
Dam: Blue Haze *FM7

Breeder:
H.J. Madders, South Zeal
Owner:
Miss S. Calmady-Hamlyn,
Pearroc Vean, Buckfast

Sire of: YEOLAND LORD NELSON b. 1939 (Little Princess *FM10)
Yeoland Horatia b. 1947 (Yeoland Lady Hamilton) FM4

————

FS4 JOLLY JANKIN 1447. Vol.19. bl. Foaled 1921. 11.3hh.
Brand MM
Sire: D.P. br. 12.1hh
Dam: D.P. bl. 12.1hh

Breeder:
Geo Mortimore Jr,
Collihole, Chagford
Owners: John Isaac
Addiscote, South Zeal and
Miss S. Calmady-Hamlyn,

Sire of: JOE III (Later YOUNG JAN) bl. 1927 (Queenie VII *FM6)
JANWYN br. 1933 (Cornwood Winnie *FM21)
Sherberton Eliza b. 1937 (Heatherbelle VI *FM8)

————

FS5 PUNCH 1726 Vol.20. br. Foaled 1925. 12hh.
Punch hole each ear   Breeder:
Sire: D.P. b. 12hh   E.W. White and Son,
Dam: Fairy III *FM4   Lambe House, South Zeal

Sire of: BOXER b. 1930 (Sparklet II) *FM5
Countess VIII b.ro.1945 (Julia IV) FM4
Queenie XXIII b.ro.1948 (Countess VIII) FM4
Molly XXI b.1949 (Countess VIII) FM4
Starlight XV gr. 1932 (Sparklet II) FM4

FS6 BROWNBERRY 2128 Vol. 23. br. Foaled 1929. 12hh.
Brand   near-side saddle   Breeder:
                                             Owner: J. Coaker,
                                             Great Sherberton

Sire of: Brownbelle II b. 1936 (Heatherbelle VI *FM8)

FS7 SAMMY II. Vol. 23. dk br. Foaled 1933. 12.1hh.
Star. Near-hind fetlock white, Brand H both sides
(only registered as a gelding)   Breeder: Sydney Horrell, Bucktor
Sire: D.P.
Dam: D.P.

Sire of: Midget V b. 1937 (Virtuous Lady) FM1

FS8 JUDE 2423 Vol. 24. bl. Foaled 1941
Sire: DINARTH SPARK (W.S.B.) gr.   Breeders: Miss N. Dawson and
Dam: Juliet IV (FM2)   Miss Calmady-Hamlyn.
                                          Owner: Miss Calmady-Hamlyn

Sire of: JOHN br. 1944 (Dora IV *FM55)
Jacaranda bl. 1951 (Mountain Sweet) FM32
OATLANDS JEREMY FISHER br. 1954 (Cherrybrook *FM36)
CRUACHAN KINGFISHER br. 1967 Oatlands Tabitha Twitchet) FM5
BLUE JOHN gr. 1955 (Belstone) FM33
PARKLANDS PARAGON b. 1967 (Red Hall Aries) FM30
Blythford Scilla bl. 1969 (Azalia) FM19
Pilgrims Progress b. 1955 (Plymouth Rock) FM32
TOFFEE II B. 1956 (Treacle *FM32)
Syrup b. 1957 (Treacle *FM32)
Jenny VII br. 1945 (Dora IV *FM55)
PETE bl. 1945 (Peewit III) FM5
JEF gr. 1946 (Judith III) FM2
STORM II gr. 1949 (Dawn V *FM12)
Coronet II gr. 1953 (Hornbeam *FM35)
JURSTON SPINDRIFT gr. 1954 (Hornbeam *FM35)
PIPIT gr. 1947 (Peewit III) FM5
JENYN bl. 1951 (Jenny VII) FM55
MICHELMASS bl. 1958 (Halloween II) FM25
EASTER bl. 1961 (Hele Juliet III) FM46
Shilstone Rocks Rainstorm bl. 1964 (Jurston Maystorm) FM6
SHILSTONE ROCKS DARKNESS bl. 1966 (Midgehope Melissa) FM4
Shilstone Rocks Dark Phantome bl. 1971 (Sh. R. Bewitched) FM62

SHILSTONE ROCKS DARKNESS continued
Sh.R Dark Mountain bl. 1971 (Huntspath Hannah) FM32
SHILSTONE ROCKS FURY b. 1971 (Fall Out) FM4
Sh,R. Another Bunch b. 1976 (Whitmore Honeybunch) FM32
SH.R. JEHOVAH bl. 1976 (Huntspath Hannah) FM32
Pantmanrs Junket bl. 1980 (Park Barn Dance) FM28
SH.R. CLOUDBURST II b. 1977 (Sh.R. Rainstorm) FM6
Sh.R. Hosanna bl. 1979 (Huntspath Hannah) FM32
WHITE WILLOWS PROSPERO br. 1979 (Spellbound) FM25
Yeoland Juliet b. 1985 (Vean Honeysuckle) FM2
LANGFIELD ROTH b. 1986 (Langfield Noilly Prat) FM43
Shilstone Rocks Whirligig b. 1972 (Sh.R. Whirlwind) FM41
SH.R BACCARAT b. 1973 (Whitmore Jokari) FM30
WHITE WILLOWS DARWIN b. 1976 (Wh.W. Radium) FM4
ALLENDALE VAMPIRE b. 1980 (Allendale Black Magic) FM59
WH.W WITCHDOCTOR b. 1984 (Wh.W. Sorceress) FM25
Wh.W Spellbound br. 1987 (Wh.W. Halloween III) FM25
Shilstone Rocks Bagatelle bl. 1974 (Whitmore Jokari) FM30
Crimchard Fantasia b. 1974 (Crimchard Fantasy) FM34
Boveycombe Bunting br. 1975 (Boveycombe Heron) FM61
SH.R EASTER DAY b. 1978 (Sh.R. Rainy Day) FM6
Stonehealed Tarantella b. 1982 (Park Barn Dance) FM28
Vean Mary Rose b. 1982 (Vean Dorelia) FM55
Vean Dorabella II bl. 1984 (Vean Dorelia) FM55
VEAN BLACK JACK bl. 1985 (Vean Dorelia) FM4
SH.R FASTNET FURY b. 1979 (Sh.R. Rockfall) FM4
Langfield Chanel b. 1982 (Blachford Brandween) FM45
LANGFIELD CANTH b. 1983 (Langfield Noilly Prat) FM43
Dykes Daisymead bl. 1986 (Stokeleigh Muffet) FM43
DYKES ACANTHUS bl. 1988 (Stokeleigh Muffet) FM43
Wendel Sea Spray b. 1988 (Langfield Green Ginger) FM18
SHILSTONE ROCKS DARK DAY b. 1982 (Sh.R. Rainy Day) FM6
Stonehealed Daydream b. 1985 (Crimchard Fantasy) FM43
Haven Halina bl. 1983 (Huntspath Hannah) FM32
Dunros Martini b. 1984 (Catesby Scrapit) FM50
Azalia bl. 1962 (Molly XIX) *FM19
Fall Out b. 1963 (Gamma Ray) FM4
Telstar b. 1964 (Gamma Ray) FM4
White Willows Radiation ch. 1965 (Gamma Ray) FM4
White Willows Radium b. 1967 (Gamma Ray) FM4
Millcroft Bewitched bl. 1967 (Rose Vean Curlew) FM54
Boveycombe Gemini b. 1959 (Fudge III *FM56)
Spellbound b. 1960 (Halloween II) FM25
White Willows Sorceress bl. 1969 (Halloween II) FM25
JESTER IV br. 1957 (Yeoland Lady Hamilton) FM4
(PIPIT) JENTYL bl. 1952 (Jenny VII) FM55
OATLANDS DIGGORY DELVET bl. 1961 (Oatlands Mrs Tittlemouse) FM36
Winkie Pop III bl. 1967 (Off Ration) FM31
Dunros Peppermint bl. 1967 (Whitestone Cornmint) FM16
Vean Honeysuckle bl. 1967 (Vean Jentylys) FM2
WHITE WILLOWS MACBETH bl. 1968 (Spellbound) FM25
RYLANDS BAYLEAF b. 1972 (Cottage Garden) FM30
Senruf Tiffany b. 1976 (Senruf Tiffin) FM56
Springs Rowan bl. 1973 (Blythford Robinia) FM19
Kilbees Skylark bl. 1963 (Dunnabridge Tansy) FM25
OATLANDS MR MCGREGOR b. 1965 (Oatlands Mrs Tittlemouse) FM36

OATLANDS MR MCGREGOR continued

    Catesby Honeypot br. 1971 (Honey Bee III) FM32
    Catesby Honeyset bl. 1972 (Honey Bee III) FM32
    CATESBY COCKSPUR b. 1973 (Catesby Orchis) FM32
     SHILSTONE ROCKS D. DAY b. 1981 (Sh.R. Rainy Day) FM6
    Oakfield Linnet b. 1974 (Ellimore Tavy) FM15
    CATESBY PIP bl. 1974 (Peppa) FM46
    CATESBY CRUSADER II B. 1976 (Busy Bee V) FM32
     Catesby Scrapit ch. 1979 (Catesby Catkin) FM50
    OAKFIELD ROBIN bl. 1978 (Whitmore Calluna) FM24
    Whinberry Truffle b. 1980 (Springs Mountain Rose) FM45
    PUMPHILL BEAU GESTE b. 1982 (Allendale Black Magic) FM59
    PUMPHILL BEAU SABREUR b. 1985 (Allendale Black Magic) FM59
    KILBEES MR JINGLE bl. 1970 (Red Hall Auriga) FM30
    Park Barn Dance b. 1975 (Hambledon Juno) FM28
    KILBEES PLANET b. 1974 (Red Hall Auriga) FM30
(PIPIT) Vean Wayzgoose gr. 1953 (Zigzag) FM2
JENSON br. 1954 (Jenny VII) FM55
 Rose Vean Teal b. 1960 (Snipe) *FM54
 PETER TAVY II b. 1960 (Jurston Mary Tavy) FM15
  Hisley Quince b. 1964 (Queenie XXIII) FM4
  HISLEY WOODCOCK b. 1962 (Dunnabridge Wigeon) FM24
   Hisley Candleight b. 1972 (Hele Judith II) FM45
   SENRUF GREBE b. 1973 (Blachford Greta) FM45
    Senruf Arabella b. 1977 (Senruf-Abelia) FM56
    MARINA HARBOUR MASTER b. 1984 (Park Blueberry) FM31
   Hisley Cherry Brandy b. 1979 (Blachford Brandween) FM45
   Hisley Polonaise b. 1982 (Torfields Pretty Penny) FM4
   HISLEY SALVO b. 1983 (Hisley Serenade) FM6
    Hisley Charisma b. 1986 (Hisley Caviar) FM45
   Hisley Stardust b. 1984 (Hisley Serenade) FM6
   CRIMCHARD BRIGHT SPARK b. 1966 (Whitmore Honeymoon) FM32
   Crimchard Fantasy b. 1970 (Fair Joanna) FM43
   CRIMCHARD FANFARE b. 1972 (Fair Joanna) FM43
   CRIMCHARD FIREFLY br. 1973 (Fair Joanna) FM43
    Senruf Astra bl. 1980 (Senruf Abelia) FM56
   Hambledon Juno b. 1966 (Sooty of the Barn *FM28)
  VEAN WILDFIRE gr. 1956 (Wild Rose IV *FM18)
  WITCHCRAFT bl. 1959 (Halloween II) FM25
   Huntspath Josephine bl. 1964 (Jacaranda) FM32
 Vean Blue Jennykin gr. 1956 (Jenny VII) FM55
 VEAN VENCOCK gr. 1957 (Zigzag) FM2
 Vean White Rose b. 1957 (Wild Rose IV *FM18)
 VEAN ZERO gr. 1960 (Zigzag) FM2
  Midgehope Japonica bl. 1969 (Sherberton Judy) FM39
 Rose Vean Curlew gr. 1961 (Snipe *FM54)
 Catesby Peewit gr. 1962 (Mola *FM50)
 Rose Vean Peewit bl. 1962 (Snipe *FM54)
 PARKLANDS PIPPIN bl. 1963 (Pilgrim's Progress) FM32
  Over the Moon br. 1966 (Oatlands Cottontail) FM5
(JUDE) JANUS bl. 1949 (Dora IV *FM55)
 ROSE VEAN JACK SNIPE b. 1958 (Snipe *FM54)
  WHITESTONE RAGGED ROBIN b. 1961 (Minerva V) FM16
   Catesby Siskin b. 1966 (Catesby Peewit) FM50
   Blytheford Robinia bl. 1966 (Azalia) FM19
   Catesby Orchis b. 1970 (Honey Bee III) FM32

WHITESTONE RAGGED ROBIN continued

   BEVERLEY PEACOCK b. 1972 (Rose Vean Peewit) FM54
   Springs Mountain Rose b. 1975 (Hele Judith III) FM45
   SPRINGS NOUGAT br. 1976 (Hele Judith III) FM45
    Moseley Springtime b. 1982 (Saucy Miss) FM60
    Moseley Miss Braithley b. 1983 (Saucy Miss) FM60
   Vean Floradora br. 1974 (White Willows Radiation) FM4
   Whitestone Rock Rose br. 1964 (Vean White Rose) FM18
(JANUS) WHITMORE ARBUTUS bl. 1959 (Honeybags) FM32
  Senruf Rose Hip br. 1962 (Syrup) FM32
  Midgehope Jonquil bl. 1964 (Sherberton Judy) FM39
  Senruf Abelia bl. 1968 (Boveycombe Gemini) FM56
  Whitmore Jigsaw b.1969 (Josie) FM30
  Whitmore Titania bl. 1969 (Imp of Tor) FM59
  Whitmore Calluna b. 1970 (Dunnabridge Ling) FM24
  Senruf Jacaranda bl. 1978 (Midgehope Japonica) FM39
  Senruf Gorse b. 1978 (Blachford Greta) FM45
  SENRUF SOLOMON br. 1980 (Senruf Susanna) FM32
  SENRUF GRADUATE b. 1981 (Blachford Greta) FM45
 Red Hall Auriga b. 1959 (Cottage Garden) FM30
 Miss Muffet of Robins bl. 1959 (Widecombe Fair) *FM43
 JASPER bl. 1959 (Mountain Sweet) FM32
  BLACK VELVET br. 1962 (Sherberton Whisky) FM8
   SHERBERTON FIGARO bl. 1977 (Sherberton Woodlark) FM8
    Sherberton Mudilake bl. 1980 (Sherberton Twinkle Again) FM8
 Whitmore Honeymoon br. 1960 (Honeybags) FM32
 Janessa bl. 1961 (Off Ration) FM31
 Whitmore Honeymead br. 1963 (Honeybags) FM32
(JUDE) JON b. 1950 (Dora IV) *FM55
 Oatlands Mrs Tittlemouse b. 1953 (Cherrybrook) *FM36
 Red Hall Hydra gr. 1959 (Belstone) FM33
 RED HALL AQUARIUS b. 1959 (Beaver) *FM11
  Shilstone Rocks Horizon b. 1968 (Jennifer IV) FM45
  SHILSTONE ROCKS ACHILLES b. 1969 (Fall Out) FM4
   Crimchard Honeylove b. 1975 (Whitmore Honeymoon) FM32
   Mistress Mary of Plovers b. 1977 (Plovers Bo-Peep) FM5
   Crimchard Fairy Tale b. 1978 (Crimchard Fantasia) FM43
  HUNTSPATH HOLLY b. 1969 (Huntspath Josephine) FM32
  ALLENDALE FLAUROS bl. 1974 (Whitmore Titania) FM59
   Hisley Serenade b. 1978 (Sweetie Pie) FM6
   BOVEYCOMBE BO'SUN br. 1979 (Boveycombe Bunting) FM61
   TORFIELDS PENNYWORTH br. 1980 (Torfields Pretty Penny) FM4
    PLOVERS TUPPENY RICE b. 1986 (Crimchard Honeylove) FM32
   Whinberry Moonlight b. 1982 (Springs Mountain Rose) FM45
   WHINBERRY QUALITY WAY bl. 1984 (Springe Quality Street) FM45
  ALLENDALE EXORCIST bl. 1975 (Whitmore Titania) FM59
  DARNBROOK DRAMATIST b. 1984 (Catesby Miss Perkins) FM32
 RED HALL PERSEUS b. 1961 (Pilgrim's Progress) FM32
 Red Hall Aries b. 1962 (Cottage Garden) FM30
 JONACA ch. 1962 (Cater's Beam) FM10
  Sweetie Pie b. 1966 (Heather Queen) FM6
  Bittleford Surprise II b. 1971 (Surprise) FM60
 Kilbees Jenny Too bl. 1966 (Vean Blue Jennykin) FM55
 Park Blueberry b. 1968 (Blue Grass) FM31
 KILBEES MR PICKWICK b. 1969 (Vean Blue Jennykin) FM55
  Kilbees Blythe Spirit bl. 1974 (Dunnabridge Tansy) FM25

KILBEES MR PICKWICK continued

    Kilbees Sirius b. 1977 (Red Hall Auriga) FM30
    KILBEES PLOVER bl. 1971 (Kilbees Skylark) FM25
(JUDE) JULUS br. 1951 (Wild Rose IV) *FM18
    LAMMERMUIR RAMBLER b. 1964 (Plymouth Rock) FM32
    HISLEY PEDLAR b. 1970 (Hisley Quince) FM4
      Torfields Pretty Penny b. 1973 (Penny II) FM4
      Hisley Caviar b. 1975 (Blachford Brandween) FM45
      HISLEY COGNAC b. 1977 (Blachford Brandween) FM45
      Langfield Noilly Prat b. 1979 (Stokeleigh Muffs Pet) FM43
      Langfield Green Ginger b. 1979 (Stokeleigh Wild Rose) FM18
      Langfield Miz Sophie b. 1984 (Ryland Castanet) FM46
      SENRUF GLADIATOR b. 1987 (Blachford Greta) FM45
    Minerva V b. 1953 (Miss Muffet VI) *FM16
    PETROC gr. 1955 (Peewit III) FM5
    Vean Petrina bl. 1960 (Jenetta) FM55
    VEAN ZAFFER gr. 1960 (Vean Zelinda) FM2
      VEAN BROWN WILLY bl. 1971 (Vean Petrina) FM55
      VEAN ZENNOR bl. 1973 (White Willows Radiation) FM4
    SHILSTONE ROCKS OKEMENT b. 1966 (Caroline II) FM8
    Shilstone Rocks Quercina b. 1971 (Shilstone Rocks Cavallina) FM4
    Shilstone Rocks Rainy Day b. 1972 (Shilstone Rocks Rainstorm) FM6
    WHITESTONE BAYARD b. 1973 (Shilstone Rocks Bay Wind) FM15
    Vean Dorelia bl. 1976 (Vean Petrina) FM55
    Yeoland May bl. 1976 (Yeoland June) FM55
    BRANDSBY TORNADO b. 1975 (Shilstone Rocks Bay Wind) FM15
    BRANDSBY CYCLONE b. 1978 (Blythford Scilla) FM19
      Brandsby Honeybunch b. 1981 (Catesby Honeyset) FM32
      NAPPA COUNTRY BOY b. 1982 (Sh. Rocks Country Bunch) FM32
      SHILSTONE ROCKS ROUGH DAY b. 1984 (Sh.R. Rainy Day) FM6
      Shilstone Rocks Cascade II b. 1987 (Fall Out) FM4
      Shilstone Rocks Musada b. 1986 (Sh.R. Dark Mountain) FM32
      Pantmanrs Jaunt b. 1985 (Pantmanrs Junket) FM28
    Stokeleigh Wild Rose b. 1975 (Whitestone Rock Rose) FM18
    Jenetta gr. 1955 (Dora IV) *FM55
    VEAN PARTRIDGE gr. 1956 (Peewit III) FM5
    Rose Vean Quail b. 1959 (Snipe) *FM54
    Blue Grass gr. 1959 (Small Fry) FM31
    Rose Vean Grilse gr. 1960 (Vean Wayzgoose) FM2
    Vean Zelinda gr. 1956 (Zigzag) FM2
    BOVEYCOMBE LEO b. 1961 (Fudge III) *FM56
    BOVEYCOMBE JOUSTER bl. 1964 (Skaigh Princess) *FM27
    Cosdon May bl. 1970 (Skaigh Princess) FM27
    BOVEYCOMBE BUCKTHORN bl. 1971 (Pillar) FM46
    Boveycombe Heron b. 1971 (Shilstone Rocks Sanduck) FM61
    WHITE WILLOWS SHYLOCK bl. 1978 (Spellbound) FM25
    CRIMCHARD FREE 'N EASY b. 1983 (Crimchard Fantasia) FM43
    Walreddon Starlight b. 1980 (Walreddon Dawn) FM1
    Senruf Juliet br. 1963 (Boveycombe Gemini) FM56
    Shilstone Rocks Windswept b. 1964 (Zippee) *FM41

FS9 JULIAN II 2469. Vol. 25. bl. Foaled 1944.
  Irregular star.   Breeder: Miss M.E. Croft
  Sire: D.P.
  Dam: Sweet Vernal *FM9

Sire of: Mayfly V b. 1949 (Wings) *FM13

FS10 CHRYS 2745. Vol. 26. b. Foaled 1947
  Star. Off hind pastern white.   Breeder: Miss M.E. Croft
  Sire: D.P.
  Dam: Fern *FM14

Sire of: Jurston Mary Tavy b. 1951 (Mary Tavy II *FM15)

FS11 FOXTROT 2845. Vol. 26. b.ro. Foaled 1946. 11.3hh.
  Brand 1.C.   Breeder: Joan Coaker,
                             Sherberton
  Sire: SMOKEY (unreg)
  Dam: Sherberton Eliza b. 1937 (Heatherbelle VI) *FM8

Sire of: QUICKSTEP ro. 1949 (Heatherbelle VI) *FM8
      Sherberton Sherry br. 1953 (Sherberton Sweet Pea) FM8
      Sherberton Heatherbelle b. 1950 (Heatherbelle VI) *FM8
      SHERBERTON TWO STEP gr. 1952 (Brownbelle II) FM8
      Sherberton Stone Chat gr. 1956 (Linnet) FM8
      SHERBERTON SILVERTIME gr. 1957 (Sherberton Lilac Time) FM37
      SHERBERTON SILVER LINNET gr. 1961 (Linnet) FM8
        SHERBERTON PENGUIN gr. 1964 (Sher. Blackbird) *FM51
        Sherberton Titanic gr. 1968 (Sher. Titania) FM38
        Sherberton Little Belle b. 1979 (Sher. Brown Belle V) FM8
      SHERBERTON SILVER TICKET gr. 1962 (Sher. Label) *FM 52
      SHERBERTON SANDMARTIN gr. 1967 (Stonemartin)
        Sherberton Bridesmaid II gr. 1979 (Sher. Bridesmaid) FM58
        Sherberton Calamity gr. 1979 (Sher. Loppy L) FM53

FS12 YEOLAND BOB-A-NOB Vol. 26. br. Foaled 1945.
  Brand PJ. near side (only reg. as a gelding)   Breeder: Miss P.E. Hyett
  Sire: D.P.
  Dam: Yeoland Pussy Willow b. (Yeoland Lady Hamilton) FM4

Sire of: ROBERT EMMET br. 1948 (Yeoland Lady Hamilton) FM4
      Dusk IV br. 1952 (Yeoland Beepety Bump) FM1

FS13 GAY BOY IV 2937 Vol. 26. br. Foaled 1948.
Brand HC near saddle   Breeder: R.H. Caunter,
                                         Dunnabridge

Sire: D.P.
Dam: Sylvia bl. (unreg. by BOXER F25)

Sire of: Dunnabridge Goose Girl br. 1951 (Gooseberry II) *FM24
Halloween II bl. 1952 (Moorhen III) *FM25
HUCCABY b. 1952 (DP)
  DUNNABRIDGE BONNY BOY b. 1955 (Moorhen III) *FM25
  Kilbees Firenzi b. 1964 (Venetia) FM55
DUNNABRIDGE b. 1958 (Wonder Why II) *FM29
  CAWSAND PRINCE br. 1961 (Skaigh Princess) FM27
  Crookety Candytuft br. 1966 (Fair Diana) FM26
  Blachford Greta b. 1967 (Blachford Brandween) FM45
  Hisley Quill b. 1962 (Queenie XXIII) FM4
CAWSAND CAVALIER br. 1960 (Betty XXI) *FM27
  CRIMCHARD PLAYBOY br. 1967 (Whitmore Honeymoon) FM32
  Cruachan Moonflight b. 1979 (Cruachan Moonbeam) FM34
  Higher Tor Bridget b. 1969 (Higher Tor Midget) FM1
CROOKETY CAVALCADE br. 1970 (Crookety Candytuft) FM26
  CROOKETY MOONSTONE b. 1981 (Sh.R. Horizon) FM45
  Senruf Jingle br. 1972 (Joybelle of Tor) FM4
  Blachford Brandween b. 1962 (Hele Judith II) FM45
                    *———————————

FS14 BELLEVER 3033. Vol.26. br. Foaled 1945.
Brand B near saddle   Breeder: Major J.C. Bulteel

Sire: D.P.
Dam: Chinkwell *FM30

Sire of: Mountain Sweet br. 1948 (Treacle) *FM32
Belstone gr. 1948 (Granite) *FM33
Plymouth Rock br. 1949 (Treacle) *FM32
                    ———————————

FS15 ICICLE 3034. Vol.26. gr. Foaled 1946. 11.3hh.
Brand S.   Breeder: Geo Smith, Hexworthy
                                  Owner: J. Coaker, Sherberton

Sire: D.P.
Dam D.P.

Sire of: COCK ROBIN II b. 1950 (Linnet) FM8
PIXIE III b. 1953 (Fay) *FM17
Mayflower X b. 1957 (Mayfly V) *FM13
                    ———————————

FS16 SILVER DOLLAR 3166. Vol.26. b. Foaled 1947. 12.0hh
Small Star. Off ear nicked. Brand M nr quarterBreeder: Mann Bros, Widecombe
                                         Owners: Mr & Mrs Reep

Sire: D.P.
Dam: D.P.

Sire of: Sherberton Whisky br. 1958 (Sherberton Sherry) FM8
Windfall of Shilstone Rocks b. 1962 (Zippie) *FM41
Lodestone of Tor gr. 1966 (Belstone) FM33
                    ———————————

FS 17 TEIGNHEAD 3402. Vol.27. b. Foaled 1948.
Brand R.   Breeder: J. Rowe,
                                  Great Frenchbeer, Chagford
                                  Owner: Mrs K.J. Jackson

Sire: D.P.
Dam: D.P.

Sire of: Gamma Ray b. 1954 (Julia IV) FM4
Caroline II b. 1954 (Chymes) FM8
BROWN BERRY III b. 1955 (Brownie XVIII) *FM23
  MOORTOWN BERRY b. 1961 (Granite II) *FM49
  MOORTOWN LAD gr. 1963 (Granite II) *FM49
  MOORTOWN ROBERT b. 1978 (Granite II) *FM49
                    ———————————

FS18 HELE ROMEO 3404. Vol.27. dk b. Foaled 1948
                                  Breeder: A. Mortimore,
                                  Brook Farm, Tavistock
                                  Owners: J.H. Stephens,
                                  Higher Hele, Cornwood.
                                  Mr. & Mrs J. Coaker, Sherberton

Sire: D.P.
Dam: D.P.

Sire of: HELE ROMEO II bl. 1954 (Hele Jenny) *FM44
Hele Judith IV br. 1958 (Hele Judith) FM45
Hele Judith II b. 1956 (Hele Judith) FM45
Hele Judith III b. 1957 (Hele Judith) FM45
Midgehope Chocolate bl. 1959 (Jurston Charm) *FM42
SHERBERTON SPARROW b. 1962 (Linnet) FM8
Sherberton Cherry b. 1964 (Sherberton Cocktail) *FM53
                    ———————————

FS 19 RANGER III 2943. Vol.26. dk b. Foaled 1947. 11.2hh.
    Brand H   Breeder: T. Holman,
                                      King's Arms, South Zeal

Sire: D.P.
Dam: D.P.

Sire of: CAWSAND BOY b. 1951 (Betty XXI) *FM27
          May Queen VII bl. 1954 (Queenie XX) FM6
          CAWSAND BOY II bl. 1955 (Queenie XX) FM6
          Skaigh Princess bl. 1958 (Betty XXI) *FM27
          Bees-Wing b. 1961 (Honey-Locust) FM32
          Honey Bee III br. 1962 (Honey-Locust) FM32

FS20 RAYBARROW POOL 3563. Vol.27. gr. Foaled 1953.
    Brand J (later gelded)   Breeder: Mrs K.J. Jackson

Sire D.P.
Dam: Chymes (FM8)

Sire of: GREY WETHERS II ro. 1956 (Granite II) *FM49
          Penny II b. 1960 (Queenie XXIII) FM4
          Betty's Star bl. 1957 (Betty XXI) *FM27
          Heather Queen bl. 1958 (Queenie XX) FM6

FS21 SHERBERTON NEWMAN 3712. Vol.28. bl. Foaled 1953.
    Brand C. nr hind and HC nr saddle   Breeder: R.H.N. Caunter,
                                    Dunnabridge
                                    Owner: Mr & Mrs J Coaker,
                                    Sherberton

Sire of: Sherberton Titania gr. 1961 (Sherberton Tempest) *FM33

FS22 TINY 2944. Vol.2b. dk br. Foaled 1948.
    Brand H nr side   Breeder: T. Holman, Kings Arms,
                                    South Zeal
                                    Owner: Maj. J.C. Bulteel

Sire: JOE (unreg)
Dam: Betty XXI *FM27

Sire of: Cottage Garden b. 1955 (Mahjong) FM30
          Small Fry b. 1952 (Burnt Sugar) *FM31

DARTMOOR FOUNDATION MARES

FM No.			
1	Polly V	32	Treacle
2	Judy V	33	Granite
3	Blackdown	34	Sweet Brier
4	Fairy III	35	Hornbeam
5	Scintilla	36	Cherrybrook
6	Queenie VII	37	Sherberton Hutch
7	Blue Haze	38	Sherberton Tempest
8	Heatherbelle VI	39	Anne's Dolly Grey
9	Sweet Vernal	40	Susan VIII
10	Little Princess	41	Zippie
11	Beaver	42	Jurston Charm
12	Dawn V	43	Widecombe Fair
13	Wings	44	Hele Jenny
14	Fern	45	Hele Judith
15	Mary Tavy II	46	Hele Juliet
16	Miss Muffet VI	47	Sherberton Black Out
17	Fay	48	Rock Rose
18	Wild Rose IV	49	Granite II
19	Molly XIX	50	Mola
20	Hildebrand	51	Sherberton Blackbird
21	Cornwood Winnie	52	Sherberton Label
22	Midnight III	53	Sherberton Cocktail
23	Brownie XVIII	54	Snipe
24	Gooseberry II	55	Dora IV
25	Moorhen III	56	Fudge III
26	Fair Diana	57	Peggy XXXIV
27	Betty XXI	58	Sherberton Molly
28	Sooty of the Barn	59	S.R. 1/11 Wobroook
29	Wonder Why II	60	S.R. 1/42 Saucy
30	Chinkwell	61	S.R. 1/185 Dunnabridge Wild Goose
31	Burnt Sugar	62	S.R. 1/159 Kanga

FM1 Polly V 2261. Vol.12. dk br. Foaled 1905. 13.0hh
Breeder: J. Hopper, Tavistock
Owner: Mr S. Horrell from 1919

Sire: D.P.
Dam: D.P.

Produce: Virtuous Lady b. 1919 (Little Star *FSI)
Bucktor Queen bl. 1924 (D.P.)
Yeoland Beepety Bump br. 1946 (YEOLAND LORD NELSON) FS3
Dusk IV br. 1952 (ROBERT EMMET) FS12
Daybreak II ch. 1956 (JON) FS8
MORNING STAR II gr. 1960 (STORM II) FS8
Walreddon Dawn br. 1969 (CAWSAND CAVALIER) FS13
Walreddon Starlight b. 1980 (BOVEYCOMBE LEO) FS8
Lakehead Velvet b. 1964 (JENSON) FS8
Midget V b. 1937 (SAMMY II) *FS7
Daybreak br. 1944 (D.P.)
Hr Tor Dawn Skies bl. 1960 (HIGHER TOR M'SMAN) FS8
Higher Tor Midget b. 1965 (PETER TAVY II) FS8
Hr Tor Bridget b. 1969 (CAWSAND CAVALIER) FS13
HR TOR SKYLARK b. 1967 (HISLEY WOODCOCK) FS8
Midget VI b. 1953 (D.P.)
HIGHER TOR MARKSMAN b. 1957 (JENYN) FS8

––––––––––

FM2 Judy V 3173. Vol.16. Foaled 1915. 12.0hh
Breeder: Edmond Northey

Sire: D.P.
Dam: D.P. ex 1970 Biddy III bl. 1903 1/2 sister to 771 Busby

Produce: Juliet IV br. 1923 (THE LEAT) *FS2
Judith III gr. 1939 (DINARTH SPARK) W.S.B.
JEF gr. 1946 (JUDE) *FS8
JUDE bl. 1941 (DINARTH SPARK) W.S.B.
Zigzag gr. 1937 (DINARTH SPARK) W.S.B.
Zog gr. 1951 (PIPIT) FS8
Vean Wayzgoose gr. 1953 (PIPIT) FS8
Rose Vean Grilse gr. 1960 (VEAN PARTRIDGE) FS8
Vean Zelinda gr. 1956 (JUDE) *FS8
VEAN ZAFFER gr. 1960 (PETROC) FS8
Vean Jentylys bl. 1962 (JENTYL) FS8
Vean Honeysuckle bl. 1967 (OATLANDS DIGGORY DELVET) FS8
Yeoland Juliet b. 1989 (WHITE WILLOWS PROSPERO) FS8
Vean Zena bl. 1964 (JENTYL) FS8
Piers Aquila br. 1975 (RED HALL AQUARIUS) FS8
Vean Vencock gr. 1957 (PIPIT) FS8
Vean Zero gr. 1960 (PIPIT) FS8

––––––––––

FM3 Blackdown 3758. Vol.16. bl. Foaled 1907. 13.0hh
Breeder: Mrs Crocker,
Plume of Feathers
Owner: H.R.H. Prince of Wales,
Duchy Stud

Sire: CONFIDENT GEORGE bl. 13.2hh (by PORTWOOD CONFIDENCE)
Dam: D.P.

Produce: THE LEAT b. 1918 (DWARKA) *FS2

––––––––––

FM4 Fairy III 4163 Vol.16 b. Foaled 1913. 12.0hh
Breeder: E.W. White, South Zeal

Sire: D.P.
Dam: D.P.

Produce: Daisy XVI b. 1923 (D.P.)
Yeoland Lady Hamilton b. 1935 (CAWSAND DINKY unreg.)
Yeoland Pussy Willow b. 1942 (BOXER) FS5
YEOLAND BOB-A-NOB b. 1945 (DP)
Yeoland Horatia b. 1947 (YEOLAND LORD NELSON)
Oatlands Rebeccah Puddleduck b. 1958 (O. JEREMY FISHER) FS8
ROBERT EMMET br. 1948 (YEOLAND BOB-A-NOB) FS12
JESTER IV br. 1957 (JENYN) FS8
Julia IV b. 1937 (CAWSAND DINKY)
Countess VIII b.ro. 1945 (BOXER) FS5
Queenie XXIII b.ro 1948 (BOXER) FS5
PUNCH IV gr. 1951 (D.P.)
Penny II b. 1960 (GREY WETHERS II) FS20
Torfields Pretty Penny b. 1973 (HISLEY PEDDLAR) FS8
TORFIELDS PENNYWORTH br. 1980 (ALLENDALE FLAUROS) FS8
Hisley Polonaise b. 1982 (HISLEY WOODCOCK) FS8
Hisley Quill b. 1962 (DUNNABRIDGE) FS13
Hisley Quince b.ro. (PETER TAVY II) FS8
HISLEY PEDLAR b.ro. (LAMMERMUIR RAMBLER) FS8
Molly XXI b. 1949 (BOXER) FS5
Midgehope Melissa bl. 1962 (WHITMORE ARBUTUS) FS8
SHILSTONE ROCKS DARKNESS bl. 1966 (EASTER) FS8
Delight of Torr br. 1958 (YEOLAND WYNBEAM) FS8
Shilstone Rocks Windrush b. 1964 (CAWSAND CAVALIER) FS13
Juliet VIII b. 1952 (D.P.)
Dartmoor's Doormouse br. 1973 (DARTMOOR'S CHILDE)
Gamma Ray b. 1954 (TEIGNHEAD) FS17
Fall Out b. 1963 (MICHELMASS) FS8
Shilstone Rocks Cavalina b. 1967 (CAWSAND CAVALIER) FS13
Shilstone Rocks Quercina b. 1971 (SH.R. OKEMENT) FS8
SH.R. ACHILLES b. 1969 (RED HALL AQUARIUS) FS8
Sh.R. Rockfall gr. 1970 (PETROC) FS8
SH.R. FASTNET FURY b. 1979 (SH.R. DARKNESS) FS8
SH.R. FURY b. 1971 (SH.R. DARKNESS) FS8
Sh.R. Cascade II b. 1987 (SH.R. ROUGH DAY) FS8
Telstar br. 1964 (MICHELMASS) FS8
White Willows Radiation ch. 1965 (MICHELMASS) FS8
VEAN ZENNOR bl. 1973 (VEAN ZAFFER) FS8

White Willows Radiation continued
          Vean Floradora br. 1974 (WHITESTONE RAGGED ROBIN) FS8
          Vean Floribunda b. 1983 (SH.R. EASTER DAY) FS8
          Vean Viola b. 1987 (WHITE WILLOWS PROSPERO) FS8
          Vean Twilight b. 1984 (SHILSTONE ROCKS EASTER DAY) FS8
          VEAN ECLIPSE b. 1987 (SHILSTONE ROCKS EASTER DAY) FS8
          White Willows Radium br. 1967 (MICHELMASS) FS8
          WHITE WILLOWS DARWIN b. 1976 (SH.R. BACCARAT) FS8
       Belle of Torr b. 1956 (CAWSAND BOY) FS19
       Joybelle of Torr b. 1964 (JENYN) FS8
       Senruf Jingle br. 1972 (CAWSAND CAVALIER) FS13

FM5 Scintilla 4253. Vol.18. gr. Foaled 1914. 11.3hh.
                              Owner: Miss S.Calmady-Hamlyn

Dam: D.P.

Produce: Sparklet II gr. 1923 (THE LEAT) *FS2
          BOXER 1930 (PUNCH) *FS5
          Starlight XV gr. 1932 (PUNCH) FS5
          Miss Muffet bl. 1936 (D.P.)
          Oatlands Tabitha Twitchit b. 1951 (JOHN) FS8
          OATLANDS TOM KITTEN bl. 1960 (OATLANDS JEREMY FISHER) FS8
          Oatlands Cottontail b. 1962 (JENTYL) FS8
          Over-the-Moon br. 1966 (PARKLANDS PIPPIN) FS8
          Plovers Bo-Peep b. 1973 (DUNNABRIDGE BONNY BOY) FS13
          Mistress Mary of Plovers b. 1977 (SH.R. ACHILLES) FS8
          CRUACHAN KINGFISHER br. 1967 (O'LANDS JEREMY FISHER) FS8
       Water Wagtail bl. 1924 (THE LEAT) *FS2
       Peewit III gr. 1939 (DINARTH SPARK) WSB
       PETE bl. 1945 (JUDE) *FS8
       PIPIT gr. 1947 (JUDE) *FS8
       May Day V bl. 1952 (JUDE) *FS8
          Cruachan Brican bl. 1963 (O. JEREMY FISHER) FS8
          Cruachan Batchelor Girl bl. 1967 (O. DIGGORY DELVET) FS8
          Higher Tor Jill bl. 1970 (HIGHER TOR SKYLARK) FS8
       PETROC gr. 1955 (JUDE) *FS8
       VEAN PARTRIDGE gr. 1956 (JUDE) *FS8

FM6 Queenie VII 4985 Vol.19. dk br. Foaled 1919. 12.0hh.
   White Spot. Brand C   Breeder: J. Cottle, S. Zeal
                                           Owner: T. Holman, S. Zeal

Sire: CANNON BALL gr.
Dam: Queenie b.

Produce: JOE III (later YOUNG JAN) bl. 1927 (JOLLY JANKIN) *FS4
          Queenie XX b. 1943 (PUNCH unreg.)
          May Queen VII bl. 1954 (CAWSAND BOY) FS19
          Jurston May Storm bl. 1960 (STORM II) FS8
          Shilstone Rocks Rainstorm bl. 1964 (EASTER) FS8
          SHILSTONE ROCKS CLOUDBURST II 1970 (SH.R. FURY) FS8
          Shilstone Rocks Rainy Day b. 1972 (SH.R. OKEMENT) FS8
          SHILSTONE ROCKS EASTER DAY b. 1978 (SH.R. DARKNESS) FS8
          SHILSTONE ROCKS D. DAY b. 1981 (CATESBY COCKSPUR) FS8
          SHILSTONE ROCKS DARK DAY b. 1982 (SH.R. DARKNESS) FS8
          SHILSTONE ROCKS ROUGH DAY b. 1984 (BRANDSBY CYCLONE) FS8
          Shilstone Rocks Rain Again b. 1976 (WHITMORE ARBUTUS) FS8
          Shilstone Rocks Wet Again dk b. 1980 (SH.R. FURY) FS8
          Jurston Springtime bl. 1962 (JURSTON SPINDRIFT) FS8
          Jurston Maytime bl. 1963 (JENSON) FS8
          Jurston Lilac Time bl. 1964 (JENSON) FS8
          CAWSAND BOY II bl. 1955 (CAWSAND BOY) FS19
          Heather Queen bl. 1958 (RAYBARROW POOL) *FS20
          Sweetie Pie b. 1966 (JONACA) FS8
          Hisley Serenade b. 1978 (ALLENDALE FLAUROS) FS8
          Hisley Salvo b. 1983 (HISLEY WOODCOCK) FS8
          Hisley Stardust b. 1984 (HISLEY WOODCOCK) FS8

FM7 Blue Haze 5037. Vol.19. gr. Foaled 1918. 11.2hh.
   Brand M and diamond offside neck. Punch Breeder: H.J. Madders, South Zeal
   hole off ear. Square halfpenny near ear   Owner: Miss S. Calmady-Hamlyn

Sire: D.P. br. 12.0hh
Dam: D.P. gr. 11.3hh

Produce: GREY WETHERS gr. 1924 (D.P.) *FS3

FM8 Heatherbelle VI 6614 Vol.22. b. Foaled 1924. 12.1hh.

Small star. Brand, plume of feathers on shoulder

Breeder: HRH The Prince of Wales
Owner: J. Coaker, Sherberton

Sire:
Dam: D.P.

Produce: Brownbelle II b. 1935 (BROWN BERRY) *FS6
Sherberton Sweet Pea gr. 1945 (SAILOR unreg)
Sherberton Sherry br. 1953 (QUICKSTEP) FS11
Sherberton Whiskey br. 1958 (SILVER DOLLAR *FS16)
BLACK VELVET br. 1962 (JASPER) FS8
Martini II br. 1963 (WITCHCRAFT) FS8
Gaulden Gin Fizz bl. 1967 (OATLANDS DIGGORY DELVET) FS8
Furry Dance b. 1946 (SAILOR unreg)
Sage gr. 1950 (FOXTROT) *FS11
SHERBERTON TWO STEP gr. 1952 (FOXTROT) *FS11
Sherberton Brownbelle b. 1958 (HELE ROMEO) *FS18
Sherberton Brownbelle V b. 1970 (BLACK VELVET) FS8
Sherberton Little Belle gr. 1977 (SHERBERTON PENGUIN) FS11
Sherberton Eliza (Elizabelle) b. 1957 (JANWYN unreg.) FS4
Linnet b. 1944 (SMOKEY Unreg)
Sherberton Stone Chat gr. 1956 (SHERBERTON TWO STEP) FS11
Sherberton Nuthatch b. 1966 (HELE ROMEO) *FS18
Sherberton Linnet b. 1969 (HIGHER TOR BOY BLUE) FS8
Sherberton Ribbon br. 1979 (BLACK VELVET) FS8
SHERBERTON PAUL b. 1987 (CROOKETY MOONSTONE) FS13
Sherberton Skylark gr. 1959 (PUNCH IV)
Sherberton Blue Tit gr. 1964 (HELE ROMEO) *FS18
Sherberton Bunting br. 1979 (SHERBERTON SPARROW) FS18
Sherberton Dusk br. 1987 (CROOKETY MOONSTONE) FS13
Sherberton Woodlark b. 1966 (HELE ROMEO) *FS18
SHERBERTON FIGARO bl. 1977 (BLACK VELVET) FS8
SHERBERTON SPARROW b. 1972 (HELE ROMEO) *FS18
Chymes gr. 1945 (SMOKEY unreg.)
RAYBARROW POOL gr. 1953 (DP) *FS20
Caroline II b. 1954 (TEIGNHEAD) *FS17
SHILSTONE ROCKS OKEMENT b. 1966 (PETROC) FS8
FOXTROT b.ro. 1946 (SMOKEY unreg.) *FSII
QUICKSTEP ro. 1949 (FOXTROT) *FSII
Sherberton Heatherbelle b. 1950 (FOXTROT) *FS11
Sherberton Twinkle b. 1954 (FOXTROT) *FS11
Sherberton Twinkle Again b. 1970 (BLACK VELVET) FS8
Sherberton Muddilake bl. 1980 (SHERBERTON FIGARO) FS8
SHERBERTON PETER b. 1981 (CROOKETY MOONSTONE) FS13

FM9 Sweet Vernal 7955 Vol. 25. lt. b. Foaled 1940. 12hh.

Brand C near saddle. Strip and nr hind, white fetlock

Breeder: Mrs M.E. Croft

Sire: D.P.
Dam: Berry

Produce: JULIAN II bl. 1944 (D.P.) *FS9
Sweet Briar II b. 1948 (D.P.)

FM10 Little Princess 8329 Vol.25. b. Foaled 1935. 11.2hh.

Brand W near side

Breeder: W. Aggett, South Zeal
Owner: F. Webber, South Zeal

Sire: BOXER FS5
Dam: D.P.

Produce: YEOLAND LORD NELSON b. 1939 (GREY WETHERS) *FS3
Cater's Beam b. 1946 (YOUNG JOE unreg.)
YEOLAND WYNBEAM b. 1955 (JENYN) FS8
JONACA ch. 1962 (JON) FS8

FM11 Beaver 8399 Vol.25 b. Foaled 1941. 11.3hh.

Few white hairs offside face. Both ears tipped, near ear nicked

Sire: D.P.
Dam: D.P.

Produce: RED HALL AQUARIUS b. 1959 (JON) FS8

FM12 DAWN V 8401 Vol.25. gr. Foaled 1938. 11.1 1/2hh.

Breeder: W. Mortimore, Lettaford, North Bovey
Owner: Mrs Croft, Quintatown, Chagford

Sire: D.P. bl.
Dam: D.P. gr.

Produce: Juliet VI gr. 1944 (D.P.)
STORM br. 1946 (JEF) FS8
STORM II gr. 1949 (JEF) FS8

FM13 Wings 8402 Vol.25. dk. b. Foaled 1943. 11.1hh.

Brand W nearside thigh

Breeder: Mr Whitley
Owner: Mrs Simmonds, Cowick Barton, Exeter

Sire: D.P.
Dam: D.P.

Produce: Mayfly V b. 1949 (JULIAN II) *FS9
Mayflower X b. 1957 (PIXIE III)
Maybelle b. 1965 (JENSON) FS8
May Tinkerbelle br. 1979 (ALLENDALE FLAUROS) FS8

FM14 Fern 8403 Vol.25. dk b. Foaled 1932. 11.2hh
                                        Breeder: Miss Croft, Chagford

Sire: D.P.
Dam: D.P.

Produce: CHRYS b. 1947 (D.P.) *FS10

FM15 Mary Tavy II 8560 Vol.26. b. Foaled 1939. 11hh.
    Small star. Brand, large C in saddle place   Breeder: C.H. Doidge, Horndon,
                                        Mary Tavy
                                        Owners: Miss Calmady-Hamlyn,
                                        Miss M.E. Croft

Sire: D.P.
Dam: D.P.

Produce: Marita II b. 1948 (D.P.)
    Jurston Sagentha br. 1958 (STORM II) FS8
    Spindle br. 1961 (JURSTON SPINDRIFT) FS8
    Jurston Mary Tavy b. 1951 (CHRYS) *FS10
    PETER TAVY II b. 1960 (JENSON) FS*
    Ellimore Tavy ch. 1968 (BOVEYCOMBE LEO) FS8
    Oakfield Linnet b. 1974 (OATLANDS MR McGREGOR) FS8
    Jurston Windrift gr. 1958 (JURSTON SPINDRIFT) FS8
    Shilstone Rocks Bay Wind b. 1966 (BOVEYCOMBE LEO) FS8
    WHITESTONE BAYARD b. 1973 (PETROC) FS8
    BRANDSBY TORNADO b. 1975 (PETROC) FS8

FM16 Miss Muffet VI 8626 Vol.26. Iron gr. Foaled 1939. 12hh
                                        Breeder: E. Rice, Peter Tavy
                                        Owner: Miss S.E. Ferguson,
                                        Worcester

Produce: Minerva V b. 1953 (JUDE) *FS8
    Whitestone Mint bl. 1959 (JANUS) FS8
    Whitestone Cornmint b. 1963 (ROSE VEAN JACK SNIPE) FS8
    Dunros Peppermint bl. 1967 (OATLANDS DIGGORY DELVET) FS8
    DUNROS CURLEW br. 1973 (OATLANDS MR McGREGOR) FS8
    WHITESTONE RAGGED ROBIN b. 1961 (ROSE VEAN JACK SNIPE)
    FS8

FM17 Fay. 8740. Vol.26. b. Foaled 1947. (Star)
                                        Breeder/Owner: Miss M.E. Croft
                                        Mrs. Simmons

Sire: D.P.
Dam: D.P.

Produce: Pixie III. b. 1953 (COCK ROBIN II) FS15

FM18 Wild Rose IV. 8911 Vol.26 dk. bay mare. Foaled 1942. 12h.h.
    White streak on head, white half-ring nr.   Breeder: G. Richards, Dousland
    fore fetlock. White hoof and sock nr. hind.   Owners: Miss P. E. Hyett,
    White spot off hind. Brand r/nr saddle.   Miss Calmady-Hamlyn

Sire: D.P.
Dam: Mischief (g. daughter of LOVE'S ROMANCE TB)

Produce: JULUS br. 1951 (JUDE) *FS8
    VEAN WILDFIRE gr. 1956 (PIPIT) FS8
    Vean White Rose br. 1957 (PIPIT) FS8
    Whitestone Rock Rose br. 1964 (ROSE VEAN JACK SNIPE) FS8
    Stokeleigh Zepherine b. 1969 (VEAN ZAFFER) FS8
    Stokeleigh Wild Rose b. 1975 (PETROC) FS8
    Langfield Green Ginger b. 1979 (HISLEY PEDLAR) FS8
    Wendel Seaspray b. 1983 (SHILSTONE ROCKS FASTNET FURY)
    FS8
    Vean Alba Rosa gr. 1968 (PIPIT) FS8
    Twylands Rosanna bl. 1963 (JANUS) FS8
    Vean Rosaura gr. 1964 (PETROC) FS8
    VEAN SWEET WILLIAM gr. 1971 (JENTYL) FS8

FM19 Molly XIX 8923 Vol.26. b. Foaled 1942. 12.2hh. Mealy nose.
    Brand WS   Owner: K.S. MacDonnell,
                                        Yelverton

Sire: D.P.
Dam: D.P.

Produce: Azalia bl. 1962 (MICHELMASS) FS8
    Blythford Robinia bl. 1966 (WHITESTONE RAGGED ROBIN) FS8
    Springs Rowan bl. 1973 (WHITE WILLOWS MACBETH) FS8
    Blythford Scilla bl. 1969 (BLUE JOHN) FS*
    BRANDSBY CYCLONE b. 1978 (BRANDSBY TORNADO) FS8
    ALEXANDER ch. 1963 (MICHELMASS) FS8

FM20 Hildebrand 8962 Vol.26. gr. Foaled 1942. 12hh.
    Brand AC (bought at Chagford as a yearling) Owner: Miss Anne Coaker

Sire: D.P.
Dam: D.P.

Produce: Sherberton Vixen b. 1952 (FOXTROT) *FS11
    DARTMOORS CHILDE b. 1964 (CAWSAND BOY II) FS11

FM21 Cornwood Winnie 5853 Vol.20. br. Tan muzzle. Foaled 1925. 11.21/2hh.

Breeder: J.H. Glover, Cornwood
Owners: Miss Calmady-Hamlyn,
Miss N. Dawson

Sire: D.P.
Dam: D.P.

Produce: Topsy II b. 1929 (JAPHET)
JANWYN br. 1933 (JOE III, later YOUNG JAN) FS4

FM22 Midnight III 8973 Vol.26. bl. Foaled 1942. 11.3hh.
Star and stripe conjoined. Near hind fetlock   Breeder: T. Dall, Widecombe
white continuing half up cannon on inside.   Owner: Miss Croft
Brand TD near saddle
Sire: D.P.
Dam: D.P.

Produce: Jurston Gidlet bl. 1961 (JURSTON SPINDRIFT) FS8
Locket of Torr gr. 1966 (JENYN) FS8
Skerraton Wheal Caroline gr. 1971 (RED HALL AQUARIUS) FS8
Skerraton Camilla br. 1978 (CRIMCHARD BRIGHT SPARK) FS8

FM23 Brownie XVIII 9186 Vol.26. dk. br. Foaled 1942.
Brand H C near saddle   Breeder: R.H.N. Caunter,
Dunnabridge
Owners: Mrs Jackson, W.J. and
J. Jordan

Sire: D.P.
Dam: D.P.

Produce: BROWN BERRY III b. 1955 (TEIGNHEAD) *FS17

FM24 Gooseberry II 9178 Vol.26. dk br. Foaled 1942.
Brand HC near saddle   Breeder: R.H.N. Caunter,
Dunnabridge

Produce: Dunnabridge Goose Girl br. 1951 (GAY BOY IV) *FS13
Dunnabridge Wigeon b. 1956 (HUCCABY) FS13
HISLEY WOODCOCK b. 1962 (JENSON) FS8
Dunnabridge Ling b. 1960 (DUNNABRIDGE BONNY BOY) FS13
Whitmore Calluna b. 1970 (WHITMORE ARBUTUS) FS8
OAKFIELD ROBIN b. 1978 (OATLANDS MR McGREGOR) FS8

FM25 Moorhen III 9183 Vol.26. bl. Foaled 1946

Breeder: R.H.N. Caunter

Sire: D.P.
Dam: Sylvia (unreg. by BOXER FS8)

Produce: Teal br. 1951 (GAY BOY IV) *FS13
Hallowe'en II bl. 1952 (GAY BOY IV) *FS13
MICHELMASS bl. 1958 (JENYN) FS8
WITCHCRAFT bl. 1959 (VEAN WILDFIRE) FS8
Spellbound bl. 1960 (JENYN) FS8
WHITE WILLOWS MACBETH b. 1968 (OATLANDS DIGGORY DELVET) FS8
WHITE WILLOWS SHYLOCK bl. 1978 (BOVEYCOMBE LEO) FS8
WHITE WILLOWS PROSPERO b. 1979 (SHILSTONE ROCKS FURY) FS8
White Willows Spook bl. 1965 (JENYN) FS8
Dunros Blythe Spirit bl. 1969 (OATLANDS DIGGORY DELVET) FS8
Chark Jubilee bl. 1973 (JANUS) FS8
White Willows Sorceress bl. 1969 (JENYN) FS8
White Willows Hallowe'en III bl. 1980 (ALLENDALE FLAUROS) FS8
White Willows Spellbound br. 1987 (WHITE WILLOWS DARWIN) FS8
WHITE WILLOWS ENCHANTER bl. 1981 (SHILSTONE ROCKS DARKNESS) FS8
WHITE WILLOWS WITCHDOCTOR b. 1984 (WHITE WILLOWS DARWIN) FS8
Dunnabridge Cool Reception b. 1953 (GAY BOY IV) *FS13
Dunnabridge Tansy bl. 1958 (DUNNABRIDGE BONNY BOY) FS13
Kilbees Skylark bl. 1963 (JENTYL) FS8
Kilbees Plover bl. 1971 (JON) FS8
Kilbees Blythe Spirit bl. 1974 (KILBEES Mr PICKWICK) FS8
DUNNABRIDGE BONNY BOY b. 1955 (HUCCABY) FS13

FM26 Fair Diana 9217 Vol.26. br. Foaled 1948. 11hh.
Brand J H   Breeder: T.W. Mead,
South Brent
Owner: Maj. Gen. G. Dalby,
'Crookety', South Brent

Sire: KING OF FOREST (unreg.)
Dam: 'XM'

Produce: Crookety Candytuft br. 1966 (CAWSAND PRINCE) FS13
CROOKETY CAVALCADE br. 1970 (CAWSAND CAVALIER) FS13
Crookety Gipsy Moth br. 1967 (CAWSAND PRINCE) FS13

FM27 Betty XXI 9223 Vol.26. gr. Foaled 1945. 11.3hh

Breeder: T. J. Holman,
South Zeal

Sire: D.P.
Dam: Pixie Belle (unreg.)

Produce: TINY br. 1948 (JOE, unreg.)
CAWSAND BOY bl. 1951 (RANGER III) *FS19
Betty's Star bl. 1957 (RAYBARROW POOL) *FS20
Skaigh Princess bl. 1958 (CAWSAND BOY II) FS19
CAWSAND PRINCE br. 1961 (DUNNABRIDGE) FS13
Cawsand Sundew br. 1962 (DUNNABRIDGE) FS13
BOVEYCOMBE JOUSTER bl. 1964 (JUDE) *FS8
Cosdon May bl. 1970 (BOVEYCOMBE LEO) FS8
CAWSAND CAVALIER br. 1960 (HUCCABY) FS13

FM28 Sooty of the Barn 9437 Vol.26. bl. Foaled 1947. 11.2hh. Mealy muzzle

Breeder: I. S. Edwards
Owners: Mrs P. Slade,
Mrs Bucknell and Mrs Rowse

Sire: D.P.
Dam: D.P.

Produce: Whitmore Juno br. 1961 (JON) FS8
Whitmore Venus br. 1972 (WHITMORE ARBUTUS) FS8
Stonehealed Minerva b. 1981 (OATLANDS Mr MACGREGOR) FS8
S'HEALED VULCAN br. 1982 (SH. ROCKS EASTER DAY) FS8
S'healed Demetria br. 1984 (SHILSTONE ROCKS EASTER DAY) FS8
Hambledon Juno b. 1966 (JENSON) FS8
Park Barn Dance b. 1975 (KILBEES MR JINGLE) FS8
Pantmant's Junket bl. 1981 (SHILSTONE ROCKS JEHOVA) FS8
Pantmant's Jaunt b. 1985 (BRANDSBY TORNADO) FS8
Stonehealed Tarrantella b. 1982 (SH.R. EASTER DAY) FS8
STONEHEALED SUNDANCE b. 1984 (SH.R. FURY) FS8

FM29 Wonder Why II 9473 Vol.26. br. Foaled 1950

Breeder: N. Caunter
Owner: Mrs Jackson

Sire: D.P.
Dam: Sylvia bl. (unreg. by BOXER FS5)

Produce: Wortleberry br. 1957 (HUCCABY) FS13
DUNNABRIDGE b. 1958 (HUCCABY) FS13
Dunnabridge Wonder Where b. 1965 (RED HALL AQUARIUS) FS8
Shilstone Rocks Why Wonder b. 1969 (SH. R. DARKNESS) FS8

FM30 Chinkwell 9551 Vol.26. br. Foaled ? 11.1hh.
Brand GH near saddle   Owner: Maj. J. C. Bulteel

Sire: D.P.
Dam: D.P.

Produce: BELLEVER br. 1945 (D.P.) *FS14
Mahjong b. 1951 (JOHN) FS8
Cottage Garden b. 1955 (TINY) *FS22
Red Hall Auriga b. 1959 (JANUS) FS8
KILBEES MR JINGLE bl. 1970 (JENTYL) FS8
KILBEES PLANET b. 1974 (JENTYL) FS8
Kilbees Sirius b. 1977 (KILBEES MR PICKWICK) FS8
Red Hall Aries b. 1962 (JON) FS8
Josie b. 1957 (JULUS) FS8
Whitmore Jokari ch. 1962 (JANUS) FS8
SHILSTONE ROCKS BACCARAT br. 1973 (SH.R. DARKNESS) FS8
Shilstone Rocks Bagatelle bl. 1974 (SH.R. DARKNESS) FS8
Whitmore Jigsaw br. 1969 (WHITMORE ARBUTUS) FS8

FM31 Burnt Sugar 9559 Vol.26. ch. Aged. 11.1hh
Star near hind. White sock Brand B   Owner: Major J. C. Bulteel

Sire: D.P.
Dam: D.P.

Produce: Off Ration br. 1951 (JOHN) FS8
Janessa bl. 1961 (JANUS) FS8
Winkie Pop III bl. 1967 (OATLANDS DIGGORY DELVET) FS8
Dream III bl. 1969 (OATLANDS DIGGORY DELVET) FS8
Small Fry b. 1952 (TINY) *FS22
Blue Grass gr. 1959 (VEAN PARTRIDGE) FS8
Park Blueberry b. 1968 (JON) FS8
MARINA HARBOURMASTER b. 1984 (SENRUF GREBE) FS8
Park True Blue gr. 1972 (VEAN ZERO) FS8

FM32 Treacle 9561 Vol.26. ch. Foaled 1942. 11.1hh
Brand M near quarter   Breeder: Mann Bros, Widecombe
                                          Owners: Major J.C. Bulteel,
                                          Earl of Wilton

Sire: D.P.
Dam: D.P. gr.

Produce: Honeybags br. 1945 (D.P.)
  Honey Locust b. 1951 (JOHN) FS8
   Bees Wing b. 1961 (CAWSAND BOY II) FS19
    Busy Bee V b. 1969 (RED HALL PERSEUS) FS8
     Catesby Miss Perkins b. 1974 (O'LANDS MR MACGREGOR) FS8
      DARNBROOK DRAMATIST b. 1984 (HUNTSPATH HOLLY) FS8
     C'SBY CRUSADER II b. 1976 (O'LANDS MR MACGREGOR) FS8
   Honey Bee III br. 1962 (CAWSAND BOY II) FS19
    Catesby Bumble Bee br. 1967 (RED HALL PERSEUS) FS8
    Catesby Orchis b. 1970 (WHITESTONE RAGGED ROBIN) FS8
    C'SBY COCKSPUR b. 1973 (O'LANDS MR MACGREGOR) FS8
    Catesby Honey Pot br. 1971 (OATLANDS MR MACGREGOR) FS8
    Catesby Honeyset bl. 1972 (OATLANDS MR MACGREGOR) FS8
    Brandsby Honeybunch b. 1981 (BRANDSBY CYCLONE) FS8
  Whitmore Honeybunch bl. 1958 (JANUS) FS8
   Shilstone Rocks Country Bunch b. 1974 (SH.R. FURY) FS8
    NAPPA COUNTRY BOY b. 1982 (BRANDSBY CYCLONE) FS8
   Shilstone Rocks Another Bunch b. 1976 (SH.R.FURY) FS8
   Shilstone Rocks Cottage Bunch bl. 1977 (SH.R. BACCARAT) FS8
  WHITMORE ARBUTUS bl. 1959 (JANUS) FS8
  Whitmore Honeymoon br. 1960 (JANUS) FS8
   CRIMCHARD BRIGHT SPARK b. 1966 (JENSON) FS8
   Crimchard Honeylove b. 1975 (SH.R. ACHILLES) FS8
    PLOVERS TUPPENY RICE b. 1986 (TORFIELDS PENNYWORTH) FS8
  Whitmore Honeymead br. 1963 (JANUS) FS8
 Mountain Sweet br. 1948 (BELLEVER) *FS14
 Jacaranda br. 1951 (JOHN) FS8
  Huntspath Josephine bl. 1964 (WITCHCRAFT) FS8
   HUNTSPATH HOLLY b. 1969 (RED HALL AQUARIUS) FS8
  Huntspath Hannah bl. 1967 (MIDGEHOPE JOSEPH) FS8
   Shilstone Rocks Dark Mountain bl. 1971 (SH.R. DARKNESS) FS8
    Shilstone Rocks Musada b. 1986 (BRANDSBY CYCLONE) FS8
    SH.R. NICODEMUS bl. 1987 (BRANDSBY CYCLONE) FS8
   SHILSTONE ROCKS JEHOVAH bl. 1976 (SH. ROCKS FURY) FS8
   Shilstone Rocks Hosanna bl. 1979 (SH.R. FURY) FS8
   Haven Halina bl. 1983 (SHILSTONE ROCKS DARKNESS) FS8
   Haven Haneena bl. 1985 (SH.R. DARKNESS) FS8
  JASPER bl. 1959 (JANUS) FS8
 Plymouth Rock br. 1949 (BELLEVER) *FS14
 Pilgrim's Progress b. 1955 (JOHN) FS8
  RED HALL PERSEUS b. 1961 (JON) FS8
  LAMMERMUIR RAMBLER b. 1964 (JULUS) FS8
 TOFFEE II b. 1956 (JOHN) FS8
 Syrup b. 1957 (JOHN) FS8
  Senruf Rose Hip br. 1962 (WHITMORE ARBUTUS) FS8
   Senruf Rosella b. 1978 (SENRUF GREBE) FS8
  Senruf Susannah b. 1974 (WHITE WILLOWS MACBETH) FS8
  SENRUF SOLOMON br. 1980 (WHITMORE ARBUTUS) FS8

FM33 Granite 9596 Vol.26. gr. Aged.
         Owner: Major J. C. Bulteel

Sire: D.P.
Dam: D.P.

Produce: Smoke gr. 1945 (D.P.)
  Belstone gr. 1948 (BELLEVER) *FS14
  The White Bird br. 1951 (JOHN) FS8
  BLUE JOHN gr. 1955 (JOHN) FS8
  Red Hall Hydra gr. 1959 (JON) FS8
  Lodestone of Torr gr. 1966 (SILVER DOLLAR) *FS16
  Skerraton Wheal Emma gr. 1971 (SH. ROCKS OKEMENT) FS8

FM34 Sweet Brier 9665 Vol.26. b. Foaled 1948
         Breeder: Mr Stockman
         Owner: Miss J. Durrant,
         Mrs J. D'Ambrumenl

Produce: Bryckden Moonbeam b. 1958 (OATLANDS JEREMY FISHER) FS8
  Cruachan Moonspinner b. 1964 (O. JEREMY FISHER) FS8
  Cruachan Moonbeam bl. 1969 (WHITESTONE RAGGED ROBIN) FS8
  Cruachan Moonflight b. 1980 (CRIMCHARD PLAY BOY) FS8
 Genevieve II br. 1956 (JENYN) FS8

FM35 Hornbeam 9757 Vol.26. b. Foaled 1945. 11.1hh. Star. Ear mark near side.
 Brand CM   Breeder: Whitley
         Owner: Miss M. E. Croft

Sire: D.P.
Dam: D.P.

Produce: Coronet II gr. 1953 (STORM II) FS8
  JURSTON REBEL gr. 1961 (STORM II) FS8
  JURSTON SPINDRIFT gr. 1954 (STORM II) FS8

FM36 Cherrybrook 10001 Vol.26. bl. Foaled 1948. 11.2hh
 Small star. Brands AC – PJ Breeder: Mrs A. Belam
         Owners: Mrs P. E. Robinson,
         Mrs Dod

Produce: Oatlands Mrs Tittlemouse b. 1953 (JON) FS8
  OATLANDS DIGGORY DELVET bl. 1961 (JENTYL) FS8
  Oatlands Thomasina Tittlemouse bl. 1964 (JENTYL) FS8
  OATLANDS MR. MACGREGOR br. 1965 (JENTYL) FS8
  OATLANDS JEREMY FISHER br. 1954 (JOHN) FS8

FM37 Sherberton Hutch 1077 Vol.26. gr. Foaled 1943.
    Brand IC   Breeder: G. Smith, Hexworthy
                                               Owner: J. Coaker

Sire: SMOKEY (unreg)
Dam: D.P.

Produce: Sherberton Lilac Time ro. 1954 (QUICKSTEP) FS11

FM38 Sherberton Tempest 10181 Vol.26. gr. Foaled 1944.
    Brand IC   Breeder: J. Coaker

Sire: SMOKEY (unreg)
Dam: D.P. (Little Pearse)

Produce: Sherberton Midsummer Night's Dream. gr. 1956 (SH. TWO STEP) FS11
             Sherberton Snow Dream gr. 1970 (BLACK VELVET) FS8
             Sherberton Blizzard Girl gr. 1977 (SHERBERTON PENGUIN) FS11
             Sherberton Snow Girl II gr. 1986 (HIGHER TOR EL CID) FS8
             Sherberton Titania gr. 1961 (SHERBERTON NEWMAN) *FS21
             Sherberton Titanic gr. 1968 (SHERBERTON PENGUIN) FS11
             Sherberton Silver Sea gr. 1973 (SH. SILVER TICKET) FS11
             Sherberton Vivace br. 1987 (HIGHER TOR EL CID) FS8

FM39 Anne's Dolly Grey 7200 Vol. 23. gr. Foaled 1924. 11.3hh.
                                     Owner: Miss A. Coaker

Sire: D.P.
Dam: Dolly Grey II (unreg)

Produce: Sherberton Wandy gr. 1938 (BROWNBERRY) *FS6
             Sherberton Cobweb gr. 1948 (D.P.)
             Sherberton Judy gr. 1954 (JUDCOCK) FS8
             MIDGEHOPE JOSEPH bl. 1963 (WHITMORE ARBUTUS) FS8
             Midgehope Jonquil bl. 1964 (WHITMORE ARBUTUS) FS8
             Midgehope Japonica bl. 1969 (VEAN ZERO) FS8
             Senruf Jacaranda bl. 1978 (WHITMORE ARBUTUS) FS8

FM40 Susan VIII 10402 Vo.27. dk. b. Foaled 1948.
    Brand C near saddle   Breeder: G. Cornish
                                        Owners: S. Horrell,
                                        W.G. Shillibeer

Sire: D.P.
Dam: D.P.

Produce: Cherub II b. 1951 (D.P.)
             Blachford Rosemary b. 1961 (JENSON) FS8

FM41 Zippie 10407 Vol.27. b. Foaled 1951. 12.2hh
                                  Owners: Mr & Mrs T. Reep

Sire: D.P.
Dam: D.P.

Produce: Windfall of Shilstone Rocks b. 1962 (SILVER DOLLAR) *FS16
             Shilstone Rocks Whirlwind b. 1965 (PETROC) FS8
             Shilstone Rocks Whirligig b. 1972 (SH.ROCKS DARKNESS) FS8
             Shilstone Rocks Giggle b. 1978 (CATESBY COCKSPUR) FS8
             Shilstone Rocks Carousel II b. 1981 (SH. ROCKS CLOUDBURST II) FS8
             Shilstone Rocks Windswept II b. 1983 (SH.R. CLOUDBURST) FS8
             Shilstone Rocks Whirlaway b. 1975 (SH.R. DARKNESS) FS8
             Shilstone Rocks Legatee bl. 1977 (SH.R. BACCARAT) FS8
             Shilstone Rocks Windfall b. 1984 (BRANDSBY CYCLONE) FS8
             Shilstone Rocks Windswept b. 1964 (JUDE) *FS8

FM42 Jurston Charm 10449 Vol.27. gr. Foaled 1949.
    Brand ♡ off saddle.   Breeder: Miss M. E. Croft
                                        Owner: Mrs. W. T. Thomson

Sire: D.P.
Dam: Skittles (D.P.)

Produce: Midgehope Chocolate bl. 1959 (HELE ROMEO) *FS18
             SENRUF AERO bl. 1969 (VEAN ZERO) FS8

FM43 Widecombe Fair 10554 Vol.27. bl. Foaled 1950.
    Brand H off quarter. S H near quarter   Breeder: Mann Bros, Widecombe
                                        Owner: Major J. C. Bulteel,
                                        Mrs Spooner

Produce: Fair Joanna br. 1956 (JOHN) FS8
             Crimchard Fantasy b. 1970 (CRIMCHARD BRIGHT SPARK) FS8
             Crimchard Fantasia b. 1974 (SH. ROCKS DARKNESS) FS8
             Crimchard Fairy Tale b. 1978 (SH. ROCKS ACHILLES) FS8
             CR. FREE 'N EASY b. 1983 (WHITE WILLOWS SHYLOCK) FS8
             Stonehealed Daydream b. 1985 (SH.R. DARK DAY) FS8
             CRIMCHARD FANFARE br. 1972 (CRIMCHARD BRIGHT SPARK) FS8
             CRIMCHARD FIREFLY br. 1973 (CRIMCHARD BRIGHT SPARK) FS8
             Miss Muffet of Robins bl. 1959 (JANUS) FS8
             Blue Bell of Robins gr. 1963 (PIPIT) FS8
             Stokeleigh Muffet bl. 1974 (VEAN SWEET WILLIAM) FS8
             Dykes Daisy Mead bl. 1986 (LANGFIELD CANTH) FS8
             DYKES ACANTHUS bl. 1988 (LANGFIELD CANTH) FS8
             Stokeleigh Muffs Pet bl. 1975 (PETROC) FS8
             Langfield Noilly Prat b. 1979 (HISLEY PEDLAR) FS8
             LANGFIELD CANTH b. 1983 (SH.R. FASTNET FURY) FS8
             LANGFIELD ROTH b. 1986 (SH.R. FURY) FS8

FM44 Hele Jenny 10689 Vol.27. b. Foaled 1950.
Brand J near side Breeder: J. H. Stephens,
Higher Hele, Cornwood

Sire: D.P.
Dam: D.P.

Produce: HELE ROMEO II bl. 1954 (HELE ROMEO) *FS18

FM45 Hele Judith 10691 Vol.27. b. Foaled 1952.
Brand J S near side Breeder: J. H. Stephens

Sire: D.P.
Dam: D.P.

Produce: Hele Judith II b. 1956 (HELE ROMEO) *FS18
Blachford Brandween b. 1962 (HUCCABY) FS13
Blachford Greta b. 1967 (CAWSAND PRINCE) FS13
SENRUF GREBE b. 1973 (HISLEY WOODCOCK) FS8
Senruf Gorse b. 1978 (WHITMORE ARBUTUS) FS8
SENRUF GRADUATE b. 1981 (WHITMORE ARBUTUS) FS8
SENRUF GLADIATOR b. 1987 (HISLEY PEDLAR) FS8
Hisley Caviar b. 1975 (HISLEY PEDLAR) FS8
Hisley Cranberry br. 1979 (ALLENDALE FLAUROS) FS8
Hisley Charisma b. 1986 (HISLEY SALVO) FS8
Hisley Charmer b. 1988 (HISLEY SALVO) FS8
HISLEY COGNAC B. 1977 (HISLEY PEDLAR) FS8
Hisley Cherry Brandy b. 1979 (HISLEY WOODCOCK) FS8
Langfield Chanel b. 1982 (SHILSTONE ROCKS FASTNET FURY) FS8
Hisley Candlelight b. 1972 (HISLEY WOODCOCK) FS8
Hele Judith III b. 1957 (HELE ROMEO) *FS18
Springs Quality Street b. 1971 (PETROC) FS8
WHINBERRY QUALITY WAY bl. 1984 (ALLENDALE FLAUROS) FS8
Springs Mountain Rose b. 1975 (BEVERLEY PEACOCK) FS8
Whinberry Truffle b. 1980 (OATLANDS MR MACGREGOR) FS8
Whinberry Moonlight b. 1982 (ALLENDALE FLAUROS) FS8
SPRINGS NOUGAT br. 1976 (BEVERLEY PEACOCK) FS8
Hele Judith IV br. 1958 (HELE ROMEO II) FS18
HELE LANCER br. 1968 (CAWSAND PRINCE) FS13
Whitmore Jubilee b. 1972 (WHITMORE BEE KEEPER) FS8
W'more Royal Birthday br. 1982 (WHITE WILLOWS OTHELLO) FS8
Springwater Ottelia b. 1988 (BRANDSBY TORNADO) FS8
Hele Judith V b. 1959 (SHERBERTON CHOIRBOY)
Jennifer IV bl. 1962 (BLUE JOHN) FS8
Shilstone Rocks Horizon b. 1968 (RED HALL AQUARIUS) FS8
CROOKEY MOONSTONE b. 1981 (CROOKETY CAVALCADE) FS13

FM46 Hele Juliet 10692 Vol.27. b. Foaled 1947.
Brand J.S. near side Breeder: J. H. Stephens

Sire: D.P.
Dam: D.P.

Produce: Hele Juliet III bl. 1952 (HELE ROMEO) *FS18
EASTER bl. 1961 (MICHELMASS) FS8
Peppa bl. 1963 (MICHELMASS) FS8
Ryland Castanet bl. 1967 (OATLANDS DIGGORY DELVET) FS8
Langfield Miz Sophie b. 1984 (HISLEY PEDLAR) FS8
CATESBY PIP bl. 1974 (OATLANDS MR MACGREGOR) FS8
Pillar bl. 1964 (MICHELMASS) FS8
BOVEYCOMBE BUCKTHORN bl. 1971 (BOVEYCOMBE LEO) FS8

FM47 Sherberton Blackout 10785 Vol.28. bl. Foaled 1950.
Brand C near hind leg Breeder: J. Roberts
Owners: J. Coaker

Produce: Black Jane bl. 1958 (JANUS) FS8
Park Just Jane bl. 1966 (JENTYL) FS8
Park Jane Again bl. 1967 (JENTYL) FS8
Park Jemima Jane bl. 1970 (PARKLANDS PARAGON) FS8
Park Lucky Jane bl. 1974 (BOVEYCOMBE BUCKTHORN) FS8

FM48 Rock Rose 10788 Vol.28. b. Foaled 1943.
Brand, heart off saddle. Owner: Miss U. C. Frankenburg

Produce: Red Hall Dorado br. 1960 (JON) FS8
HOPELAWS KAZEK b. 1984 (CRUACHAN KINGFISHER) FS8

FM49 Granite II 10815 Vol.28. ro. Foaled 1953.
Breeder: W. J. Jordan

Produce: GREY WETHERS II gr. 56 (RAYBARROW POOL) *FS20
MOORTOWN BERRY b. 1961 (BROWNBERRY III) FS17
MOORTOWN LAD gr. 1963 (BROWNBERRY III) FS17
MOORTOWN ROBERT b. 1978 (BROWNBERRY III) FS17

FM50 Mola 10824 Vol.28. bl. Foaled 1947.

Brand D.R. near saddle

Breeder: D. Radmore
Owners: Miss N. Nicholls,
Mrs Hollingworth

Sire: D.P.
Dam: D.P.

Produce: Dunros Little Mo b. 1967 (WHITESTONE RAGGED ROBIN) FS8
MORSTONE MULBERRY b. 1979 (O'LANDS MR MACGREGOR) FS8
Catesby Peewit gr. 1962 (PIPIT) FS8
Catesby Siskin b. 1966 (WHITESTONE RAGGED ROBIN) FS8
Catesby Catkin ch. 1972 (OATLANDS MR MACGREGOR) FS8
Catesby Scrapit ch. 1979 (CATESBY CRUSADER II) FS8
Dunros Martini b. 1984 (SHILSTONE ROCKS DARKNESS) FS8

FM51 Sherberton Blackbird 10982 Vol.28. bl. Foaled 1952.

Brand C near hind leg

Breeder: J. Roberts
Owner: J. Coaker

Produce: SHERBERTON PENGUIN gr. 1964 (SHERBERTON SILVER LINNET) FS11

FM52 Sherberton Label 10987 Vol.28. gr. Foaled 1952.

Brand C near hind leg. AP off side.
Top cut near ear

Breeder: L. Palmer
Owner: J. Coaker

Produce: SHERBERTON SILVER TICKET gr. 1962 (SHER. SILVER TIME) FS11

FM53 Sherberton Cocktail 10454 Vol.27. b. Foaled 1950.

Brand D near saddle

Owner: J. Coaker

Sire: D.P.
Dam: D.P.

Produce: Sherberton Cherry B. b. 1964 (HELE ROMEO) *FS18
Sherberton Loppy lt gr. 1970 (SHERBERTON PENGUIN) FS11
Sherberton Calamity gr. 1979 (SHERBERTON SANDMARTIN) FS11
Sherberton Volante br. 1987 (CROOKETY MOONSTONE) FS13

FM54 Snipe 11009 Vol.28. b. Foaled 1954.

Owner: Miss S. E. Ferguson

Produce: ROSE VEAN JACK SNIPE b. 1958 (JANUS) FS8
Rose Vean Quail b. 1959 (VEAN PARTRIDGE) FS8
KILBEES JAMES BOND b. 1964 (DUNNABRIDGE BONNY BOY) FS13
KILBEES BONNIE PRINCE CHARLIE b. 1965 (D'BRIDGE B.B.) FS13
Rose Vean Teal b. 1960 (JENSON) FS8
Rose Vean Curlew gr. 1961 (PIPIT) FS8
Millcroft Munchkin b. 1966 (CAWSAND CAVALIER) FS13
Millcroft Bewitched bl. 1967 (MICHELMASS) FS8
Rose Vean Peewit bl. 1962 (PIPIT) FS8
BEVERLEY PEACOCK b. 1973 (WHITESTONE RAGGED ROBIN) FS8

FM55 Dora IV 11250 Vol.29 gr. Foaled 1938.

Breeder: Miss S. Calmady-Hamlyn
Owners: Miss S.
Calmady-Hamlyn, Mrs W. E.
Robinson

Produce: JOHN br. 1944 (JUDE) FS8
Jenny VII br. 1945 (JUDE) FS8
JENYN bl. 1951 (PIPIT) FS8
JENTYL bl. 1952 (PIPIT) FS8
JENSON br. 1954 (PIPIT) FS8
Vean Blue Jennykin gr. 1956 (PIPIT) FS8
Kilbees Jenny Too bl. 1966 (JON) FS8
KILBEES MR PICKWICK b. 1969 (JON) FS8
JANUS bl. 1949 (JUDE) *FS8
JON b. 1950 (JUDE) *FS8
Jenetta gr. 1955 (JUDE) *FS8
Vean Petrina bl. 1960 (PETROC) FS8
VEAN BROWN WILLY bl. 1971 (VEAN ZAFFER) FS8
Vean Dorelia bl. 1976 (WHITESTONES BAYARD) FS8
Vean Mary Rose b. 1982 (SHIL. ROCKS EASTER DAY) FS8
Vean Dorabella II bl. 1984 (SH.R. EASTER DAY) FS8
VEAN BLACK JACK bl. 1985 (SH.R. EASTER DAY) FS8
Vean Gentian gr. 1961 (JENTYL) FS8
Yeoland Belinda br. 1967 (VEAN ZAFFER) FS8
Yeoland June bl. 1972 (VEAN ZAFFER) FS8
Yeoland May bl. 1976 (WHITESTONE BAYARD) FS8
Yeoland Buttercup b. 1981 (SH.R. FURY) FS8
Yeoland Daisy bl. 1980 (ALLENDALE FLAUROS) FS8
YEOLAND JUNIUS bl. 1988 (SH.R. EASTER DAY) FS8
Vean Pasque Flower ch. 1956 (JUDE) *FS8
Venetia ch. 1960 (VEAN VENCOCK) FS8
Kilbees Firenzi b. 1964 (DUNNABRIDGE BONNY BOY) FS13

FM56 Fudge III 11309 Vol.29 br. Foaled 1955.
    Mealy nose   Breeder: Mann Bros, Widecombe
                                     Owner: Mrs Gould, Lustleigh

Sire: D.P.
Dam: D.P.

Produce: Boveycombe Gemini b. 1959 (JENYN) FS8
          Senruf Juliet b. 1963 (JUDE) FS8
          Senruf Tiffin b. 1965 (TOFFEE II) FS8
          Senruf Tiffany b.76 (RYLAND BAY LEAF) FS8
          Senruf Abelia bl. 1968 (WHITMORE ARBUTUS) FS8
          Senruf Arabella b. 1977 (SENRUF GREBE) FS8
          Senruf Astra bl. 1980 (CRIMCHARD FIREFLY) FS8
          BOVEYCOMBE LEO b. 1961 (JUDE) FS8

FM57 Peggy XXXIV 11391 Vol.29 b. Foaled 1948.
    Brand AB near saddle   Owner: W. G. Shillibeer

Produce: Bellever Belle b. 1958 (SHERBERTON NEWMAN) *FS21
          Lakehead Pepita b. 1964 (BLUE PETER)
          Lakehead Promise br. 1966 (HISLEY WOODCOCK) FS8
          Lakehead Peggy b. 1967 (JESTER IV) FS8
          Peggy XXXVIII bl. 1972 (WHITMORE ARBUTUS) FS8

FM58 Sherberton Molly 10183 Vol.26. dk b. Foaled 1939
                                    Owner: J. Coaker

Sire: BROWNBERRY *FS6
Dam: D.P.

Produce: Sherberton Carol Singer br. 1952 (ICICLE) *FS15
          Sherberton Bridesmaid br. 1960 (HELE ROMEO) *FS18
          Sherberton Bridesmaid II gr. 1979 (SHER. SANDMARTIN) FS11
          Sherberton Susan b. 1986 (HIGHER TOR EL CID) FS8

FM59 Wobrook SR1/11 b. Foaled 1956.
    Half take right ear. Brands S left saddle,   Breeder: G. Smith, Hexworthy
    M right saddle   Owner: Miss G. May

Produce: Fiesta b. 1960 (JENYN) FS8
          Imp of Tor br. 1963 (OATLANDS TOM KITTEN) FS8
          Whitmore Titania bl. 1969 (WHITMORE ARBUTUS) FS8
          Allendale Black Magic bl. 1973 (HUNTSPATH HOLLY) FS8
          ALLENDALE VAMPIRE b. 1980 (WHITE WILLOWS DARWIN) FS8
          PUMPHILL BEAU GESTE b. 1982 (O'LANDS MR M'GR') FS8
          PUMPHILL BEAU SABREUR b. 1985 (O'LANDS MR M'GR) FS8
          ALLENDALE FLAUROS bl. 1974 (HUNTSPATH HOLLY) FS8
          ALLENDALE EXORCIST bl. 1975 (HUNTSPATH HOLLY) FS8

FM60 Saucy SR1/42 b. Foaled 1957.
    Star   Breeder: Mrs P. Coaker,
                                      Bittleford Farm, Poundsgate

Produce: Surprise b. 1962 (SILVER DOLLAR) *FS16
          Bittleford Surprise II b. 1971 (JONACA) FS8
          Saucy Miss b. 1975 (BLACHFORD IMPRINT) FS13
          Moseley Springtime b. 1982 (SPRINGS NOUGAT) FS8
          Moseley Miss Braithley b. 1983 (SPRINGS NOUGAT) FS8

FM61 Dunnabridge Wild Goose SR1/185 gr. Foaled 1960.
    Two white patches right side of body   Breeder: R.H.N. Caunter
                                         Owners: Mr & Mrs T. Reep

Produce: Shilstone Rocks Sanduck b. 1965 (RED HALL AQUARIUS) FS8
          Boveycombe Heron b. 1971 (BOVEYCOMBE LEO) FS8
          Boveycombe Bunting br. 1975 (SHILSTONE ROCKS DARKNESS) FS8
          BOVEYCOMBE BOSUN br. 1979 (ALLENDALE FLAUROS) FS8
          Boveycombe Redwing b. 1976 (SHILSTONE ROCKS FURY) FS8

FM62 Kanga SR1/59 bl. Foaled 1960.
                                        Breeder: Mrs Kerr
                                      Owners: Mr & Mrs T. Reep

Sire:
Dam: S.R.I. Trixie

Produce: Shilstone Rocks Bewitched bl. 1964 (WITCHCRAFT) FS8
          Shilstone Rocks Enchanted b. 1969 (RED HALL AQUARIUS) FS8
          Shilstone Rocks Planchette bl. 1970 (PETROC) FS8
          Shilstone Rocks Witching Hour b. 1979 (SH.R. FURY) FS8
          Shilstone Rocks Dark Phantome bl. 1971 (SH.R. DARKNESS)

Dartmoor ponies at the Shilstone Rocks Stud, Widecombe